Greece

www.baedeker.com

Verlag Karl Baedeker

SIGHTSEEING HIGHLIGHTS ✶✶

The list of attractions in Greece is very long, but what are the real highlights on the mainland and on the islands? Whether fantastic beaches, important excavation sites or picturesque towns, we have compiled everything you should not miss!

1 ✶✶ Corfu
Green is the colour that dominates the landscape on this Ionian island, which in no way means you have to do without magnificent coastlines and beaches. ▶ page 232

2 ✶✶ Ioánnina
Víkos Gorge, one of the world's deepest, reaching a depth of 600 m/2,000 ft, and the longest on the Greek mainland, is located near the capital of the province of Epiros. ▶ page 308

©Baedeker

1 Corfu
2 Ioánnina
3 Áthos
4 Metéora Monasteries
5 Delphi
6 Athens
7 Olympiá
8 Corinth
9 Mycenae
10 Epidaurus
11 Aegina
12 Mystrá
13 Chíos
14 Mýkonos
15 Délos
16 Pátmos
17 Rhodes
18 Santorini
19 Crete

BAEDEKER'S BEST TIPS

We have gathered together for you the most interesting of the Baedeker's Tips in this book. Experience and enjoy Greece at its best.

⚠ Byzantine culture
The Byzantine Museum in Athens provides a comprehensive picture of the culture of the Byzantine Empire.
▶ **page 70**

⚠ Sirtos and pidik dances
The famous Athenian Dora Stratou Dance Theater performs traditional Greek dances. ▶ **page 74**

⚠ Holiday in the »White House«
The »White House« located on the beach in Kalámi on Corfu can be rented.
▶ **page 91**

⚠ Swimming, splashing about, sliding ...
The giant water slide in »Aegina's Water Park« is fantastic fun not only for children. ▶ **page 99**

⚠ Simply delicious!
Greek yogurt is a special delicacy available in various forms. ▶ **page 107**

⚠ Border river trip
A trip on the border river of Evros passes near Dadia through Greece's largest wooded area with its rare species of birds. ▶ **page 148**

⚠ Up on Kríkelo
A hike up 826 m/2,710 ft Kríkelo on the island of Amorgós is a fantastic experience, especially in spring when everything is turning green and in blossom.
▶ **page 162**

⚠ Coastal serenity
The deserted coast between the tiny villages of Páleros und Astakós near Árta is incomparably beautiful.
▶ **page 172**

⚠ The most beautiful view ...
... of the Acropolis is from Filopáppos Hill. ▶ **page 182**

Always in view
The 156 m/512 ft high Acropolis can be seen from almost any spot in Athens.

■ Archaeology in the Metro

Numerous remnants dating back to past ages were uncovered during the construction of the Metro. The finds can be admired at selected Metro stations.
► page 200

■ Harbour trip

Do not even try to penetrate the confusion of one-way streets and narrow, steep lanes of Piraeus by car. We recommend taking a ride on the water.
► page 214

■ View of the monasteries

If the lengthy procedure of gaining admittance to Mount Áthos is too daunting or you happen to be female and are not allowed to enter, an impression of the monasteries can be had from aboard ship. ► page 221

■ »Orestes«, »Oedipus« and »Antigone«

It is a thrilling experience – and not just for theatre lovers – to see a tragedy by Euripides or Sophocles in the »original setting«, in the famous Theatre of Epidaurus. We tell you how to get tickets.
► page 297

■ »High Alpine« mountain ride

A narrow, picturesque road leads from Gýtheio to the northeast into the mountain world of the 1,935 m/6,348 ft Mt Párnon. There is a lot to discover along the way.
► page 304

■ Typical souvenirs

Beautiful wrought silver and embroidery work are produced in Ioánnina. Where to buy such souvenirs can be found on
► page 308

Pandelimonos monastery
One of the 20 major monasteries of the Autonomous Monastic Republic of Áthos

Dexia Bay on Itháki
It is thought that the Phaeacians set Odysseus on land here. Located above the bay is a dripstone cave that almost exactly matches the cave described in the »Odyssey«.

⚠ Itháki's most beautiful beach ...
... is the small pebble beach at Aspros Makrýs Gialós. some 200 m/220 yd long and up to about 25 m/30 yd wide
▶ **page 316**

⚠ Mountain train ride
A 23 km/14 mi ride can be taken on a narrow gage, cog-wheel train from the coastal town of Diakoftó to Kalávryta through fascinating mountain scenery of sheer rock faces and deep valleys.
▶ **page 325**

⚠ Surrealistic Greece
The painter Minás Vláchos exhibits his own work and the work of artist friends in the Kárpathos Arts Centre in Pigádia.
▶ **page 328**

⚠ Fascinating play of light
There is a 75 m/250 ft long and 35 m/115 ft high grotto on the south coast of the small island of Kastellórizos, the Fokaliá Grotto, known for its stalactites and the fantastic way light plays on the water.
▶ **page 331**

⚠ Off to Odysseus' island
A trip to Itháki, or Ithaca, the »Island of Odysseus«, can be taken in the morning from Sámi or Fiskárdo on Kefalloniá. The ferry returns in the afternoon, providing time enough to gain an impression of the island and to take a dip in one of the beautiful coves. ▶ **page 340**

⚠ Paradise for hobby ornithologists
Some 280 varieties of birds nest on Lésbos or use the island as a stopping-off place on their long journeys between northern and southern climes. We give you tips where the best places for bird-watching are.
▶ **page 374**

🔳 Hot sounds around a cool pool

Among the most popular night time venues on Mýkonos is the »Hard Rock Café«, some 4 km/2.5 mi from Mýkonos Town. At night, parties are thrown around the pool.   ► page 405

🔳 Cyclades en miniature

The hobby craftsman, Benétos Skiadás, has a private museum with over 80 handmade models of typically Cycladic buildings.   ► page 434

🔳 Celebrity vineyard

Lovers of fine wine should not miss taking a tour of the traditional vineyard, Achaia Clauss. Many celebrities, including Gary Cooper, have bought wine here in Greece's largest winery.   ► page 442

🔳 Sound and light

An especially spectacular sound and light show is presented at the Grand Master's Palace in Rhodes Town.   ► page 458

🔳 Folklore museum in a holiday village

If you want to have a taste of how life once was on Sámos, the holiday resort of Dóryssa Bay is the right place. The extensive resort was built to resemble a Samian village and a museum shows the tools used by farmers, basketmakers, fishermen and beekeepers. It is occasionally possible to watch a potter, smith or barber at work in the old workshops.
► page 469

🔳 Cave trip

The three sea caves, Skótini Spiliá, Galázia Spiliá and Halkini Spiliá on Skiáthos can be explored by swimming into them – an impressive experience!   ► page 487

🔳 Fun and action ...

... can be had in »Waterland« in Taga-rades, outside the gates of Thessaloníki, one of the country's largest recreational parks with a 200 m/220 yd slide and a pool with »real« ocean waves.
► page 510

Holiday mood
Mýkonos is Greece's party island.

Fabulous coves...
...like Anthony Quinn Bay on Rhodes are plentiful in Greece
► page 461

BACKGROUND

PRACTICALITIES

Legendary commander
His campaigns of conquest took him all the way to India.
► page 77

Greek wine
Songs have been written about Greek wine and today wines from Greece are enjoyed around the world.
► page 109

TOURS

SIGHTS FROM A to Z

Price categories

Hotels
Luxury: from €100
Mid-range: €50 – 100
Budget: less than €50
Double room overnight for two persons

Restaurants
Expensive: from €18
Moderate: €12 –18
Inexpensive: less than €12
Menu with appetizer, main course and dessert (no drinks)

Fascinating
*The Blue Grotto near Kastellórizo
is a real must-see.*
▶ **page 287**

Metéora
*It is impossible to imagine how the
building materials were transported up
this 300 m/1,000 ft rock.*
▶ **page 388**

Cult sites
The Apollo temple in Delphi is only one of many examples of imposing structures that were constructed in ancient Greece.
► page 278

Background

BRIEF AND CONCISE, CLEARLY WRITTEN, AND QUICK AND EASY TO CONSULT; FACTS WORTH KNOWING ABOUT GREECE, ABOUT THE COUNTRY AND ITS PEOPLE, ITS NATURAL BEAUTY AND WILDLIFE, ITS ECONOMY AND EVERYDAY LIFE.

LAND OF THE SUN

Even if the great German writer Goethe stood »upon the shore«, his »soul still seeking for the land of Greece«, you do not have to. How fortunate we are today because we have the possibility of exploring Greece, the cradle of European civilization, as the country is popularly and justifiably called, and of discovering all its many and varied facets.

You will be carried away by the great variety of enchanting landscapes, discover idyllic, rustic villages, dive merrily into the blue waters of the sea, take a break from the hectic of everyday life on a wide beach and drink a toast with Dionysus, the god of wine, to this totally fabulous country with all its sights, both ancient and new. For many decades now, Greece's major economic assets have been the sun, endless beaches, the inviting, gleaming seas and, not forgetting, the innumerable ancient archaeological sites that impressively attest to the country's five thousand years of history. It can easily be seen that Greece is an exceptional country; for which region on earth can boast of over 4,000 km/ 2,485 mi of mainland coast and some 2,000 islands, 160 of which are inhabited, give or take a few? There is something for every taste here, from the large island of Crete, which can almost be considered, economically and culturally, a continent of its

Fun in the sun *can be had (almost) always and everywhere in Greece with its 15,000 km/ 9,000 mi of coastline.*

own, down to the tiniest, almost deserted islet. Experience fantastic, expansive beaches, secluded picturesque rocky coves, untouched fishing villages or lively tourist centres. There is something to satisfy the needs of all sun-hungry holiday-makers, big and small: Mýkonos or Amorgós, Chalkidikí or Outer (Exo) Máni – and that's a guarantee! Initially, it was the fantastic ruins of Greek Antiquity that attracted an enthusiastic bourgeoisie. It was considered very chic in their circles to simply »have seen« Greece, the cradle of Western civilization. And even today, the world famous sites, such as the impressively beautiful Acropolis high above the pulsating metropolis of Athens, the ancient Oracle of Delphí, the Theatre of Epidauros and the huge palace in Knossós are major attractions. By taking a little time, amazing things can be discovered. It is well worth taking a

Farmer's salad
It is part of every meal and is often offered as »Greek salad«.

History
The Greeks, like this stonemason at work in Epidaurus, spend a lot of time, money and effort preserving the legacy of their ancestors.

Not just gýros
Lovers of fresh fish and seafood will discover Greece to be their own personal paradise.

Tremorous islands
Although it poses no danger to explore the 30 m/100 ft deep Stéfanos crater on the Aegean island of Nísyros, the volcano is still not completely dormant.

Souvenirs
Souvenir hunters get their money's worth everywhere in the country, like here in the labyrinth of the old part of Kos Town.

Surfing, diving and much more
Whether on, in or under the water, the Greek mainland and the islands offer a wealth of ways to indulge in one's favourite sport.

closer look around the ruins and museums, at the impressive artistic power and technical achievements, and perhaps gain a feeling for the spirit of the place. The architectural legacies of later centuries are much more numerous and these are what characterize the image of Greece today. But alongside these architectural highlights, Greece has some of the most beautiful and impressive scenery in Europe. Choose between the lush, verdant, subtropical Ionian Islands and the impressive, bleak landscapes of the Cyclades. The mainland, too, holds many lesser-known treasures best exploited in spring or autumn; such as the wonderful mountain world of Epiros with its snow-covered peaks and the interesting and bustling Thessaloníki, the gorgeous dune coasts and river biotopes with their uncommon flora and fauna.

Greece would not be Greece without its own characteristic way of life, which can be enjoyed everywhere, as it requires no more than a shady square and a »kafés«. You will find Greece an extremely hospitable country. Wherever you go you will feel welcome and be greeted with open arms. Visitors to the islands, above all, have the impression that the pace of life is slower. »Live and let live« is the motto here. To have all the time in the world, to be able to talk with others at length and to have fun together – there is no doubt that this constitutes a great deal of the charm of the country, of the fascination that it exerts on visitors. No matter whether you are on the mainland or the islands, the hallmark of Greece is an irresistibly attractive Mediterranean way of life. Enjoy this lightness of being and open your heart to it! Have fun on your journey of discovery through Greece – to experience the country and its people with all your senses is truly rewarding!

Island-hopping

The lonely and romantic coves still exist, but they can usually only be reached by boat.

Facts

Greece is full of contrasts, from the big-city bustle in Athens and overrun tourist strongholds to secluded mountain villages and near-to-deserted islands with fabulous coves. This section offers things worth knowing about the country and its people.

Natural Environment

Greece, dominated by sea and mountains, can be divided into three **Major regions** major geographiczones: the Greek **mainland**, the large, hand-shaped **Peloponnese Peninsula** and the Greek **islands**. About two-thirds of the land area is occupied by mountain ranges, about a sixth is low-lying and another fifth is constituted by the islands. The heart of the Greek mainland is formed by the Pindos Mountains, rising up to a height of 2,637 m/8,652 ft. The country's highest elevation, however, is Mount Olympus in Thessaly; the »Mountain of the Gods« is 2,917 m/9,570 ft high.

The present state of Greece's natural landscape is the result of com- **Geology** plicated processes stretching back into geological time. The geologic substructure in the east of the country is largely composed of ancient landmasses or mountains sunken for the most part below sea level. The Dinaric-Hellenic system of folded mountains in the west was formed in the Cretaceous Period, which began about 140 million years ago, up until the Tertiary, which ended some two million years ago, with the **Pindos Mountains** being among the youngest of the mountain ranges. This mountain chain stretches from the north of Greece to the southern tip of the Peloponnese, where it sinks into the sea, turns eastward and continues above the surface as the major islands of Crete and Rhodes. Deep bays have formed where the – younger – mountain ranges run out into the sea, as can be seen by the »fingers« of the Peloponnese. In many places today in the interi-or, fertile hill and alluvial terrain stretch between the heavily karstic calcareous massifs. The more ancient folded mountain chains in the mainland now turn eastwards, forming the diversified coasts of east-ern Greece. The Tertiary Period, about 65 million years ago, saw the sinking of the old Cycladic mountain system, whose peaks jut out of the Aegean Sea to form the Cyclades. The fertile landscapes of Mace-donia, Thessaly, Boeotia and Argolis in the east and northeast of the Greek mainland were also formed in the recent geological past through the process of lowering; on the other hand, mighty ancient massifs like Olympus also tower up there. Far to the north, the foot-hills of the Rhodope Mountains spread down into Greek territory.

The earth's crust in the whole of the Mediterranean region is still to- **Earthquakes and** day in a state of unrest. Seismic activity can be more or less clearly **volcanism** registered almost daily, occasionally with catastrophic consequences. These earthquakes are triggered by the constant movements of the continental plates. In Greece's case, the African plate is moving northward at a speed of about 2.5 cm/1 in a year and is pushing

← *Large and small islands just made for relaxation and exploration – for example »Mouse Island« off Corfu.*

Facts and Figures Greece

Greek national flag

► Bordering states: Albania, Macedonia, Bulgaria, Turkey
► International country vehicle code: GR

Population
► 10.5 million
► Population density: 79.5 per sq km/206 per sq mi

Language
► Modern Greek

Religion
► c. 97% of the population belong to the Greek Orthodox Church.

State
► Hellenic Republic (Elliniki Dhimokratia)
► Form of government: parliamentary democracy
► Parliament: 300 members
► Chief of State: President Karolos Papoulias (since 2005)
► Head of Government: Prime Minister Kostas Karamanlis (since 2004)
► Administrative structure: 13 regions, each with several prefectures, and the autonomous region of the Monastic Republic of Mount Athos
► National Holiday: March 25

Economy
► Gross national product: € 163.9 billion
► Per capita income: € 14,850
► Unemployment rate: 11.5%
► Most important trading partners: Germany, Italy, France, Russia

Location
► Southeast Europe
► Between 36° and 41° latitude north and 20° and 26° longitude east

Area and territory
► 132,000 sq km/50,965 sq mi (mainland: 107,000 sq km/41,300 sq mi, island area: 25,000 sq km/9,650 sq mi)
► Coastline: 15,000 km/9,320 miles (mainland coastline: 4,100km/2,548 miles)
► Islands: more than 2,000 (c. 150 inhabited)
► Highest elevation: Mt Olympus (2,917 m/9,570 ft)
► Capital: Athens (pop 777,000; greater metropolitan area of Athens/Piraeus: pop. c. 3.2 million)
► Largest cities: Thessaloniki (pop. 385,000), Piraeus (pop. 180,000), Patras (pop. 153,000), Heráklion (Crete; pop. 115,000)

underneath the Aegean microplate in a subduction zone marked by increased volcanism. The Aegean microplate, in turn, covers a part of the Eurasian major plate. The volcanism thus released, and at present probably only dormant, produced the islands of Aegina, Mílos and Santorin.

Northern Greece

Northern Greece stretches south to the level of the Ambracian Gulf on the west coast and the Gulf of Lamia on the east coast. The Píndos Mountains form its spine, the highest elevation being the 2,637 m/8,652 ft high Mt Smolikas. Spreading out to the west of the Píndos massif toward the Ionian Sea is the charming hill country of **Epiros**. Further northeast of the Píndos range is the fertile bay of Thessaloníki, framed by Macedonia's mountain ranges. Adjoining to the east is **Chalkidikí Peninsula**, known for its beautiful bathing beaches, and whose »fingers«, Kassándra, Sithonía and Áthos, reach out into the northern Aegean. Far to the northeast, Greece has a share of the historic region of Thrace, embraced by the southern foothills of the Bulgarian Rhodope Mountains and the floodplains of the Nestos and Evros rivers. Even today, the landscape is still largely marked by tobacco cultivation. Rising up to the southwest of Thessaloníki is the ancient massif of Olympus, while the fertile **Thessaly basin** stretching to the south of it is bounded in the west by the Píndos Mountains and in the east by the coastal mountains of Thessaly.

Even snow-covered mountains can be found in Greece, like here in the Erymanthos range.

Greece's coastline is about 15,000 km/9,000 mi long.

Central Greece   The ancient landscape of **Thessaly** provides the transition from north to central Greece. Central Greece, bordered to the south on the one hand by the lengthy Gulf of Pátras and on the other by the Gulf of Corinth, is the heartland of Greece with its capital, Athens, and includes the Attic Peninsula, as well as the limestone mountains of Giona (2,510 m/8,235 ft) and Parnassus (2,457 m/8,061 ft) looking down on the basins and plains of Boeotia, Phocis, Locris and Aetolia. Also considered part of central Greece are the Gulf of Attica and the island of Évia, separated from the mainland by a narrow channel.

Southern Greece   Southern Greece, that is to say the **Peloponnese**, is connected to the heartland by the narrow Isthmus of Corinth, which is bisected by a canal. The central area of the Peloponnese is **Arcadia**, whose highest point reaches 2,500 m/8,202 ft and from which steep limestone mountain ranges reach out into the sea to the south and southeast like the fingers of a hand.

Ionian Islands   The Ionian Islands lie off the west coast of the Greek mainland at the outlet of the Adriatic Sea. The most famous of these islands, named »Eptanissia« (the »Seven Islands«) by the Greeks, is Corfu. The number seven refers to the short interlude around 1800 when the Ionian Islands comprised the independent **Septinsular Republic** (Republic of the Seven Islands).

Stretching out to the east and south of the Greek mainland almost to the coast of Asia Minor are several groups of islands that together constitute the Aegean Islands.

Aegean Islands

The core of the Cyclades Islands is composed of some three dozen larger and smaller islands clustered around Délos, an island considered sacred in Antiquity. A number of these barren islands have long since become extremely popular holiday destinations, among them Mýkonos, Páros, Náxos and Santorin.

◄ Cyclades

Despite what the name suggests, there are a couple more (uninhabited) islands than just twelve that belong to the Dodecanese, lying off the coast of Asia Minor. The best-known are Pátmos, Kálimnos, Kos and Rhodes. The Sporades, whose most charming scenery is considered to be on the island of Skópelos and are counted as part of Central Greece, lie off the major island of Euboea (Évia).

◄ Dodecanese

◄ Sporades

The largest of the Greek islands is Crete. It forms the southern edge of the Aegean Sea. The island is some 300 km/186 mi long and is about equally distant from Attica and the coast of North Africa, with Asia Minor also not too far away. This bridging function explains why Crete is considered to be, in a cultural sense, **the cradle of Europe**.

Crete

Flora and Fauna

Flora

In terms of plant geography, Greece is one of the most interesting regions in Europe. About a seventh of all of Greece's indigenous plants are endemic, which means they are only found here. In addition, vegetation of southeast European, Near Eastern and North African origin grows in Greek soil.

About one half of the country is covered by Mediterranean sclerophyllous and shrub vegetation that is termed **frygana**. This vegetation cover is similar to the Italian macchia and the garrigue of southern France. Included in frygana are evergreen und kermes oaks, arbutus trees, olive trees, laurel, gorse, myrtle, rosaceous plants, juniper, spurge and numerous other plants. In the humid west of Greece, this form of vegetation extends up to the higher regions. The further south, the scantier the frygana becomes. Eventually, it changes into sparse, dry vegetation consisting

? DID YOU KNOW …?

■ … that more than 800 different species of herbs and plants, almost 20 percent of all of the country's flora, are to be found growing in the great pine forests of the 1,413 m/4,636 ft Mt Parnes (Parnitha), Attica's highest mountain?

Olive groves are unfortunately becoming a rarity.

almost exclusively of juniper bushes, thistles, thyme, peppermint and water retentive succulents, including cacti, agave and opuntia.

Forests Greece lies within the range of the **Mediterranean broad-leaf and mixed forest zone**. Millennia-long over-exploitation of the once rich primordial forests is the reason why there are no longer any forests or just scanty remains in many areas of Greece. There are still mixed forests in the coastal regions and basins with various species of oak, pine, plane, carob and olive trees and other diverse growths. Cypress and eucalyptus are typical of the landscape. Mixed deciduous woods of beech, chestnut, plane, elm, walnut and maple trees can be found in the north of Greece and in the mountain regions of Central Greece up to an elevation of 1,500 m/4,921 ft. Coniferous forests dominate the landscape at elevations between 1,700 m/5,577 ft and 2,000 m/6,562 ft with diverse species of pine and fir. Even further up, bleak alpine meadows unfold, interspersed with stunted conifers.

Cultivated plants **Olive groves**, **fig crops** and **vineyards** are characteristic of Greece. Some of these fields have been cultivated since Antiquity. As not much money can be earned nowadays with wine, olive oil and figs, more and more once-cultivated land is lying idle, and is gradually being taken over by frygana. Recently, attempts have been made to reforest such areas. Today, plantations in the particularly fertile regions are being managed according to the latest methods. Diverse varieties of vegetables and fruit, tobacco and cotton are being cultivated on a large scale. Sugar beet, potatoes, wheat, barley, maize and rice are also being grown.

Animals

The widespread devastation of the original plant cover has had a very **Wild animals** negative effect on the biodiversity of the animal world. A considerable population of red deer and wild boar can still be found only in secluded mountain regions. Seen more often are sheep, goats, donkeys and mules, as well as hares and rabbits, hunted by foxes, badgers, martens and feral cats. There are still some wild goats (Capra aegarus) on Crete.

Even the reptiles are being increasingly pushed back. This is particu- **Reptiles** larly true of **Hermann's tortoise** and the **loggerhead turtle**, the sea turtle that lays its eggs on various sandy beaches and lets the sun incubate them. In 1999, the famous »turtle beach« in Laganás Bay on the island of Zákynthos was declared a nature-protection zone. Geckos and various other species of lizard can still be seen quite regularly, on the other hand. Beware of snakes, particularly venomous **vipers** and the now rigorously protected **blunt-nosed viper**, not only in frygana undergrowth, but also in gardens and other warm places.

Greek birdlife is very diverse; after all, this southeastern European **Birds** country is an important land bridge for many migrating birds. A great number of **diurnal birds of prey**, including eagles, the Eurasian black vulture, the bearded vulture or lammergeier, peregrine falcons and hawks can still be found in the mountain regions and especially on the Evros. Partridge and quail as well as lapwings and magpies can be seen quite often. Black-and-white oyster-catchers, terns, European rollers and several species of gull circle in the air near to the coasts. The nuthatch, especially the pygmy nuthatch, as well as buntings and the colourful European bee-eater are also widespread. Pelicans can still be found only in a few reserves.

The insect world in Greece is highly diverse. This is particularly true **Insects** in spring when myriads of butterflies and bees swarm out to the flowers and cicadas stage their ear-splitting chirping concerts. Keep an eye out for the poisonous rogalida spider, as well as scorpions.

The fauna in Greek waters has surprisingly few species, which can be **Marine life** attributed to overfishing and water pollution. Among the relatively widespread species of fish are grey mullets, barbel mullets, mackerel, dentrex, perch, European hake, sardines, anchovies, Adriatic fish of the triglidae family and tuna fish. Squid, octopus, different species of molluscs, lobster, langouste, shrimp and crabs are also still plentifully represented. Watersports enthusiasts should watch out for aggressive sharks and moray eels, particularly in the rocky areas of the coast. Sea-urchins and stinging jellyfish can also dampen the joy of bathing. Now and again, **dolphins** can be observed from a ship or boat. The Mediterranean monk seals, which usually seek out secluded sections of rocky coastline, are one of the world's most endangered mammals. The coral cover and sponge colonies have been greatly reduced by water pollution.

Population · Politics · Economy

Population

Settlements About 28 % of Greece's population live in rural settlements. Drinking-water is a decisive factor in the location of a settlement. The towns, mostly small and middle-size, are primarily located on the eastern half of the mainland. There are very few major cities. Athens, the country's capital, and the neighbouring port of Piraeus form together with their suburbs a unified area with some 3.2 million inhabitants. Dominating in the north is Thessaloníki with 380,000 inhabitants. The largest town of the Peloponnese is Pátras with 153,000 inhabitants.

? DID YOU KNOW ...?

■ ... that in Greece the expression »we'll call that loaf of bread a roll« gently alludes to a possible coming catastrophe?

Rural exodus and emigration Most of the islands, in contrast to the cities, are seeing a steady decline in population. The barren soil and the fragmenting of estates through the division of assets have made life so difficult that young people frequently prefer to look around for better ways to make a living on the mainland, in the industrialized nations of Western Europe or overseas, especially in the USA. About 4 million Greeks live abroad. Recently though, there has been a turnabout trend because many young Greeks, disappointed with city life, are returning to the countryside.

State and Society

State form Following the fall of the military dictatorship in 1974 and a plebiscite on the fate of the monarchy in which a large majority of the people spoke out for the abdication of the exiled King Constantine II, Greece adopted a constitution in 1975 that provided for a **parliamentary democratic republican** form of state and government.

National flag First raised in 1822, the flag displays a Greek cross in the upper left corner with nine blue and white stripes corresponding to the nine syllables of the Greek battle cry »Freedom or Death« used in the War of Independence from Turkish domination. The colours blue and white were those of Otto I, the first modern king of the Hellenes, who came from Bavaria.

Two generations, two different worlds

The parliament, elected every four years in free and secret elections, consists of 300 members, who in turn select, by a three-quarter majority, the president for a term of five years. The head of government is the prime minister.

Constitutional organs

The territory of the Republic of Greece is divided into **thirteen administrative regions**, which are in turn subdivided into more than 50 prefectures (»nomí«). The Nomí are composed of almost 150 provinces (»eparchíes«). The **Autonomous Monastic State of the Holy Mountain** (Mount Athos) on the eastern »finger« of the peninsula of Chalkidikí in northern Greece, with its 20 Greek Orthodox monasteries, enjoys complete internal self-government.

Administrative divisions

Religion

Almost the total population (c. 97 %) belongs to the **Greek Orthodox Church** because every child of Greek Orthodox parents is automatically made a member and there is no formal means of leaving the church. The remaining three percent is made up of Muslims, Protestants, Roman Catholics and Jews.

Religious affiliations

State church ▶ The Greek Orthodox Church has been autonomous since 1833 and the state church since 1864, with parliament deciding on its interests. The Archbishop of Athens functions as its head; only the islands of the Dodecanese and the Monastic Republic of Áthos are under the direct jurisdiction of the Patriarch of Constantinople. Crete, as a semi-autonomous ecclesiastical province, also has a special position.

Priests Greek Orthodox priests (»pappás«) with their black cassocks, long hair and characteristic beards are a common sight on the streets and village life is hard to imagine without them. They are allowed to marry, although only before their ordination. If the wife of an ordained priest dies, he may marry again. Married priests, however, are allowed neither to join a monastery nor to hold higher ecclesiastical office. As the Orthodox Church is the state church, pappás have the status of government employees, albeit with a relatively meagre salary. They can supplement their income through donations or fees for performing church services, such as baptisms, marriages and funerals.

Easter The Feast of the Assumption of the Virgin (August 15) and Easter are the **most important religious holidays**. Easter is traditionally a family-centred celebration. Its festivities begin with the procession on Good Friday, during which the entombment of Christ is recreated with the worshippers accompanying the flower and embroidery-bedecked casket of Christ. The faithful gather in the church about an hour before midnight on Easter Eve. When the priest announces the resurrection of Christ at midnight, the Easter light is lit and all the members of the congregation pass the flame from candle to candle. A large bonfire is lit in many villages and Judas symbolically burned. Following the midnight service, the families gather to partake of the first Easter meal after the period of fasting. Traditionally, this is **magiritsa**, a soup made with the offal of a lamb.

? DID YOU KNOW ...?

■ ... that on Corfu it is the custom to drop clay pots out of house windows and from balconies on to the street on Easter Saturday?

The Feast of the Assumption The Assumption of the Virgin Mary is celebrated on 15 August. Many Greeks return to their villages and their hometowns on this day – the big cities are left almost deserted. The focus of the festivities is the Church of the Virgin Mary on the island of **Tínos**, one of the Cyclades, where thousands of the faithful gather after a long period of fasting to fulfil an oath or to pray for intercession.

Christmas Christmas plays a role of lesser importance than Easter in the Greek Orthodox religion. On 24 December, groups of children parade from house to house singing and are rewarded with money, fruit or sweets. The feast is usually celebrated in the villages with a mass and

The kafenion – where men prefer to congregate

MALE COFFEE TALK

The kafenion, the traditional Greek café, is the place where men meet, read, chat and play cards or tavli – usually over a cup of Greek coffee or an ouzo.

The kafenion is a **man's world**. This is where mostly older men meet and »palaver« about »major« and »minor« political issues, as well as what's new in the village. They also play cards or tavli, a Greek version of backgammon, or read the newspaper. Or the men absentmindedly finger a komboloi, a chain of pearls, olive wood, amber, silver or gems, which was adopted from Islam. The most important beverage in all of this is Greek coffee, the **kafés ellinikós**, ordered without sugar (sketos), with a little sugar (métrios) or sweet (glikós). Only sips are taken of the coffee and that over a long period of time, even when it has long since got cold. Whoever does not feel like a coffee can order either an ouzo or a »gliko tu kutaliosis«, a syrupy mass with preserved fruits, e.g. cherries or quinces.

Women meet elsewhere

There is no drink minimum; nobody is given dirty looks when they sit for hours over a single coffee or a game of tavli. Business deals are also made here, sealed with a handshake. No one can afford to be dishonest. The guests in the kafenion all share the same political views as its landlord. The kafenia are often plain and simply decorated, which is why younger Greeks prefer more stylish cafés and bars.

Greek patriarchalism is particularly evident in the kafenion. Women are not forbidden to enter, to be sure, but they are supposed to meet in other places. Women meet each other in front of their houses or while shopping. There are also kafenia – and this is little known – where whole families gather in the evenings.

song and dance. Most city-dwellers have adopted the Western Christmas rituals, decorating their homes, setting up a Christmas tree and enjoying the usual celebrations. One essential difference remains: only the children receive presents.

Economy

Services The most important sector by far in the Greek economy is the service industry. More than half of all those working are employed in the areas of trade, hospitality and catering, transport, communications, real estate and financial services.

Tourism ► Greece is one of the world's »classic« travel destinations and tourism has always been an important source of revenue. The number of visitors to Greece had already broken the million mark by the 1960s. About 14 million tourists were tallied in 2004. A majority of all holidaymakers in Greece come from EU countries, primarily from Germany and Britain.

Agriculture Although agriculture makes only a small contribution to the gross national product, it remains an important pillar of the Greek economy. Even though hardly a third of the land is used for agriculture, Greece is one of Europe's most important suppliers of olives, grapes, fruit and vegetable. Despite EU restrictions, **wine growing** is still pursued on a major scale in Attica, in the Peloponnese and on Crete. A part of the production also goes into table grapes, raisins, currants and sultanas for export. The major industrial crops are sugar beet, cotton and tobacco. For the most part, they are further processed in Greece. The agricultural sector is dominated by small, indeed mini, operations. Mechanization is little developed because of the small size of the farms, the modest income and the hillside location of many fields. Animal husbandry is extensive in the mountain regions. In most cases, the sparse vegetation allows only the keeping of sheep and goats.

Fishing The catch has been drastically reduced in recent decades because of overfishing and water pollution. Despite considerable expansion, domestic fishing is not able to meet the demand, particularly that of tourists. For this reason, many businesses are running marine fish hatcheries – particularly for bream and monkfish – and farming shellfish so that almost half of the fish processed in the country is farmed. Sponge fishing, once a highly profitable source of employment in the Aegean, is almost insignificant today.

Industry The manufacturing industries, which in Greece include the mining, energy and processing sectors, have developed quite rapidly since the 1970s. Their share of the gross national product lies at about one-third. The main branches are the textile, food, metal-working and chemical industries and oil refining. The industrial centres are

A fisherman preparing his nets for the catch

Athens, Thessaloníki and Pátras; currently more than half of all of Greece's industrial companies are located in greater Athens.

Mining

Greece has a variety of mineral resources whose exploitation was not economic for a long time. Chief among the raw materials are lignite and bauxite, which is largely exported. At present, more than two dozen different types of ores are being mined, including iron, silver, nickel, copper, chromium, lead and zinc. Added to that is a considerable amount of marble.

◄ Petroleum

Greece has been a petroleum exporting country since 1981. Two years earlier, »black gold« had been discovered off the northern Greek island of Thassos. Natural gas is being exported along with the oil. Since then, further lucrative petroleum and natural gas fields have been surveyed on the Asiatic continental shelf of the Aegean Sea. Both Greece and Turkey are claiming these deposits, though, which has also caused tension between the two nations. An important fossil energy source is the lignite mined in the north and north-west of the Greek mainland and on the island of Euboea.

History

Greece has had a decisive influence on European history from the Minoan culture – Europe's first advanced civilization – and the powerful city-states of Antiquity down to the present. After all, it was the ancient Greeks who founded democracy and gave our continent its name.

Prehistory · Minoan Culture

7th millennium BC	First settlement in the Aegean region
3300–2100 BC	Early period of the culture on Crete named after King Minos
2000–1700 BC	First high point of the Minoan Culture
12th BC	Fall of the Minoan civilization after the destruction of the Palace of Knossós

Archaeological finds confirm settlements in the Aegean area since the 7th millennium BC. Common characteristics indicate a connection to civilizations in the Middle East, so that we can speak of a **Neolithic cultural area** extending over the whole region. The excavation of axes, knives and pottery attest to a Copper Age culture centred in the Argolis (eastern Peloponnese) during the 3rd millennium BC.

First settlement

The Minoan culture, named after the legendary King Minos, developed around huge palace complexes. Seals, copper and bronze daggers and gold jewellery from the early period of the 3rd millennium BC have survived in the ports in the east and in the vaulted tombs on the plain of Messará

Prepalatial

An urban civilization was grouped around the royal court during the first cultural flowering called the Old Palace Period after the **palaces of Knossós, Mália** and **Festós**. The economic basis was intensive wine and olive-oil cultivation and metalworking. The settlement on Crete appears during this phase to have been a relatively self-sufficient society that had little contact with other peoples, making it apparently unnecessary to fortify the palaces and cities. Examples of crafts of outstanding quality from this time have survived in the form of thinly walled vases painted in bright colours named Kamáres pottery after the site where they were first discovered.

Protopalatial (Old Palace Period)

An earthquake probably destroyed the Cretan palaces around the middle of the 17th century BC. Their reconstruction marks the beginning of the Late Minoan Period. Particularly Knossós was rebuilt on a more magnificent scale. Interest now shifted abroad, to the Mycenaean mainland and especially to the New Kingdom in Egypt. Trade and contact with neighbouring peoples brought the Linear script, which replaced the old pictographic system of writing. Religious and social structures bore matriarchal characteristics. A flowering of pottery and fresco painting in the so-called palace style developed in Knossós.

Neopalatial (New Palace Period)

← *Traces of the past are present everywhere in Greece – these are the ruins of the Palace of Knossós on Crete.*

Fall of the The Mycenaean conquerors advanced to Crete around 1400 BC. The
Minoan Culture final **destruction of Knossós** in 1200 BC ended the Minoan civilization – whether by some kind of natural catastrophe or foreign inva-
sion is unknown.

Mycenaean ·
Early Greek Archaic Period

1400 to 1150 BC	Mycenae develops into the most powerful principality of the Greek mainland.
10th century BC	Dorians settle on the Greek mainland.
c. 850 BC	Development of the Greek alphabet
c. 750 to 500 BC	Greeks found over 700 colonies and cities.

Mycenaean A number of different principalities were formed on the Greek main-
Period land with the influx of new ethnic groups during the middle of the
2nd millennium BC. The most powerful was in Mycenae. In contrast
to the initially peaceful and self-sufficient Crete, it was dominated by
a hierarchical aristocracy of warriors under the leadership of a king,
preoccupied with competition and seizing and settling land. Monumental fortresses, protected by massive walls, stood not only in Mycenae, but in Tíryns, Thebes, Iolcos and on the Acropolis of Athens
as well. During the 15th century BC, the Greeks in the Peloponnese
extended their sphere of influence all the way to Asia Minor, Crete
and Melos. Extraordinary works of art were produced through a
mingling with the Minoan culture in the Late Mycenaean period
from 1400 to 1150 BC. Beehive tombs with their burial offerings and
fortifications are evidence of this still today.

Dorian The movement of Illyrians into the northwest of the Balkans at the
Invasion end of the 2nd millennium BC triggered a migration of the Dorians
living in the west and south of the Balkans. To avoid this threat, the
peoples that had been living in the Greek region until then moved to
Asia Minor and the Aegean islands, where they experienced a cultural flourishing through their contact with the East. The Ionian **Pre-
Socratic** school of philosophy was the cradle of Western philosophy.

First Greek In the first half of the 8th century BC, the Dorians established urban
Colonization centres at cult sites on the mainland such as Dodóna, Delphí and
Olympía. The cities usually developed around a fortified elevation,
the acropolis. Greece's particular geographic location meant that the
migration did not take place as one great flood but rather in small
spurts. Little by little, families and tribes pushed their way into the

fertile plains. This meant a splintering and breaking apart of old tribal and defence unions in favour of a single state in which the new and promising **polis** form of state could develop.

After the storm of the Dorian invasion, things in Greece were quiet for about 400 years, between the 9th and the 6th centuries. It was during this time that the **core of Western culture** developed. The Greek alphabet emerged around 850 BC, including not only consonants but, for the first time, vowels as well. The Homeric epics composed in the 8th century achieved a complexity hitherto unattainable and made the transition from oral tradition to literature.

The basic geographic conditions, i.e. the limited possibilities of urban development and the supply problem resulting from a shortage of fertile land, were of defining consequence for the further development of Greece. A wave of colonization resulted from the numerous wars among the cities and the difficulty many cities had in providing their citizens with sufficient land. New territory was conquered from the sea and was only cautiously expanded inland. As a rule, settlement was confined to coastal areas. Among the most important new settlements were Taranto (c. 700 BC, colonized by Sparta), Syracuse (settlers from Corinth, c. 730 BC) and Massilia (colonists from Phocaia, c. 600 BC). From the heartland regions like Attica all the

The Mycenaeans built enormous fortress complexes.

way to such distant colonies as Massilia (Marseilles) and Al Mina in Syria, the Hellenes were able to distinguish themselves as a unified cultural community through a common language, shared lifestyles, shrines, feasts of sacrifice and games. By the end of the colonization period, the Greeks had founded over 700 cities all around the Mediterranean.

Sparta

c. 900 BC	Founding of the city-state of Sparta
740–720 BC	First Messenian War
650–633 BC	Second Messenian War
c. 550 BC	Founding of the »Peloponnesian League«

Fortified city-state During the course of the gradual conquest of the fertile Eurotas plains in the southern Peloponnese around 900 BC, Dorian bands of warriors subjugated a large number of non-Dorian communities in the neighbourhood of Amykles and, with the unification of four villages, formed a city, Sparta. A special feature of Sparta was that the subjugated population was many times the size of the free population. To keep this power structure stable, the city-state had to be particularly defensively organized and equipped. Sparta conserved the political structure from the period of immigration and continued the kingship in the form of a **dual monarchy**. The rigorous social stratifi-

Only scattered ruins remain of once mighty Sparta.

cation into Spartiates, perioikoi (free mercenaries, tradesman, merchants) and helots (state-owned serfs), however, stirred up unrest and revolts.

When a shortage of land developed in the last third of the 8th century BC, Sparta undertook a campaign to the west and conquered Messenia. At first, the doubling of arable land brought riches and security. Every Spartan now received enough land and serfs so that his family was provided for even during active military service. With prosperity, culture also thrived in Sparta. Literature, poetry and music came to life and the young Spartiates dominated the Olympic Games. As was generally the case in Greece, the tendency of the time to weaken kings in favour of the free citizenry can also be seen in Sparta's development. However, unlike Athens, it was not the will of the citizens that became decisive in Sparta, but rather that of a small military and political elite.

First Messenian War

◀ Sparta's golden age

The resistance to the Spartan state in suppressed Messenia increased so much during the course of the 7th century BC that it finally led to the Second Messenian War from around 650 until 633 BC Sparta was able to defeat Messenia once and for all with the help of new military tactics like the phalanx, a unit of heavily-armed infantry.

As a result of the great effort expended in subduing the Messenians and after unsuccessful campaigns of conquest, Sparta attempted to secure its territory through alliances with the states and tribes in the north of the Peloponnese and to expand its sphere of influence over the whole of the peninsula with the aid of its allies. Although the **Peloponnesian League**, formed around 550 BC, left the cities outside Sparta's sphere of influence their independence, it backed up Sparta's position of military supremacy in Greece.

Second Messenian War

◀ Alliance policy

Athens

624 BC	Draco codifies Athenian law
594 BC	Solon elected archon and gains dictatorial powers
From 560 BC	Peisistratos ruled as tyrant in the city-state with few interruptions until his death in 528 BC.
c. 510 BC	Cleisthenes expels the tyrant Hippias and reorganizes Attica's territorial and political structure.

The countryside of Attica remained untouched by the wave of Dorian immigrants. During the course of the first millennium BC, the tribal structure dwindled in importance in favour of an urban society, with the old kingship being modified to a religious office with

Beginnings

The Temple of Athena on the Acropolis is more than 2,500 years old.

annual tenure. The actual government lay in the hands of the **archons**, who, as annually elected chief magistrates, formed the council of the »**nine archons**«. After their term of office, they automatically became members of the **areopagus**, the influential council of elders and, at the same time, the highest court of appeal.

Draco A source of unrest was the fact that almost the whole country was owned by the aristocracy and the farmers increasingly found themselves in debt bondage. When a bloody family feud cause an uproar in Athens in the mid-7th century BC, Draco, one of the **thesmothetes** (lawgivers), seized the opportunity to undertake a partial codification of the law around 624 BC.

Solon In 594 BC, Solon (►Famous People) was elected archon and invested with dictatorial powers to overcome the smouldering social conflicts and avert the threatening civil war. Solon sought to create a balance between the aristocracy and farmers with a comprehensive, codified law. The laws were written on tablets and displayed publicly so that the population, which was divided into four classes, could avail themselves of their guaranteed rights.

Those among the aristocracy who sought to restore their powers initiated violent unrest, resulting in Peisistratos seizing power as a tyrant in 560 BC. This introduced into Athens as well the extreme of aristocratic power known as **tyrannis**, or tyranny, which was the form of rule dominant in most Greek cities from the middle of the 7th century to the 5th century BC. The fortunes of a state were dependent on the person of the tyrant alone. Peisistratos pursued a wide-scale »middle class policy« that brought about an upswing in commerce and the arts. Athens became a gathering place for Greek artists and a lively building programme developed. Surviving from this time are the remains of the Olympieion and the temple to Athena on the Acropolis.

Peisistratos

Cleisthenes, the head of the long-banished aristocratic Alcmaeonidae dynasty, took over the leadership of a popular revolt against the tyranny of the sons of Peisistratos with his ideas for reform. With Sparta's help, he was able to expel the tyrant Hippias, Peisistratos' second son, in 511/510 BC Cleisthenes rearranged Attica's territorial and political structure. Although the aristocracy continued to rule because of their wealth, education, and influential connections, the new guiding concept of **»isonomy«** – equal rights for all citizens – made it possible for all male citizens to have an equal say in political life.

Cleisthenes

Classic Period

490 – 479 BC	Persian Wars: the Greeks defeat the Persian army in the Battle of Marathon and the naval Battle of Salamis
478/477 BC	Founding of the Delian League
432 – 404 BC	Peloponnesian War
371/370 BC	Sparta loses its position of supremacy on the Peloponnese

As a result of his campaigns of conquest, all of Asia Minor had fallen into the hands of the first **Persian Great King, Cyrus**, by the mid-6th century BC. At the beginning of the 5th century, the Persians demanded recognition of their suzerainty from the Greek city-states, which especially Sparta and Athens rejected out of hand. In response, the Persians sent a military expedition fleet to Erétria and Attica that was only stopped by the Athenians in 490 BC at the **Battle of Marathon**. This defeat launched a monumental re-armament in Persia under **Xerxes**. Opposing this was the Greek front, which was in no way united because some of the cities were thinking of coming to terms with the Persians. Sparta was finally able to weld the (by now

Persian Wars

heavily armed) city-states into a fighting alliance by the autumn of 481 BC. The Persian campaign, however, was able to penetrate a long way toward Thessaly and Attica before the Greeks won the **naval Battle of Salamis** in 480 BC. A year later, the Persian land forces were also defeated by the Greek alliance at Plataea in Boeotia.

Athens as a major power

Within a few years after winning the Persian Wars, Athens gained a position of supremacy in Greece. The basis for this was primarily the decision to build a fleet and the uniting of all the major Greek cities in the **Delian League** in 478/477 BC to continue the campaign against the Persians. As Sparta had no interest in a policy of revenge against the Persian Empire, Athens took over the initiative of continuing the war and was able to bring those Greek cities that were formerly dependent on the Persians into her sphere of influence and bind them to her. And so an empire grew that included almost all of the Greek city-states of the Aegean, a major part of the Mediterranean area and the Black Sea region.

Age of Pericles

Around 450 BC, a change in Athenian politics developed. The newly elected **strategos** (general) Pericles (► Famous People) distanced himself increasingly from expansionist policies and intensified the democratization of the state. After the aristocracy, who had dominated the areopagus until then, had been deprived of power, the rights of the areopagus itself were curtailed in 462/461 BC. Almost all of the governmental decisions were made by the assembly, which had an adjunct council composed of 500 members elected annually and an army of officials assigned to it. The democratic principle of equality for all citizens, which however never applied to women, slaves or foreigners, was most clearly expressed in the principle of drawing lots, which determined the nine archons, the highest magistrates. There was still a political elite, however, that grew out of the circles of aristocrats and large landowners and whose members held

Cultural golden age ►

the office of the strategos in their hand. The expansionist foreign policies and the »democratic« domestic policy brought Athens an extraordinary cultural development. Craft and commerce were taken to undreamt of heights with goods from Attica being exported throughout the Mediterranean region. The Parthenon and the Propylaea were erected during Pericles' rule and **Phidias**, the most important sculptor of classical Greece, created the monumental statues of Athena and Zeus.

Sparta versus Athens

The differences between Sparta and Athens intensified in the 5th century BC. Sparta, which saw itself and its Peloponnesian allies increasingly threatened by Athenian power politics, declared war on Athens in 432 BC. Between 431 and 421 BC there were skirmishes,

Peloponnesian War ►

conquests and devastation in various locations throughout the whole of the Greek region without one belligerent or the other gaining any advantage. When Athens attempted to take Syracuse, Sparta came to the aid of the beleaguered city and inflicted a great defeat on the Athenian fleet. Finally, in 404 BC, Athens was forced to capitulate. Although the city remained independent and was allowed to retain its Attic lands, it was »demilitarized« and forced to replace its »democratic« system with an oligarchy. But over time, Sparta by itself was not up to its role of leadership in Greece. The rigid social structure had led to a drop in the number of full citizens (spartiates) during the previous two hundred years from 8,000 to 1,500. So it is certainly no surprise that resistance to Sparta's absolute rule soon began to stir. A Persian-supported alliance of Thebes, Argos, Corinth, Athens and the central Greek cities inflicted a devastating defeat on the Spartan army in 371 BC at Leuktra in Boeotia, destroying the myth of Sparta's invincibility. Theban forces even advanced to the city of Sparta itself and in the autumn of 370 BC forced the warrior city-state to relinquish its almost 300-year hegemony in the Peloponnese.

Hellenism

338 BC	Battle of Chaironeia
336 BC	Following the murder of Philip II, his son, Alexander, assumes the throne of Macedonia.
323 BC	Death of Alexander the Great
3rd century BC	The empire of Alexander the Great crumbles during the Wars of the Diadochi.

The old, traditional tribal structures still existed in the north of Greece in the 4th century BC. Rural tribes lived there with a king at their head. One of these tribal leaders, Philip II, was able to establish a powerful kingdom within a few years through territorial expansion and consolidation of his status as ruler of Macedonia. In 340 BC, the Macedonians moved against central Greece. A coalition of the major free city-states under the leadership of Athens had to admit defeat in the summer of 338 BC at the **Battle of Chaironeia**. Philip II prepared to conquer the Orient and in the spring of 336 BC crossed the Hellespont, but soon afterwards he was assassinated in the city of Aigai, the capital of Macedonia.

Philip II of Macedonia

After the murder of Philip in 336 BC, his son, Alexander (►Famous People) ascended to the throne and continued the campaign his father had begun, after crushing revolts with calculated brutality and prevailing against competition in Greece. When Alexander died at the age of 33 in 323 BC, he left behind to his rivalling successors, the **Diadochi**, territorial dominions that stretched from the Danube to the Nile and from the Adriatic to the Indus River. With all his en-

Alexander the Great

The larnax of Philip II is on display in the archaeological museum in Thessaloniki.

deavours to conquer the world, Alexander was left little time to order the conglomerate of subjugated countries into a unified state.

Alexander's legacy Even if Alexander's empire fell apart during the **Wars of the Diadochi**, his military campaigns had spread Greek culture and language over all of the Middle East and Egypt. Hellenism, characterized by a refining of the arts and a specializing in the sciences, left its mark on the ancient world of the time. Up until the time Rome intervened at the end of the 3rd century BC, a number of small dynasties and countless autonomous cities had been able to establish themselves, after years of violent power struggles, alongside three great monarchies, the Antigonides in Macedonia, the Seleucides in the Near East and the Ptolemies in Egypt.

Roman Domination

148 BC	Macedonia is incorporated as a province of the Roman Empire.
146 BC	Roman victory over the Achaean League
63 BC	Greece is made a Roman province.

The First Macedonian-Roman War (215–205 BC) ended in victory for King **Philip V** and strengthened his position of power in Greece; the Second Roman War (200–197 BC) put an end to Philip's aspirations of expansion. At first, under his son and successor, **Perseus** (179–168 BC), there was a balance in foreign affairs, but Rome's growing mistrust of Perseus finally lead to the Third Macedonian-Roman War, which ended in defeat for Perseus and his death. After a temporary period of autonomy, Macedonia was incorporated in the Roman Empire in 148 BC. Only two years after Macedonia's defeat, the fate of all of Greece was decided with the defeat of the **Achaean League**, an alliance of twelve Peloponnesian city-states that had opposed Rome's imperialist designs.

Conflicts, rapprochement and incorporation

Rome's goal was to occupy and transform the autonomous Greek city-states into a Roman province. When Athens sided against Rome in its war against the king of Pontus in northern Asia Minor, **Mithri-**

Greece becomes a Roman province

The remains of a Roman aqueduct on Lésbos

dates VI, the Roman general **Pompey** took away its special position in 63 BC and placed it under Roman provincial administration. The yoke of Roman exploitation only became lighter during the imperial period, when Augustus fostered governmental practices that stabilized the social structures of the Greek cities in favour of an aristocracy that was submissively dependent on Rome. Although the city-states had lost their power, Greece was able to preserve its cultural achievements and its influence had more of an effect on the neighbouring super-power than ever before.

The Eastern Roman/ Byzantine Empire

AD 395	The division of the empire by the Byzantine Emperor Theodosius seals the end of the Roman Empire.
527 – 565	Justinian I consolidates the Byzantine Empire.
7th century	Arabs conquer a major part of the Byzantine Empire.
c. 900	Greece comes under the hegemony of the Bulgars.
1054	Final break between the Orthodox and Roman Catholic churches
1204	Byzantine Empire divided up after Crusaders and Venetians take Constantinople
1453	Byzantine Empire falls to the Ottoman Turks

Fall of the Roman Empire

The Roman Empire was divided in the 4th century A.D. From the day in the year AD 330 when the first Eastern Roman and Christian emperor, **Constantine I**, chose the ancient city of Byzantion (Latinized Byzantium) to be his capital, until the end of the 14th century, Greece was part of the Eastern Roman Empire. The administrative division between the Eastern and Western empires had been made by Emperor Diocletian in around AD 300, and the two halves had gone their separate ways. The differences culminated in an issue of belief; Byzantium separated itself from Rome and introduced Christianity as the state religion in 391. The end of the Roman Empire came with its formal division in 395 by **Theodosius**. The Latin language and the Roman concept of empire increasingly lost importance and Byzantium was defined as the successor to the Greek culture of Antiquity. The onslaught of Germanic tribes that destroyed the Western Roman Empire also threatened Byzantium. In the early part of the 5th century, the Visigoths conquered Thrace, Macedonia, Thessaly, central Greece and the Peloponnese. Further danger in subsequent decades came from the raids of the Vandals, Ostrogoths and Huns.

Barbarian invasions ►

It was not until **Justinian I** (527 – 565) that the Byzantine Empire was secured outwardly and peace and order were restored internally. The Byzantine Empire also reached its greatest size in the decades of his rule. This splendour was past soon after Justinian's death. Once again, a time of changing influences and power relationships began for Greece when the Slavs allied themselves with the Avars and were able to settle the whole Balkan Peninsula.

The Arabs invaded the eastern Mediterranean in the 7th century, taking control of a large part of the Byzantine Empire and advancing as far as Crete, which remained Arab for almost a century and a half. Around 900, the Bulgars besieged the empire. Czar **Simeon I** advanced to the Gulf of Corinth. At the beginning of the 11th century, **Basil II**, the »Bulgar Slayer«, was able not only to win back Greece but also make West Bulgaria into a Byzantine province. The final schism between the Orthodox and Roman Catholic churches came in 1054. The death of Theodora in 1056, with whom the Macedonian dynasty also died out, plunged the empire into a violent crisis accompanied by civil

The monasteries of Metéora came into being during the Byzantine period.

wars. Its borders were also crumbling. Asia Minor became Turkish, the Normans conquered southern Italy and crossed over to Epiros. A military aristocracy took over power with the regency of **Alexios Komnenos** (1081 – 1118). But even they were unable to slow down the increasing loss of power of the central administration, the collapse of the economy and the signs of disintegration on the empire's borders. Alexios won the battle against the Normans only with the support of the Venetians. The country experienced a cultural flowering under his successor, **John II Komnenos** (1118 – 1143), but by the close of the 12th century the territorial disintegration of the empire could no longer be stopped. The Balkans once and for all slipped out from under Byzantine hegemony during the reign of Manuel I (1143 – 1180). There were revolts in Asia and, after taking Thessalonica in 1185, the Normans once again stood at the gates.

Late Byzantine Period In 1204, the soldiers of the Fourth Crusade, together with the Venetians, captured Constantinople. That was the end of the era of the Byzantine Empire, which the conquerors divided up amongst themselves. In the first quarter of the 13th century, during the reign of **Theodore I**, the **Empire of Nicaea** was built up. In 1254, a major part of the Aegean region was incorporated into this successor state of the Byzantine Empire. In 1261, **Michael VII** was finally able to recapture Constantinople. Once again, a Byzantine empire was created, but only for a short while. After the Ottoman Turks had occupied almost the whole of the Balkan Peninsula and had attempted numerous times to take Constantinople, the centre of the Byzantine Empire fell once and for all into the hands of Sultan **Muhammad II** in 1453.

Ottoman Domination

14th/15th centuries	The Ottoman Turks conquer Greece.
1571	Battle of Lepanto
1821–1827	Greeks struggle for independence from Turkish domination
1822	Greece's independence proclaimed at the first National Assembly of Epidauros
1830	The Ottoman Empire recognizes the independence of the Kingdom of Greece at the London Conference.

Conquest of Greece by the Ottoman Turks The expansion of the Ottoman Empire changed what until then had been a world of small and medium-sized Islamic and Aegean states into a unified sphere of Turkish power. Large parts of Greek territory had already come into Ottoman possession by the 14th century. The fall of Athens in 1456 marked the end of Turkish conquests.

Battle of Lepanto The Venetians became the Turks' most important opponents in the Mediterranean. For a century they fought over maritime trading privileges and Greek territory. Although a Venetian and Spanish alliance dealt the Turks a crushing defeat in the naval Battle of Lepanto in 1571, the Sultan was able to secure possession of all of Greece in the Treaty of 1573 because the victorious alliance showed itself to be in disaccord and Venice proceeded tactically with great caution. Like all other nations dominated by the Ottoman Turks, the Greeks also had the status of semi-citizens. This meant extensive religious freedom and the preservation of cultural identity. The Muslim ruling dynasty was able to integrate the subjugated peoples into their empire through a so-called **blood tax** (a levy of young men), who were raised to be a leadership elite in the military (the Janissary Corps), in the court and administrative apparatus.

While the first decades of Ottoman rule were marked by a prosperous economy, the tax burden greatly increased in the 16th century as a result of internal crises in the Turkish Empire. In order to evade the increasing exploitation of the rural Greek population by the Muslim ruling class, large numbers of villeins and dispossessed formed robber bands. Sultan Suleiman used Christian militia to fight them, out of which the future military leadership developed. They were to have a leading role in the Greek struggle for independence in the 19th century.

The resistance against the sclerotic Ottoman regime was organized in secret societies, the Hetairia Philike. Supported by Greek merchants in Constantinople, the Fanariots, and the Orthodox Church, they initiated a national uprising. Particularly the society of Philikes, founded in 1814 in Odessa and led by Prince Alexandros Ypsilanti, actively promoted revolts. In 1821, he crossed the Pruth River into Turkish territory with his voluntary corps, giving the signal for the national uprising against the sultan. Despite initial failures, the movement proclaimed a **Declaration of Independence** in 1822 at the first National Assembly of Epidauros. The intervention of Britain, Russia and France finally proved decisive in the battle. This alliance managed to utterly destroy the Ottoman-Egyptian fleet in 1827 at the battle of Navarin. **Count Kapodistrias**, who was in

The conquest of Rhodes Town by the Turks in 1522.

the diplomatic service of the czar and who gave up his office because of his commitment to the Greek nation, was elected the first Greek head of state and began building up the country's administration from out of Nauplion. The Ottoman Empire recognized the independence of the Kingdom of Greece at the **London Conference** of 1830.

... and reintroduc- tion of the monarchy ▶ publican parties found themselves in the minority against the conservative-royalist »People's Party«. Venizelos attempted in 1935 to regain power with a coup d'état, but failed. His only recourse was to emigrate to Paris. The army now seized the rudder. The monarchy was reintroduced under General **Ioannes Metaxas** with the help of a rigged referendum and, after twelve years, King **George II** once again sat on the throne. With the king's acquiescence, Metaxas took over the government in 1936 and dissolved parliament.

Second World War In order to avoid an Allied southern front, German forces invaded from out of Bulgaria in April 1941 and occupied Greece. Pogroms, mass executions and ruthless exploitation during the **Black Winter** of 1941/1942, when in Athens alone 50,000 people died of hunger, aroused the resistance of the population. The partisan war was shouldered primarily by the communists, the National Liberation Front (EAM) founded in 1941 and its military formations, and the

Territorial development of modern Greece

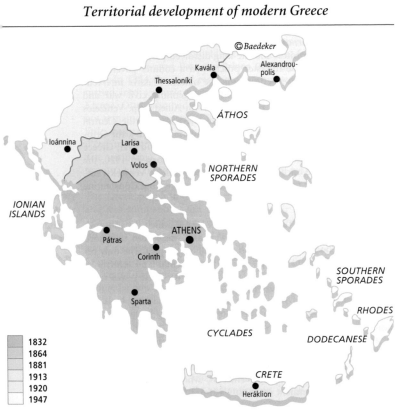

© Baedeker

Kavála
Alexandroupolis
Thessaloníki
ÁTHOS
Ioánnina
Larisa
Volos
NORTHERN SPORADES
IONIAN ISLANDS
Pátras
ATHENS
Corinth
SOUTHERN SPORADES
RHODES
Sparta
CYCLADES
DODECANESE
CRETE
Heráklion

1832
1864
1881
1913
1920
1947

Greek Liberation Army (ELAS) until the last German unit left Greece in November 1944.

After the withdrawal of the German occupiers, a conflict that had **Civil war** long been smouldering between the old political cliques and the communists flared into a civil war. The British intervened in December 1944 and helped the conservative National Guard win. The royalists gained the majority in the 1946 parliamentary elections and King **George II** returned from exile in Romania.

The Paris Peace Treaties of 1947 regulated the territorial claims in **Postwar years** the Balkans. Italy, which had occupied the islands of the Dodecanese since the Balkan Wars of 1912/1913, was forced to return them to Greece, thus giving Greece its present territorial extent. Domestically, the prime ministers of the subsequent years, **Alexandros Papagos** (1952 to 1955), **Konstantinos Karamanlis** (1955 – 1964) and **Georgios Papandreou** (1964 to 1967), pursued a Western orientation. Greece joined NATO in 1952 and in 1961 Karamanlis signed a treaty of association with the EEC.

> **? DID YOU KNOW …?**
>
> ■ … it was not until 1952 that women were allowed to vote in Greece?

The army staged a putsch on 21 April 1967. Colonels **Papadopoulos** **Dictatorship of** and **Pattakos** established a terror regime in Greece that elicited **the Colonels** growing protests at home and abroad. A counter-putsch by King Constantine II failed in December 1967. Against the provisions of the constitution, Papadopulos ordered the abolition of the monarchy in 1973. He proclaimed a republic and named himself president. A budding economic upswing collapsed altogether in the oil crisis and worldwide recession of 1973. Violent student unrest in Athens induced the fall of the dictatorship. The attempt to bring Cyprus com- ◄ Cyprus Crisis pletely under Greek control provoked Turkey's intervention. On 24 July 1974, in the face of a threatening war, the military turned over the power of state to former prime minister **Karamanlis**, who had been called back from exile in Paris.

New Republic

1975	Greece's new democratic constitution is ratified.
1981	Greece becomes member of EC
2002	Euro made official currency
2004	The Nea Dimokratia wins the parliamentary elections; Karamanlis becomes prime minister

Referendum for the republic

The political situation normalized with Karamanlis' »government of national unity«. The 1952 constitution was reinstated, with the exception of the provision on the form of state. On 8 December 1974, the Greeks decided in a free election for the parliamentary monarchy to be replaced by a republic. Still in the same year, Greece withdrew from NATO on the grounds that the alliance had been unable to prevent the Greek and Turkish conflict over Cyprus. June 1975 saw the ratification of a new democratic constitution that embodied basic rights. In 1979, the Greek government concluded a membership agreement with the EC that took effect in 1981. Greece once again became a full member of NATO in 1980.

1980s and 1990s

The Pan-Hellenist Socialist Movement (PASOK) led by **Andreas Papandreou** (► Famous People) won the parliamentary elections of 1981. By the end of the decade, the problems with the EC's open market gradually disappeared. The economy became stable, aided by a flourishing tourist trade and merchant fleet. After a four-year phase of transitional governments of varying coalitions led by the second largest popular party, the Nea Dimokratia (New Democracy), PA-

Konstantinos Simitis and his PASOK party emerged victorious in the close election of 2000.

SOK was able to regain a majority of votes in the parliamentary elections of 1993. In March 1995, the parliament elected independent **Konstantinos Stephanopoulos** as the new president. For reasons of health, Prime Minister Papandreou resigned in January 1996 and his successor, **Konstantinos Simitis** was able to secure a governing majority for PASOK in autumn 1996.

PASOK, led by **Simitis**, was able to stay just ahead of the ND in new **2000 – 2005** elections in 2000 with 43.8 % of the votes and an absolute majority in parliament, and was able to form a government. The euro was introduced as the official currency in Greece on 1 January 2002. The ND gained the majority in the March 2004 elections and **Kostas Karamanlis** became prime minister; **Karolos Papoulias** has been president since March 2005. In 2004, Greece's national soccer team, trained by the German Otto Rehhagel, won the UEFA European Football Championship.

The worst **forest fires** in decades raged in the Peloponnese in August **2007** and September, but Attica and Euboea were also badly affected. Seventy people lost their lives, 110 villages were destroyed and 260,000 ha/650,000 acres of land were laid waste – about the area of Luxemburg. In most cases, the fires were assumed to have been set by building speculators and fanned by hot temperatures. The conservative government of Karmanlis came in for criticism and was accused of passively standing by. The government promised funds as well as reconstruction and reforestation. Although Karamanlis and his ND lost votes in the **parliamentary elections** on September 16, he was able to defend his slim majority.

Art and Culture

Two of the ancient Seven Wonders of the World were in Greece: the Colossus of Rhodes and the statue of Zeus by Phidias in the Temple of Zeus at Olympia. But Greece is not just the homeland of famous statues; even today, the works of ancient Greek dramatists are being performed, Homer's »Odyssey« is being read and the myths of the Greek pantheon are being told.

Mythology

At almost all of the ancient sites visited in Greece, the visitor will come across the names of the gods venerated there, or the legends and myths linked to each of the places. The Greeks of Antiquity believed in a large number of deities who intervened in the affairs of men and even displayed astoundingly human characteristics. The origins of Greek mythology reach back into the 2nd millennium BC. The mythology of the gods was taken in part from other cultures, with recognizable Oriental, Aegean and Indo-Germanic influences.

The poets **Homer** and **Hesiod** brought the Greek gods into genealogical order. Uranos (heavens) and Gaia (earth), the primordial gods, ruled first; from them were descended the divine race of Titans (Oceanus and Thetys, Hyperion and Theia, Cronus and Rhea, Coeus and Phoebe). Zeus, the son of Cronus and Rhea, ended the reign of the »dark powers« by subduing the Titans and founding the rule of the Olympian gods. They took their name from the highest mountain in Greece, **Olympus**, which Homer had described early on as the abode of the gods.

Titans

> **? DID YOU KNOW ...?**
>
> ■ ... that the name Europe is derived from the Phoenician princess, Europa, who was abducted by Zeus while in the form of a bull?

Ruling along side Zeus, the almighty ruler of fate, was Poseidon, the god of the seas and Hades, the god of the underworld. Zeus' wife Hera was the goddess of marriage and birth. Among Zeus and Hera's progeny were Pallas Athena the goddess of wisdom, Apollo the god of light and prophecy, Artemis the goddess of the hunt, Ares the god of war, Aphrodite the goddess of beauty, Hermes the messenger of the gods and the god of trade, Hephaestus the god of fire, the forge and crafts, and Hestia the goddess of the hearth. Minor gods include the love god Eros, the nine muses (Clio, Melpomene, Terpsichore, Thalia, Euterpe, Erato, Urania, Polyhymnia and Calliope), the Charites or Graces, Themis and the Hores, Nike the goddess of victory, Iris the messenger of the gods, Hebe goddess of youth and Ganymede cupbearer to the gods. In addition, the sky deities, Helios (sun), Selene (moon) and Eos (dawn), can be added, as well as Asclepius, the god of medicine, Nemesis (punishment) the goddess of fate, and Tyche (fortune), plus the three Fates or Moirae: Clotho, Lachesis and Atropos. Among the earth gods were primarily Dionysus the god of wine, the nymphs, the satyrs and Silenus, as well as Pan the god of shepherds and flocks, and Demeter the goddess of fertility.

Olympian gods

← *Vase painting in old Corinth is a craft with a history going back thousands of years.*

Heroic legends Legends were not only woven around the gods, but also around heroes. In contrast to the gods, the heroes, usually the product of a mating of a god and a human, were mortal, but they possessed super-human abilities. The prime example of a hero of Antiquity is Heracles, but Perseus, Oedipus, Orpheus and Theseus are also famous figures of legend. The heroic legends are often based on historical fact and refer to actual persons. The Trojan epic cycle describes the battle for the city, the return home of the Greeks (»Odyssey«, ▶Baedeker Special p. 318) and Aeneas' escape from Troy (»Aeneid«).

Ancient Greek Art History

Early History

Neolithic period and the Bronze Age The oldest evidence of the production of art within the territory of present-day Greece dates back to the Neolithic period and the Bronze Age. It is attributed to two cultural areas, one in the southeast that includes Crete, the Dodecanese, the Cyclades and Sámos and one in central and northern Greece called the **Sesklo culture** after its most important excavation site, Sesklo, in Thessaly. Representative of this culture are polished red and black vessels, occasionally also exhibiting an incised pattern, painted crockery and idols formed of fired clay with clearly emphasized female sexual characteristics.

The **Dimini culture**, which started in Thessaly from 2900 BC and exhibited a close relationship to the Danubian countries, produced pottery that started narrow at the bottom and flared out to the top and was decorated with spiral patterns. During the transition from the Neolithic period to the Bronze Age, between 3200 and 2000 BC, an independent and very advanced culture developed on the Cyclades. The most famous artefacts of this early Cycladic period of art are the marble idols, characterized by slim figures and greatly simplified, geometric facial features.

Minoan Art
(c. 3300 – 1400 BC)

Early Minoan Period The Bronze Age civilization on the island of Crete is named after the legendary **King Minos**. Among the important cultural achievements of the Early Minoan period (about 3300 – 2100 BC), also called the **Protopalatial**, are the production of bronze artefacts and the introduction of the potter's wheel. Alongside simple houses, there were also already one to two-storeyed, palatial buildings. The dead were buried in chambered graves with some being richly provided with grave gifts.

Remains from the Minoan Protopalatial period: the west wing of the Palace of Knossós

The first great palace was built on Crete in the time from 2100 to 1750 BC in the Middle Minoan period. Profound political and economic changes on the island and the development of a priest-kingship were the social prerequisites for the creation of these monumental buildings that can be admired in **Knossós**, **Festós**, **Mália** and **Káto Zákros**. Besides the Minoan palaces, there are also grand villas, presumably used as summer residences, that have partially survived on Crete. **Gourniá**, in the eastern part of the island, conveys a vivid image of a Minoan city. The houses formed irregular city blocks transversed by narrow lanes.

Middle and Late Minoan Periods

Shaft graves, passage tombs and chambered graves dating from the Minoan period have been discovered on Crete in the vicinity of large settlements. The most elaborate tomb structures are the two-storeyed **temple tomb near Knossós** and the **royal tomb at Isopata**.

◄ Tomb Structures

In contrast to the cultures of the same period in Mesopotamia and Egypt, the sculptural work of the Minoans was limited to small items, i.e., pottery, goldsmithery, works in ivory and gem cutting and seal engraving. Ceramic art is comparatively well documented. The potter's wheel, introduced from Anatolia, and new firing techniques made the production of jugs with spouts possible.

◄ Crafts

Mycenaean Art
(1600 – 1150 BC)

During the heyday of Minoan civilization on Crete, the Peloponnese, above all the thickly populated region of **Argolis**, started developing

Palatial citadels

along its own lines. Mycenae, a city stronghold on the northern edge of the region, had held a position of supremacy in the Peloponnese since about 1600 BC. The culture, named after the fortress of Mycenae, exhibits recognizable Egyptian influences, as well as a close contact with the Minoan culture on Crete. Besides **Mycenae** itself, other important excavation sites are **Tíryns**, **Árgos**, **Asine** and **Pýlos**.

The most significant legacy of Mycenaean culture consists in the palatial citadels erected on commanding locations. In Mycenae and Tíryns, they were monumental, surrounded by walls built in a style called »cyclopean« because of the immense size of the stones used, whereas Pýlos has no fortification at all.

Graves ► There were **vaulted tombs** in many other places in the Peloponnese and on the Greek mainland besides Mycenae. Weapons and gold jewellery were enclosed with the dead in the 14th century BC **shaft graves** of Mycenae, including the famous gold mask discovered by Heinrich Schliemann preserved today in the National Museum in Athens.

The ruins of the palace fortress of Mycenae give only a hint of its former size.

The connection to Minoan art was very close in all areas of craftwork ◄ Crafts
– gold jewellery, face masks, clay, gold and bronze vessels, weapons
and armament, etc. – and above all in **pottery**. Pottery was imported
from Crete and imitated. Along with the shapes of vessels borrowed
from Crete, there were also characteristic local types like the Vafio
cup, a beaker with a profiled ring and a spiral decoration. A new, individual style developed about 1450 BC which also introduced figures into the ornamentation.

Geometric Art
(1050 – 700 BC)

Although individual technical skills and artistic traditions survived   **Vase painting**
the fall of the Mycenaean culture, the art that developed in direct
connection with the Dorian invasion (c. 1200 BC) in Greece represents a new beginning. The start was the »Geometric« art that is
named for its geometric lineal pattern. The Geometric style of art
knew no monumental buildings and no large sculptures; the artistic
development primarily took place in pottery painting. Circumferen-
tial ribbons of patterns consisting of concentric circles or semicircles
are typical.

Later, the meander, along with triangular and rhombic friezes, developed into the most important ornamental pattern. During the course
of the 8th century BC, in the **Late Geometric style**, pictures of people and animals appeared increasingly alongside the purely geometric
patterns, gradually supplanting the latter. The scenes depicted primarily had a connexion to death, like entombment and lamentation
of the dead, but there were also hunting and battles scenes and pictures of gymnasts, dancers and musicians.

Archaic Art
(700 – 500 BC)

Greece has the Archaic Period to thank for the introduction of life-   **Monumental**
size **statues** and **relief sculpture**, executed in marble or limestone,   **sculptures**
and usually painted in colour. The artists found inspiration for these
monumental sculptures in Egypt and in Oriental countries with
which the Greeks traded.

Large-scale sculpture developed into two special types of figures   ◄ Large-scale
called the **kore**, the clothed female, and the **kouros**, the naked youth.   sculpture
The three-dimensional and anatomically correct working of the body
increased in the later period even though the frontal, slightly for-
ward-stepping stance of the figure with the arms held to the side of
the body and fists clenched remained obligatory until the 6th century
BC.

When stone became established as the building material of temples   ◄ Pediment sculp-
and treasuries during the 7th century BC, large-scale relief figures al-   ture, tomb reliefs
so developed as building decoration for pediments and entablatures.

The **Temple of Artemis** in **Corfu**, erected around 600 BC, already had two sculpted pediments and metopes with reliefs. Characteristic of this early phase of relief sculpture is that the figures were in relatively flat relief. By the close of the Archaic Period, the sculptors had imbued their figures with three-dimensionality and freedom of movement, as can be clearly seen in the figures of the **Temple of Apollo** in **Erétria**. Relief also fulfilled an important function in the burial cult, which included full-length reliefs of the deceased decorating the narrow grave steles.

Vase painting

Pottery production presented a widely diverse picture at the start of the Archaic Period. There was a vast number of workshops, schools and artist signatures. Corinth, the Cycladic Islands, the eastern islands including Rhodes, as well as Athens and Attica, were centres of ceramic art. The **black-figure pottery** technique, i.e. a pale background with black human or animal figures, was first introduced in Corinth. The details and the drawing within the contours of the silhouette figures, in part very delicately executed, were engraved with a hard stylus. Usually scenes from mythology were the focus of the pictures. Not only were several figures represented, but different

Red-figure vase painting; Dionysus and his entourage

scenes were juxtaposed, frieze-like, with the heads on an equal level. Before the Attic black-figure vase painting style was replaced in the early 6th century by a new style, it reached a new zenith in the work of the potter and painter **Exekias**. Nine of his signed works have survived.

The new **red-figure** style developed while Exekias was creating his last works. Now the background was covered in black and the figures retained the reddish colour of the clay. The drawings within the contours were no longer incised but rather rendered in glossy black or diluted matt lines. The figures of such illustrations gain in plasticity compared with the black-figured silhouettes.

◄ Red-figure pottery

The Greek Temple

The beginnings of temple construction date back to the 9th century BC. The simplest form of temple – not a gathering place for the faithful but rather a place for cult images – derived from a basic form typical of Greek dwellings. The windowless, rectangular inner chamber of the temple, called the **naos** or **cella** (Latin for small chamber), stood in the early temples on a base of undressed stone. The entrance to the cella was usually located on the east side with the image of the deity opposite. The inner support, the pillars, beams and roof with gables on the narrow sides, were of wood and the flat saddle roof was decked with clay tiles. It was not until the second half of the 7th century BC that marble or limestone were used for all parts of the structure.

Development of temple building

The simplest of the various types of temple forms is the **templum in antis**, in which the porch, the pronaos, was formed by the protruding walls of the naos, called antae. Two columns supporting the pediment stood between the antae. An example of this form of temple is the **Treasury of the Athenians** in Delphí. If the rear of the naos also had a porch or opisthodomos, then it becomes a double anta temple, e.g. the Aphaia temple on Aegina. When the porch of such a temple has a row of columns in front of it supporting the pediment – as can be seen on the Acropolis in Athens in the east cella of the **Erechtheion** – then it is termed a prostylos or prostyle temple. If the row of columns is repeated at the rear of the structure, it is then called an amphiprostylos. An example of this is the **Temple of Nike**, likewise on the Acropolis in Athens.

Temple Forms

The most striking form of Greek temple after the second half of the 7th century BC is the peripteros, where the cella is surrounded on all sides by a colonnade, the peristasis. The classic proportions, used since the 5th century BC, called for the long side having twice the number of columns of the short side, plus one. The ratio in the Athenian Parthenon is 8 : 17, and in the Temple of Zeus at Olympía 6 : 13. The circular temple or **tholos** is a special form of secondary importance. It consists of a cella with a perfectly round ground plan,

◄ Peripteros

◄ Circular temples

Basic forms of Greek Temples

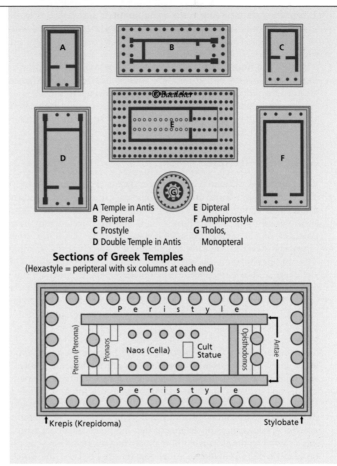

A Temple in Antis E Dipteral
B Peripteral F Amphiprostyle
C Prostyle G Tholos,
D Double Temple in Antis Monopteral

Sections of Greek Temples
(Hexastyle = peripteral with six columns at each end)

Peristyle

Pteron (Pteroma)

Pronaos

Naos (Cella) Cult Statue

Opisthodomos

Antae

Peristyle

Krepis (Krepidoma) Stylobate

surrounded by a circle of columns. Examples of this can be found in Delphi and in Epidauros.

Orders

The oldest of Greece's stone temples, like the Heraion in Olympía built around 600 BC, follow the Doric order.

Doric order ►

Characteristic of these buildings is an impression of being ponderous and squat. This is due in part to their relatively thick columns, tapering toward the top with between 16 and 20 flutings in their shafts and standing without a base directly on the stylobate, the top step of the temple foundation. The Doric capital, consisting of a circular convex moulding, the **echinus**, and a square slab, the **abacus**, bear the **architrave beams** with the frieze of sculpted triglyphs and flat or sculpted metopes. The triangular pediment consists of the **tympanum** framed by horizontal and raking (diagonal) cornices. Reliefs are found on the metopes and on the tympanum. The Ionic form of   ◄ Ionic temple is particularly suited for large temples as found on Sámos   order and at Ephesos, Sardes and Didyma in Asia Minor. An Ionic temple comes across as more gracile and more elegant than a Doric temple. The columns stand on a base, while narrow ridges between the fluting stress their vertical character. The characteristic elements of the capitals are the scrolled **volutes**.

The Corinthian order is the same as the Ionic, except for the capital.   ◄ Corinthian The Corinthian capital's sculpted decoration is in the form of large,   order deeply lobed **acanthus leaves** that encompass its round body, with tendrils swinging up to the corners of the concave abacus. The Corinthian order was particularly widespread during the time of imperial Rome.

Art of the Early Classical Age (490 – 450 BC)

The Doric style first appeared in its full flowering in the **Temple of**   **Architecture** **Zeus** at **Olympía** (470 – 456 BC). Along with the Parthenon in Athens, the Temple of Zeus, designed by the local architect, **Libon of Elis**, is considered to be one of the two most important temple buildings of the Greek Classical period. The dimensions of all its components are strictly based on a basic unit of measurement corresponding to the distance between two columns. The columns are twice as tall as the width of the bay between them. The outside colonnade with its 6 x 13 columns exhibits the classical proportions (1 : 2 + 1).

The first phase of Classical Greek art is also known as the »**Severe**   **Sculpture** **style**«, a term derived from the characteristics of the sculpture of this period. As most of the larger sculptures of the Classical Period have only survived as Roman copies, the smaller pieces, particularly the numerous **bronze statuettes**, are of great importance in the evaluation of the Severe style in art history. For example, the austere frontal position gave way to a slight turn of the head to the right. The eyes in the now empty sockets were originally of a different material that gave the statues a life-like expression.

One of the few original bronze statues to have survived from the   ◄ »The Charioteer Classical Period is the larger than life-size statue of a driver of a four-   of Delphi« horse chariot that is preserved today in the museum in Delphi and was created in all probability after one of the chariots belonging to the Sicilian tyrant **Polyzalus** won a victory at the Pythian games held in Delphí in 474 BC. Despite the stiff, stylized posture, a slight turning of the body foretells the departure from frontality and the three-dimensional working of the details heralds a new language of form.

Vase painting By the beginning of the 5th century BC, the black-figure vase painting had been almost completely supplanted by the Attic **red-figure pottery**. During the whole of the 5th century, Athens was the undisputed centre of pottery production in Greece. The red-figure style of painting offered far greater possibilities for drawing within the figure than the traditional black-figure technique, making the figures appear more three-dimensional. The painting style used on vessels connected with burial rituals, known as **lekythos** developed its own technique. Slender oil jars with long necks were decorated with pastel-like polychrome paints applied to a white background. The figures are drawn with delicate, almost fleeting brushstrokes and the gestures and facial expressions betray a high degree of emotional involvement.

Painting Vase painting was greatly influenced by wall painting. In the first half of the 5th century BC, **Polygnotus of Thassos**, whose works have only survived in descriptive references, was the most important representative of this art form. Among Polygnotus' innovations was to distribute his figures freely about the picture instead of positioning them all on one line; each figure had its own perspective.

Relief art As early as in the Archaic Period, narrow steles with flat reliefs were occasional replaced by free-standing funerary statues. The tradition of funerary reliefs continued in the Severe style, although with some innovations. When two figures were depicted in a relief, they were no longer placed one behind the other, but rather facing each other. The plasticity with which the figures emerge from the surface increased, as did the refining of the facial expressions and gestures.

High Classical Period (450 – 400 BC)

Architecture and sculpture Under the political leadership of **Pericles**, Athens rose to become the leading power in Greece around the middle of the 5th century BC Art, which stood in the service of politics and was fostered by it, also experienced a golden age in the time of Pericles. The **Acropolis**, which was destroyed by the Persians in 480/479 B.C, was redesigned as part of a gigantic building programme in Athens. Within about 50 years, the Parthenon, the Propylaea, the Temple of Athena Nike and the Erechtheion were erected on the rocky outcrop of the Acropolis.

Parthenon ▶ The Parthenon (447 – 438 BC) was the start, in which the Doric style was already being merged with Ionic elements. The columns are more slender than before and the interval between the columns was shortened at the corners so that the temple appeared as a whole better proportioned, streamlined and lighter than the only slightly earlier temple of Zeus. The cella was to receive the huge image of Athena Parthenos fashioned of gold and ivory created by the Athenian sculptor and architect **Phidias**. Pericles had charged him with the

Many famous works were created in the workshop of the sculptor Phidias in Olympía.

overall direction of the building of the temple in the 440s BC. He designed all of the sculptural decoration for the Parthenon – 92 metopes, a 160 m/525 ft frieze and the two immense pediment reliefs. But Phidias garnered most of his fame for his monumental statue of Zeus for the Tempel of Zeus in Olympía – one of the Seven Wonders of the Ancient World – and for the statue of Athena Parthenos, of which only Roman copies are still extant.

Late Classical Period
(400 – 330 BC)

The depiction of human beings in sculpture and vase painting became more differentiated; idealization and the monumental made way for an increase of interest in spiritual and psychological expression. In general, the late style of the Greek Classical period is termed »painterly«. What is primarily indicated by this term are formal qualities like integrating the figure into a spatial background and the enlivening of the surface through light and shadows. Praxiteles' career as a sculptor lasted from about 360 to 330 BC. His works are known only through Roman copies, except for one original, **Hermes and the Infant Dionysus**, from the Temple of Hera in Olympía. The

Sculpture, vase painting

◀ Praxiteles

sculpture is »painterly« insofar as it was conceived for viewing only from the front. Praxiteles went his own way, not only in design but also in his interpretation of the subject. He represents Apollo as a scarely-grown youth still playing childish games. With his statue of **Aphrodite of Knidos**, of which there are some 50 copies extant, he dared to be the first in Greece to portray a goddess naked. The leading sculptors of the Late Classical Period besides Praxiteles were Timotheos, Bryaxis, Skopas and Leochares. **Timotheos**, who created the marble acroterial figures on the pediment of the Temple of Asklepios in Epidauros around 380/370 BC, is considered the main master of the transitional period. **Skopas** was not only a sculptor but also an architect. Around 340 BC, he supervised the rebuilding of the temple of Athena Alea in Tegea that had burned down in 395 BC. The original bronze of »Apollo Belvedere« (Rome, Vatican Museum) was probably made by **Leochares**. **Bryaxis** was a pioneer in his youth of a modern style composed in diagonal axes. All four sculptors were involved in a building that, because of its great importance, was counted among the Seven Wonders of the Ancient World, namely the no longer extant **»Mausoleum«** of Mausolos, the king of Caria, erected in 353 BC at Halicarnassus (present-day Bodrum) on the coast of Asia Minor.

Lysippus ► Lysippus (c. 395 – 300 BC) is considered to be the one who perfected Late Classical sculpture and, at the same time, a forerunner of Hellenism. He is said to have produced over 1,500 works, although all that has survived are Roman copies. This is true even of his most famous work of an athlete cleaning himself with a scraping tool after a competition, **»Apoxyomenos«** (Rome, Vatican Museum). Lysippus does not show the glorious victor, but rather an exhausted competitor with a melancholy look on his face. With its relatively small head and heavily-built body, the statue conveys a realistic image of an athlete.

Funerary reliefs ► The figures of 4th century BC Attic funerary reliefs became more and more isolated from each other and emerged, statue-like, from the background of the relief. The architectural framing of the reliefs' images also gained in three-dimensionality.

Painting A new feeling of style that preferred painting over lineal drawing appeared in the monumental painting of the late 5th century BC and above all in the 4th century BC, but the works are only known from contemporary descriptions, vase paintings and copies. Illusionistic painting developed that simulated subtle depth through a representation of perspective and modulation with the aid of light and shadow.

Vase painting The Attic red-figure style of vase painting remained widely popular as well in the 4th century BC. Another technique, **Apulian vase painting**, named after the site in southern Italy where most of the vases were found, also developed parallel to it. Characteristic of this technique is the use of opaque white, red with a yellowish coloured glaze. The style developed in monumental painting is reflected here more than in Attic vase painting. But vase painting declined with the rising importance of panel and monumental painting and its production had almost come to a complete stop by the end of the 4th century BC.

Circular buildings were characteristic for temples in the Late Classical Period. The oldest is in the district of Athena Pronaia in Delphí. It is followed by the co-called Thymele of Epidauros. An outer ring of Doric columns and an inner ring of Corinthian columns were used in both buildings.

Temple architecture

Hellenistic Art
(323 – 27 BC)

The cultural period between the death of Alexander the Great (323 BC) and the creation of the Roman province of Achaia (27 BC) is designated as Hellenistic. During these three centuries, Greek art spread out as far as the Orient and was in turn permeated by Oriental influences. Emerging as the new centres of art along side the cities of the Peloponnese were the flourishing capitals of the newly independent parts of Alexander's empire, chiefly **Alexandria** and **Pergamon**.

Sculpture went through a change in style from the Late Classical to the Hellenistic periods under **Lysippus** and his school. A typical work of the early phase of Hellenistic art is the portrait statue of Demosthenes (Rome, Vatican Museum) created in 280 BC by **Polyeuktos** that is still distinguished by a realistic facial expression, a relatively austere, concentrated composition and a hard modelling. An increased amount of psychologising and dramatising in sculpures becomes noticeable in the course of the 3rd century BC. This can especially be observed in famous works like the figure of a dying Gaul, part of a large votive offering that **Attalos I of Pergamon** provided for the celebration of his victory over the Gauls in 230 BC (copy in the Capitoline Museum, Rome).

Sculpture

An even stronger impression of movement is given by the »Winged Victory of Samothrace« (190 BC; Paris, Louvre), which is thought to have originally been a monument celebrating the victory of Rhodes over Antiochos III of Syria. A spiral twisting of the body of **Nike, the winged goddess of victory**, takes place at the same time as its forward motion, leading the viewer around the statue, while the wind presses her thin garment to her body, allowing her contours to vividly emerge.

◄ »Winged Victory of Samothrace«

Architecture and architectural sculpture meld in the monumental Zeus Altar of Pergamon into a unique artistic whole (Berlin, Pergamon Museum). It was erected during the reign of **Eumenes II** (197 – 159 BC). A relief frieze, with turbulent scenes illustrating the

◄ Zeus Altar of Pergamon

battle of the Greek gods against the giants, runs around the complete base of the altar, which is surrounded by colonnades.

»Venus de Milo«, »Laocoön and his Sons« ▶

The frieze on the Pergamon Altar marks the high point and turning point in Hellenistic sculpture. The two major branches of the following period are represented by two world-famous works, »Venus de Milo«, created at the end of the 2nd century BC (Paris, Louvre), and »Laocoön and his Sons«. The bronze original of »Laocoön and his Sons« from around 140 BC has not survived, but the marble copy made in the 1st century BC by the three sculptors of the isle of Rhodes, **Hagesandros**, **Polydoros** and **Athanodoros** (Vatican Museum, Rome) has. The »Venus de Milo« goes back to the composition scheme of the Greek High Classical Period, whereas »Laocoön and his Sons« unites principles of the Classical approach, e.g., frontal positioning, with inner and external dynamics typical of Hellenistic statuary.

Architecture

The trading cities and their Hellenistic rulers, wanting a lavish display of their power, were the motor for the creation of Hellenistic architecture. Marketplaces, the focus of city life, were now laid-out according to plan and decorated with public buildings. Newly developed buildings were added like libraries and the stoa, a hall open on one of its sides with one or several rows of colonnades.

Roman Art
(2nd / 1st century BC – 4th century AD)

The Romans had begun »importing« and imitating Greek art and culture as early as the 2nd century BC. This did not change, not even after Greece was incorporated into the Roman Empire and the Hellenic city-states had become politically of no consequence.

Sculpture

Portrait sculpture developed more and more into a specialized »Roman« genre. What in Greek portraiture until then was usually a statue of a complete person and, as a rule, more or less in a stylized form, the sculptors now began working more toward modelling the facial features as individual and realistic as possible.

Relief

During the Roman period, relief art, as well as the statues of emperors and great generals, were intended to pay tribute to the Roman Empire. An example is the **Arch of Galerius**, erected around 300 B.C in Thessaloníki, on which the victorious Roman army is immortalized in battle and marching scenes.

Architecture

A number of architectural styles were slightly modified under Roman rule. So it was that the odeon, for example, developed from the Greek theatre. Also a number of typical Roman structural forms, like the triumphal arch, aqueduct and baths, were adopted. Moreover, the Roman understanding of vaulting techniques made larger and

The style of Roman living on Kos: the Casa Romana Villa in Kos Town

more daring structures possible than during the era of Hellenism. Greek Classical forms, however, remained the favoured style.

Marvellous Roman mosaic floors have survived not only on the Greek mainland, but also on the larger islands. As wall paintings in private dwellings have been lost, the mosaics alone convey an impression of domestic life in Roman cities and country residences.

Mosaics

Byzantine Art
(4th – 15th century AD)

The founding of Constantinople in 330 BC and the division of the Roman Empire into East and West 65 years later brought the eastern Mediterranean region a new cultural heyday that lasted until the Byzantine Empire fell in 1453. The architects, painters and sculptors of the Byzantine Era no longer sought and found their inspiration in ancient Greek art, but rather in the Christian art of Late Antiquity.

The first churches were built on Greek soil when Christianity was adopted as the state religion in the 4th century. The dominant style of early Christian church buildings was the **basilica**. In this type of building, which had developed out of the Roman market basilica, the nave is accompanied by one or two lower flanking aisles. The church has a particular orientation: the altar is in the east and the entrance

Architecture

Dome-crossing
Church ►

with a narthex in front of it, often with an atrium, in the west. In the course of the centuries, the ecclesiastical building developed more and more away from an oriented and towards a centrally planned structure with equal-length axes. A new type became established in the 9th century throughout the Byzantine trading area, the church with a dome crossing. Above the crossing of the transepts, which were usually equally long and decked with barrel vaulting, sat a central dome born by supports or pillars. The sanctuary is separated by a stone barrier which later evolved into the **iconostasis** (picture wall). On either side are two smaller apses liturgical purposes, called the **prothesis** and the **diaconicon**. Accordingly, the church has, as a rule, three apses on the east side. The decorating of the church was governed by an iconographic scheme guided by the concept that the church interior should reflect the heavenly hierarchy.

Painting

Byzantine painting ranges from monumental to miniature, from icons to frescoes and mosaics. Early Byzantine painting was already strongly intertwined with cult practices and had been dedicated to portraying humans from the beginning. Strict frontal positioning established itself in the 4th century. In the depiction of groups, the heads of the people shown were all at the same height with the main figure rendered larger than the minor figures. The **Iconoclastic Controversy** of the 8th/9th centuries temporarily ended this tradition. The banning of illustrations of Christ and the saints allowed only ornamental designs. The dominant form of panel painting was the **icon**. The transportable cult images with pictures representing the saints and biblical scenes are to this day a main pillar of the Orthodox faith. They are to be found not only in churches, but also in the private homes of the believers. Originally, only priests were allowed to produce icons because icon painting was considered to be a **liturgical act**. The main subject matter was and is the portrayal of the Madonna and Child with composition, colours and material subject to fixed guidelines.

Ottoman Period (15th – 19th centuries)

The almost 400-year rule of the Ottoman Turks in Greece began in 1456 with the capture of Athens and the subsequent taking of the whole of the Peloponnese. Post-Byzantine art on the Balkan peninsula no longer had anywhere near the importance it had had in past

*The icon of Mary from the Skiádi monastery
»travels« from one village to another during
Lent and is honoured everywhere with
processions, masses and festivals.*

SACRED IMAGES

Icons, which are objects of special veneration by believers and often associated with old legends, form an essential part of the tradition of popular Orthodox beliefs.

The **transportable cult images** with the representations of saints and Biblical scenes are called icons (images) in the Orthodox Church. Along with the Holy Scriptures, they remain even today a pillar of the Orthodox faith. Besides in churches, they can also be found in many homes and vehicles. They are adorned with gems, costly draperies, rings and clocks, taken along on trips and the destination of pilgrimages.

Bringing the saints near

Icons bring the saints close to mankind, which is why they enjoy great veneration. This veneration is not directed at the image, but rather at the saint who is identified with the icon. In the churches, icons are arranged according to a specific pattern on the **iconostasis**, a high, wooden screen separating the chancel from the congregation. The icon of the saint whose feast day it is is displayed on the stand in the centre.

Artistic restrictions

The painting of icons is regarded as a liturgical act, which originally only priests were allowed to perform. The icon's composition, colouring and materials are precisely prescribed so that the painter has hardly any freedom in the design of the illustrated

*Icons are a pillar
of the Orthodox Church*

work and cannot develop an individual style. The painter may not put any personal expression in the pictures and remains nameless. His job is to maintain the tradition. That is why many icons look the same, regardless of which century they date from.

The **unique colouring** of the pictures, achieved through a complicated production process, draws the viewer closer. The technique is usually mineral paint on wood, which is covered with a layer of boiled linseed oil. This guarantees an incredible durability, particularly since the icons are not only looked at, but also kissed, touched and passed around. Many ancient founding legends are woven around miracle-working icons.

The Suleiman Mosque, a relic from the Ottoman period

centuries, but Turkish rule allowed enough latitude for Byzantine-influenced art to continue. The most prominent examples of the continuation of its architecture during the Ottoman period are the **Monastery of Metéora**, the monastic buildings on the Holy Mount **Áthos** and the numerous churches built in the northern Greek city of **Kastoriá**.

Modern Greek Art History

Architecture

Traditional building methods

The traditional methods of building in Greece was characterized primarily by the climatic conditions and the materials available on site. Thus stone houses are typical in Epirus, clay structures in Thessaly, wood-covered façades with bay windows in Thrace and white-washed cube-shaped houses on the Cyclades. On the other hand, the various occupying forces also left their mark on the country's architecture. Anatolian building methods can be seen predominantly in the north of the country and the influence of the former Frankish masters is apparent in the old part of town on the Cycladic island of Náxos, and the construction methods of the English and French are evident in the Ionian Islands, especially on Corfu. The founding of the modern state of Greece in 1832 was not only a political turning-point, but also had an effect on urban development. Greece came

Urban development ►

under the influence of Western Europe and its culture. This was most distinctly manifested in the two largest cities of the country, **Thessaloníki** and **Athens**. The way the cities look today did not evolve over centuries but is the product of the last 200 years. A large part of Thessaloníki's buildings were destroyed in a great fire in 1917. Before King Otto arrived in 1833, Athens was an insignificant provincial town with nothing much left of it after the War of Liberation. So the city planners, above all **Leo von Klenze**, had a free hand in every

i **Modern Greek Art**

■ The National Gallery in Athens (open Mon and Wed 9am – 3pm, 6pm – 9pm, Thu – Sat 9am – 3pm, Sun 10am – 2pm) and the beautifully designed Vorres Museum in Peanía, not far from Athens (open Sat and Sun 10am – 2pm) offer an overview of Greek art work of the last 100 years.

respect in implementing **Neo-classicism** in numerous official buildings, including the parliament building, the academy and the university.

Visual arts

The establishment of an art academy and a school of applied arts in Athens provided for the development of visual arts in the modern state of Greece in the second half of the 19th century. Along with representatives of the traditional monument art and history painting, there were also a handful of artists who developed their own style and form of expression, like the sculptor **Giannoulis Chalepa** (1851 – 1938), whose works encompass styles extending from Realism to Expressionism, and **Michael Tombros** (1889 – 1974), whose palette of expression ranges from Naturalism to an abstract, expressive style. **Georgios Gounaropoulos** (1890 – 1977) was a member of the »Generation of the 30s«, who attempted to present what was typically »Greek« in art. After the Second World War, the Greek art scene was decisively influenced by the styles of Western Europe and North America. Because of political and social conditions, though, many young artists found themselves compelled to leave their homeland in the 1950s and 60s to realize their ideas elsewhere. Among them were the internationally renowned sculptors **Takis** (born 1925) and **Giannis Kounellis** (born 1936; ►Famous People). Takis ended up in Paris in the 1960s where he worked on objects with magnetic fields and sounds, and kinetic sculpture.

Customs and Folklore

Even if the Greek national costume has more or less disappeared from everyday life, it is still occasionally possible to see people wear- **National costumes** ing it on festive occasions, particularly in rural areas. One component of the men's folk dress is the **foustanélla**, a short kilt trimmed with small bells and coins, usually worn together with a white shirt and an embroidered waistcoat. On Crete, men still often wear the characteristic pleated, black baggy trousers, the **vráka**, and tie on a black headscarf. Old costumes are also sometimes worn on Kárpathos, in the south of Rhodes and on Corfu, as well as in the Píndos mountains of central Greece. The colourful uniform of the former royal bodyguard, the **Evzones** – the »finely girded« – which was derived from the Albanian folk costume, is still worn today by, among others, the Athenian Parliament guard of honour.

! **Baedeker** TIP

Sirtos and Pidik Dances
Authentic Greek folk dances are performed by the famous Athenian Dora Stratou Dance Theatre, residing in the Filopáppos Theatre (May – Sept Thu – Sun 10.15pm, Wed and Sun also c. 8.15pm; tickets: Skoliou 8, Pláka, tel. 21 09 24 43 05).

Folk dances Music and dance have always gone hand-in-hand in Greece. Ancient vases show a profusion of dancers and, according to legend, Zeus'

The traditional costumes are worn these days almost only on holidays.

mother, Rhea, personally taught her priests the original dance figures. Choreographically there are two major dance forms today, the **sirtos dances** with more moderate dance movements and the tempestuous, occasionally almost acrobatic **pidikhtos dances**, with each island and every region of the mainland having developed its own style and variations. They are fostered today by clubs and folk dance groups and performed on festive occasions. The Greek circle dances in which the dancers hold hands or a handkerchief have only recently been danced by mixed couples; originally they were performed with the sexes separated.

Famous People

Whoever hears the word Greece automatically thinks of great philosophers like Aristotle und Plato, the poets Homer and Sappho or the military commander, Alexander the Great. But it was not just in ancient times that there were Greeks who shaped the image of their country, and also the world.

ΑΡΙΣΤΟΤΕΛΗΣ

Aeschylus (525 – 456 BC)

Aeschylus is the founder of the tragedy in the modern sense. Origi- **Poet**
nally, tragedies were, as their name says, cultic »goat songs« in honour of the god Dionysus (»trágos« = goat and »oidé« = song). Aeschylus revolutionized the form of tragedy by having two actors appear
along with the chorus instead of only one, which was traditional until then. This made dialogue and real dramatic action possible for the
first time. From that point, the chorus only had the function of in-
terpreting the actors' dialogue. The main subject of the tragedies of
Aeschylus is the fateful tension between gods and men who are heading toward certain downfall if they rebel against the gods. Only seven
of Aeschylus' 90 tragedies have survived, among them »The Persians«, »Prometheus Bound« and »The Oresteia«.

Alexander the Great (356 – 323 BC)

The son of and successor to the Macedonian king Philip II launched **Military leader**
a »Pan-Hellenic campaign of revenge« against the Persians as the
commander of the Greeks in 334 BC. He defeated the Great King of
Persia, Darius III in 333 BC at the Battle of
Issos (Turkey). This opened the way to
Egypt, where Alexander founded the city of
Alexandria and had his divine lineage and
right to rule confirmed by the Oracle of Zeus
(Amun). From Egypt, Alexander marched
his army to Babylonia and then on to Persia.
His Indian campaign (327 – 325 BC) took
him to the river Hyphasis and to Beas in
what is now the Punjab. The goal of the rest-
less conqueror, to meld the heterogeneous
parts of his newly created empire culturally
and politically, was condemned to fail: The
empire immediately fell apart under the Diadochi, his direct successors.

Archimedes (around 287 – 212 BC)

Archimedes, a Greek born in Syracuse on Sicily, left to posterity a **Mathematician**
whole series of fundamental contributions to the fields of mathematics and applied mechanics, and he not only expanded abstract
mathematics, including the measurement of geometric planes and
the volume of solid objects, but also practical engineering. The devi-
ces he constructed, such as the pulley and diverse war machines including a crane-like arm with a grappling hook and an improved cat-

← *The philosopher Aristotle lived for a time at the court of Philip II of*
Macedonia as tutor to the prince, Alexander (the Great).

apult, appeared to his contemporaries like technical marvels. A statement Archimedes made about an immersed body's buoyancy has been known ever since as »Archimedes' Principle«.

Aristotle (384–322 BC)

Philosopher Aristotle went to Athens at the age of 18 and was a member of Plato's academy for about two decades. After Plato died in 347 BC, he settled in Assos in Asia Minor and later in Mytilene on the isle of Lésbos. In 343 BC, he was called to the Macedonian court by King Philip II to tutor his son, Alexander. In 334 BC, Aristotle returned to Athens where he founded a school of philosophy. After Alexander the Great died, he was accused of not holding the gods in honour and fled to Chalcís on the island of Euboea, where he soon died. Of his very considerable œuvre, a number of his systematic treatises have survived. They cover the fields of logic, natural sciences, metaphysics, ethics, politics and art theory. Turning his back on the dualism in Plato's thought, Aristotle attempted to order empirical knowledge into a universal system, bringing together all fields of science of his time.

Bouboulina (1771–1825)

Freedom fighter Many legends have grown up around the famous heroine of the Greek War of Independence. Laskarina Bouboulis, known by her nickname »Bouboulina«, lost two husbands in the war against Algerian pirates. The pugnacious widow bought her own ship, the »Agamemnon«, with the sizable fortune she had been left and sailed off to do battle against the Ottomans in the naval blockade of Nafplion. Her turbulent life – it is said she had innumerable love affairs – also did not end without drama. She died in her house in Spétses during a violent family quarrel, by a gunshot to the head.

! **Baedeker TIP**

Greek Heroine

Those interested in the remarkable freedom fighter, Bouboulina, and her adventurous life should not miss the museum dedicated to her on the Island of Spétses.

Maria Callas (1923–1977)

Singer No singer of the 20th century is more deserving of the title of »Primadonna assoluta« than Maria Calogeropoulos, known as Maria Callas. Prized by music experts and the tabloid press alike, she remained nonpareil for over 20 years on the opera stages of the world. The daughter of a pharmacist who had emigrated to the USA, she began her career in 1938 in Athens, where she had studied under Elvira de Hidalgo at the Athens Conservatoire. Her breakthrough came in 1947 in the Arena di Verona with the title role in »La Gioconda«

by Amilcare Ponchielli. Although critics found fault with a certain inconsistency in her voice, she sparkled with an incomparable coloratura technique and acting presence. Along with her activities as a singer, she also worked as a teacher and film actress and director. Thanks to her committed efforts, a number of operas that had disappeared from the repertoire of the world's opera houses were performed once again.

Maria Callas and Aristotle Onassis (left), an ideal couple for the popular press

Odysseas Elytis (1911 – 1996)

Poet

Odysseas Elytis was born in Iráklion, Crete, and spent his childhood in Athens where he studied law and remained until his death. He belonged to the group that had gathered around Giorgos Seferis, who had renewed modern Greek poetry in the 1930s. Elytis wrote surrealistic poems marked by an affinity to nature. His major work, »To axion esti«, a volume of poetry published in 1959, was set to music by Mikis Theodorakis. He received the Nobel Prize for Literature in 1979.

Euripides (c. 485 – 406 BC)

Tragedian

Euripides is regarded as the founder of the psychological drama, the character tragedy. His dominant theme was Protagoras' aphorism, »Man is the measure of all things«. In his tragedies, the gods no longer control the destiny of man, but rather man acts independently, lives his own life and struggles through completely personal conflicts. Of his 90 or more dramas, 18 have survived intact and are performed to this day, including »Alcestis«, »Electra« and »Orestes«. Almost all of Euripides' great dramas have served as the basis for modern works by, among others, Corneille, Racine, Goethe, Schiller, Grillparzer and Sartre.

El Greco (around 1541 – 1614)

Painter

El Greco (Spanish »The Greek«) was born as Domenikos Theotokopulos around 1541 on Crete. He learned icon painting as a child in his homeland. As a young man, he went to Venice where he also worked in Titian's studio. Later he lived in Rome and, after 1577, in Toledo. Along with his religious works, he created numerous compelling portraits and landscapes. His style is characterized by elongated, sinuous figures, expressive colouring and unreal light effects that imbue his paintings with an impression of the ethereal and the supernatural.

Herodotus (c. 490 – c. 425 BC)

Historian Herodotus, whom Cicero referred to as the »Father of History«, was born in Halicarnassus, present-day Bodrum, Turkey. He critically observed the countries he travelled through as well as writing political reports. The highpoint of his work is his portrayal of the Persian wars. Herodotus's narrative account, whose reliability has been frequently substantiated, is not only an impressive document about Greek Asia Minor, where he lived, but also a source of valuable ethnological and geographical information about the countries of Asia Minor and Africa.

Hippocrates (c. 460 – c. 370 BC)

►Baedeker Special p. 353

Homer (c. 8th century BC)

Smyrna, today's Izmir in Asia Minor, claims, probably rightly, to be the birthplace of Homer, the legendary first epic poet of the Western world. Even today, it cannot be said with certainty that the creator of the »Iliad« and the »Odyssey« was actually an historical person or a

Homer, the fabled author of »The Illiad« and »The Odyssey«

kind of collective term for the older Greek epics. The prevailing opinion today is that Homer existed as an actual person and lived on the west coast of Asia Minor. He probably composed his great works by using older and shorter oral folk epics. The »Iliad« and the »Odysse«y were subjected to all kinds of alterations and enhancements in subsequent years. Furthermore, the »Homeric Hymns and Epigrams«, the comic epic of the imbecile »Margites« and the »Batrachomyomachia«, or the »Battle of Frogs and Mice«, are also attributed to Homer.

Nikos Kazantzakis (1883 – 1957)

The writer, Nikos Kazantzakis, was born in Iráklion on the island of **Writer** Crete and studied law in Athens and afterwards philosophy and political science in Paris. He returned to Greece after his studies and held a ministerial post from 1945 to 1946. His literary works – descriptions of his many travels, stories, novels and poems – are marked by penetrating descriptions, fresh, original language, abundant lyricism and profound philosophical insight. Kazantzakis gained international fame with his 1946 novel »Alexis Sorbas«, which is set on his home island of Crete (►Baedeker Special, p. 260).

Giannis Kounellis (born 1936)

Giannis Kounellis takes an important place among the contemporary **Artist** Greek artists that have made the leap into the international art scene. Kounellis, who has lived in Rome since 1956, became known worldwide at the end of the 1960s as one of the leading proponents of Arte Povera. During this period of his work, he often combined animals with impoverished environments to stress the contrast between living nature and a meagre art object. Historical cultural connotations have become an essential part of his installations since the 1970s. Everyday articles and ancient materials are combined in his works with pathos formulae of art history, e.g., gold paint, plinths or Classical sculptures.

Melina Mercouri (1925 – 1994)

The title Melina Mercouri gave her 1971 autobiography says it all, »I **Actress,** was born Greek«; the military junta had just taken away her Greek **politician** citizenship while she had been abroad passionately spreading propaganda against the dictatorship of the Colonels. Melina Mercouri was already a famous actress and a distinguished chanson singer when the military staged their putsch in 1967. The daughter of a former minister of the interior and granddaughter of a long-time mayor of Athens had her greatest success under the direction of her husband, Jules Dassin, in 1959 with the film »Never on Sunday«. She played the spirited and warm-hearted prostitute, Ilya, and sang the song

»Never on Sunday« that became a huge hit. After her return from exile, she became involved in politics and was in the PASOK cabinet for two legislative periods as minister of culture.

Aristotle Onassis (1906 – 1975)

Shipping magnate His immense wealth made Aristole Onassis a legend even during his lifetime. Accounts of his life in the jet set, about the tragedies in his family, his affair with opera singer Maria Callas and his marriage to Jacqueline Kennedy, the widow of John F. Kennedy, filled the gossip columns of the popular press during the 1960s and 70s. The nucleus of the Onassis empire was the shipping firm he founded in 1932/1933, which was supplemented later by Olympic Airways and international banking and real estate businesses. The first film about the life of the shipping magnate appeared only two years after his death in 1977 with the title »The Greek Tycoon«, which had Anthony Quinn taking on the role of Aristotle Onassis.

Andreas Papandreou (1919 – 1996)

Politician Andreas Papandreou stands equally for a new self-confident Greece after the régime of the colonels, as well as for old style autocracy. Before he became the defining political personality of the 1980s, politician Georgios Papandreou's son led a chequered life. While he was studying law and economics in Athens, he had already become active against the dictatorship of General Metaxas. He was arrested in 1939 and emigrated the following year to the USA, where he taught at a number of colleges until 1960. He was a member of the Greek parliament from 1964 until 1967 and was a minister in his father's cabinet in 1965. After going into exile again during the military dictatorship, Papandreou founded the Pan-Hellenist Socialist Movement (PASOK). Burdened by scandal and charges of corruption, Papandreou was forced to resign as prime minister in 1989. He was cleared of the accusations in 1992 and helped PASOK to regain a parliamentary majority in 1993.

Pericles (c. 490 – 429 BC)

Statesman Greece's Classical period is inseparably linked with the name of the great Athenian statesman. Under Pericles, Athens rose to become a major power and the cultural centre of Greece. Pericles was the leader of the democratic party from 461 BC on and, after 443 BC, he was first the elected strategos (military leader) and then the sole leader of the state. Among his domestic reforms were the introduction of a daily expense allowance for the council and people's court and the admittance of citizens of the lowest census class to almost all offices. Pericles was a great patron of the arts and sciences and under him the Acropolis in Athens was given its classic form.

Plato (427 – 347 BC)

Philosopher

Plato, a native of Athens, was one of the most significant philosophers of ancient Greece, and possibly the greatest. He was of Attic aristocratic lineage, was a student of Socrates for eight years, then travelled throughout lower Italy and Sicily and finally ended up in Athens again as a freed slave. In the 380s BC he founded his own school there, the Academy, where the philosopher Aristotle was trained. The core of Plato's philosophy is the »Theory of Forms«. Plato expanded on the philosophy of his teacher, Socrates (who introduced a number of general concepts for behaviour, including justice), to include everything that has to do with man. There is a »generic term« for everything that exists, an archetype, an idea. Plato's philosophical works have survived almost without exception. Not all of the writings that bear his name, however, were really written by him. Socrates, who had exercised a decisive influence on Plato, is the central figure in the famous dialogues that contain dialectic discussions of values.

Pythagoras (c. 570 – 496 / 497 BC)

Mathematician

Who does not know the mathematical theorem, $a^2 + b^2 = c^2$, named after the famous philosopher, but probably known before his time? Pythagoras himself left behind no writings and his students were sworn to secrecy. He left his birthplace, Sámos, around 530 BC, allegedly to escape the tyranny of Polycrates, and founded a philosophical and religious society of Pythagoreans in Croton in lower Italy. He was venerated by his disciples even during his lifetime as a perfect sage. The Pythagoreans considered numbers to be the essence of all things, as the principle of a »world harmony«. It is likely that the theory of the transmigration of the soul can be traced back to Pythagoras.

Pythagoras – mathematician, philosopher or actually more of an »ancient guru«?

Sappho (7th / 6th centuries BC)

Sappho, the Greek **poet** born about 600 BC on the island of Lésbos, is considered to be the greatest female lyric poet of Classical

Antiquity. Plato counted her as the tenth of the nine muses and Horace named the »Sapphic stanza« after her. She headed a society in Mytilene, the capital city of Lésbos, in which young women were instructed in the art of poetry and dance before their marriage. When aristocrats were banished from Lésbos, she went temporarily to Sicily. She is said to have thrown herself from the Leucadian cliffs out of an unrequited love for the handsome Phaon. Sappho's rich lyrical works – primarily hymns to the gods as well as wedding and love songs – have only survived in fragments.

Giorgos Seferis (1900 – 1971)

Writer The writer Giorgos Seferis was born in Smyrna, present-day Izmir, in Asia Minor as the son of a university professor. He studied jurisprudence in Athens and Paris and joined the Greek diplomatic service. He was his country's ambassador in London, among other places. The beginning of modern Greek poetry is connected to the publishing of his first volume of poetry »Strofi« (»Turn«) in 1931. At first oriented toward pure symbolism with T. S. Eliot as a model, Seferis soon found his own language. This is clear in his volume of poetry published in 1935, »Mythistórima« (»Tale of Legends«), in which he brings to mind the fateful afflictions suffered on Greek territory. Seferis was awarded the Nobel Prize for Literature in 1963.

Socrates (c. 470 – 399 BC)

Philosopher The Greek philosopher Socrates is regarded as one of the pivotal figures in Western philosophy. Plato's teacher left behind no writings;

his teachings have only survived in the writings of his students. Socrates taught by discussing his thoughts while taking walks and in small discussion groups. His basic assumption that man knows nothing about himself ran counter to the wisdom of the sophists that was in vogue at the time and led the way to Plato's »Theory of Forms«. Socrates was convinced that wise thinking necessarily produces ethically correct action. The fact that he himself acted according to this maxim did not always earn him goodwill. In 399 BC, Socrates was brought before a court for allegedly corrupting the minds of the youth of Athens. He was sentenced to death and died by drinking a cup of hemlock.

Solon (c. 640 – after 561 BC)

The name of the statesman and poet Solon is closely tied to the development of democracy in the city-state of Athens and the levelling of the social classes. As the highest magistrate with almost dictatorial powers (archon), he settled the disputes between the aristocracy and the farmers in 594 BC and to a great extent abolished debt bondage. In his major reform work, Solon, who is counted among the Seven Sages of Antiquity, reorganized measurements, weights and coinage and created the foundation for a code of laws.

Statesman

Solon was instrumental in the »democratization« of Athens.

Mikis Theodorakis taught himself how to compose and write songs as a child. He then gave his first concert at the age of seventeen.

Sophocles (c. 495 – c. 406/405 BC)

Tragedian Sophocles, along with Aeschylus and Euripides, was one of the most successful of the Attic tragedians. He increasingly reduced the appearance of the chorus in his plays and introduced a third actor, enabling him to develop real characters to a greater extent, although they were still subject to the will of the gods, whose omnipotence only becomes clear to man at the end of a painful process of recognition. Sophocles also held high offices. He was strategos from 441 until 439 and a member of the oligarchical government from 413 until 411. Of his 130 or so plays, only seven have survived, including »Antigone«, »Oedipus the King« and »Electra«.

Thales (c. 625 – c. 545 BC)

Philosopher, The Greek philosopher, astronomer and mathematician, Thales of
mathematician Miletus – one of the Seven Sages of Antiquity – founded Ionian naturalistic philosophy, according to which water constituted the principle of all things. He assumed that inorganic material has a soul and that animation, or the power to act, can be traced back to the actions

of a soul that controls everything. Knowledgeable in astronomy, it is said he predicted the solar eclipse of 585 BC. The theorem in geometry named after him (»Thales' Theorem«) – any triangle in a semicircle with the diameters as the base has a right-angle – was already known to the Babylonians.

Mikis Theodorakis (born 1925)

The Greek composer and singer, Mikis Theodorakis, studied in Athens and Paris under the composer Messiaen. He was a member of the Greek parliament for the United Democratic Left from 1963 until 1967 and was imprisoned for three years after the 1967 putsch. Living in exile from 1970 to 1974 in Paris, Theodorakis tried to enlist support for the democratic movement in his homeland in numerous political solidarity rallies and concerts. He returned to Greece in 1974 after the end of the military dictatorship and continued his work as a member of parliament in the 1980s. His musical work, which is strongly influenced by Greek folk music, is marked by his political commitment. Theodorakis' compositions include orchestral works, stage and film music, songs and oratorios.

Composer

Eleftherios Venizelos (1864 – 1936)

The lawyer and statesman, Eleftherios Venizelos, is greatly adored among his fellow Cretans because of his struggle to bring about the union of Crete and Greece. He founded the Greek Liberal Party and became prime minister of his country for the first time in 1910. He created the modern Greek state through far-reaching domestic political reforms. Internationally, he worked for the union of all Greeks and the territorial expansion of Greece by military means. The two Balkan wars (1912/1913) actually did bring about a considerable increase in territory and the ultimate annexation of Crete. His further attempts at expansion failed, due to the resistance of the Turks.

Politician

Practicalities

WHAT ARE TYPICAL GREEK
DISHES? WHERE ARE THE
MOST INTERESTING AND FUN
FESTIVALS CELEBRATED? AND
HOW DO YOU SAY »HELLO« IN
GREEK? – IT'S ALL HERE AND IT IS
BEST TO LOOK IT UP BEFORE YOU GO!

Accommodation

Camping

Greece has a large number camping sites, located for the most part along the coastlines and on the beaches. Most of the sites have minimal facilities; some even offer small cottages for hire. Overnighting outside of the camping sites, on the streets, in picnic areas, lay-bys, parking sites or in the open countryside, is absolutely not allowed.

Detailed tips on camping sites in Greece can be found at www.camping-in-greece.gr and at www.panhellenic-camping-union.gr.

Hotels

There are more hotels in Greece than you can count, ranging from exquisite luxury hotels to the simplest of private rooms. Recently though, visitors have been complaining of high prices, bad service, meagre, uncared for and dirty facilities and negligent management. All in all, the value-for-money ratio is not balanced.

Blue as far as the eye can see – Grecotel El Greco on Crete

Information on **private rooms** can be obtained from the local tourism centre and from the tourist police; reservations can be made with travel agents. Visitors arriving by ferry are offered rooms as they step off the boat. When planning a trip to Greece during high season (from June to September), it is advisable to book rooms ahead of time.

Hotels are officially divided into six **categories**. They range from luxury hotels (L) to comfortable hotels (A) and middle-class hotels (B, C). At the bottom of the scale is basic accommodation (D, E).

During the high season, the **prices for accommodation** in Greece are at the level of central European holiday destinations and in the low

► **ADDRESSES**

CAMPING

► **Greek Camping Association**
Solonos 102
GR-10680 Athens
Tel. / Fax 21 03 62 15 60
Information is also available in the information offices of the Greek Tourist Board, from the local tourist police and the office of the automobile club, ELPA, in Athens (► Transport).

HOTELS

► **Chamber of Hotels**
Stadiou 24
GR-10564 Athens
Tel. 21 03 31 00 22 / 6
Fax 21 03 23 69 62
www.grhotels.gr
Reserve hotel rooms at least a month before trip.

YOUTH HOSTEL

► **Athens International Youth Hostel**
Victor Hugo 16, GR-104 38 Athens
Tel. 21 05 23 41 70
Fax 21 05 23 40 15

! *Baedeker* TIP

Holiday in the »White House«

In the 1930s, the English writer Lawrence Durrell lived on Corfu in the »White House« located on the beach in Kalámi. Durrell described his impression of Corfu with great empathy in his novel »Prospero's Cell. A guide to the landscape and manners of the island of Corcyra«. Whoever would like to vacation in these beautiful, unaltered surroundings, can rent the »White House« through CV Travel (www.cvtravel.net).

season they are below it. Prices must be displayed in the hotel rooms and no more may be demanded than is posted. The prices for categories L, D and E vary from place to place.

Youth Hostels

At present, the only youth hostel officially registered with the International Youth Hostel Federation (IYHF) in Greece is in Athens. Information on reasonably priced accommodation in guesthouses is obtainable from the offices of the Greek Tourist Board (► Information).

Information

Arrival · Before the Journey

How to Get There

There are a number of ways of travelling to Greece from western Europe. You can choose between a direct flight to Thessaloníki or

Athens, travelling there by car through the Balkans, taking the car or train to an Italian Adriatic port and then crossing by ferry to Igoumenítsa, Pátras or Athens (Piraeus) and finally by coach.

By air Most European cities have regular daily flights to Thessaloníki or Athens. Daily low-cost and charter flights are available from, for example, London Gatwick during the season to other destinations, including Corfu, Heraklion and Kos. www.olympicairlines.com provides details of flights between Greece and Britain or North America. Also check flights operated by Aegean Airlines (www.aegeanair.com). Greece's most important airport for commercial traffic is the **Eleftherios Venizelos International Airport in Spata**, 27 km/17 mi east of Athens.

Domestic flights ▶ Besides its major airports, Greece has 22 regional airports handling a very tight network of inland flights. The most important islands can be reached from Athens with Olympic Airlines. AirSea Lines flies amphibian planes from out of Lavrion to a number of islands.

By car The route on the Balkan highway (Autoput) travels through Slovenia, Croatia, Serbia and Macedonia to Greece. Transit visas for Serbia and Montenegro can be obtained from their respective diplomatic missions (▶Information). EU citizens require no visa for travel through Slovenia, Croatia and Macedonia, but must present a passport.

By train If you are already on the continent, there is a train connection from Munich via Budapest to Thessaloníki and on to Athens (travel time app. 50 hrs). There are regular trains from Vienna via Budapest and Belgrade to Athens.

Travelling in
Greece ▶ The rail network of the OSE, the Hellenic Railways Organization, has almost 2,600 km/1,615 mi of track with a third of that alone taken up by the main route between Thessaloníki and Athens. Less than a third of the network is electrified. Despite that, the rail network covers a major part of the mainland.

Discounts ▶ Ticket discounts are offered to students, groups, families, senior citizens, plus there are weekly and monthly passes available.

By bus Eurolines, operated in the UK through National Express (see: www.nationalexpress.com/eurolines) operate bus services to Greece. Greece has an extensive network of bus routes. Its centre is Athens with three bus stations offering travel into the provinces at reasonable rates. Other bus centres are Thessaloníki and the provincial capitals. Departure times are available at the bus stations.

By ferry There are a great number of ferries plying between Italy and Greece that can be taken by those wanting to travel by car. Corfu, Igoumenítsa and Pátras can be reached from the Italian Adriatic ports of Ancona, Bari, Brindisi, Trieste and Venice. The shortest crossing between Italy and Greece is from Brindisi to Igoumenítsa.

It is possible to travel any way to Greece, by land, by water or by air.

Ferries sail regularly between the mainland and the islands and between the islands. Piraeus is the largest and most important port of departure for the islands of the Aegean. There are ferries crossing over to some of the Cyclades Islands, to Euboea and to the Sporades from the smaller ports of Lávrio, Rafína, Agía Marína and Ágios Konstantíno. You have the choice between ordinary ferries and hydrofoils, the Flying Dolphins, which are faster but more expensive. Timetables are available at the Greek National Tourism Organization central office (►Information). Also, one can inquire in the port authority offices. Travel offices and agents at the harbour and directly on the pier can provide tickets.

◄ Travel by ferry within Greece

◄ Timetables and tickets

Persons arriving from abroad in their own yachts wishing to cruise Greek waters must first of all be equipped with a customs clearance and put in at a major port classified as a port of entry and departure. Boats from EU member states are not subject to inspection by port officials. Boats from outside the EU, however, are subject to this inspection and require a transit log that gives entitlement to six months of sailing in Greek waters. A passport control is carried out on all passengers arriving by private yacht from abroad, with foreign passengers classified as »in transit«. Boats imported overland are subject to the same formalities as those from non-EU countries.

By private boat

Only males may visit the Autonomous Monastic State of the Holy Mountain and only for a period of four days. Reservations are re-

Travelling to Mount Athos

Travel Insurance

Health insurance   For EU citizens, the European Health Insurance Card, EHIC (for details, UK residents should consult www.dh.gov.uk/en/Healthcare/Healthadvicefortravellers/index.htm, Irish residents www.ehic.ie) can be used for emergencies and chronic illnesses. In case of illness, the patient can present the card at any branch office of the **Greek Social Insurance Institute, I.K.A.**, where he/she will be referred to a panel doctor on their list. The I.K.A. will provide a health insurance certificate booklet (Bibliario, pronounced »vivliário«). The patient is required to pay 25 % of the costs for pharmaceuticals; remove the coupons on the packaging and stick them onto the prescription. Any physician or hospital can be sought out in case of an emergency; they will then settle the costs through the I.K.A.

In cases where the EHIC is not accepted, the costs incurred are to be paid by the patient and the bill presented to the patient's medical insurance, hence **travel health insurance** in Greece is also urgently recommended because I.K.A. processing is so complicated that many physicians only accept private patients and compensation will not be paid on the EHIC basis. Non-EU residents should arrange for private medical insurance.

Beach Holidays

Greece has some 1,900 beaches along its mainland coast and on its islands. The **bathing season** is from April to November; the average water temperature from June till September (whether southern or northern exposure) is between 19 and 23°C/66 and 73°F. As the evening breeze can often be quite fresh, it is recommended to take some warm clothing along.

Natural beaches   These open beaches lack any kind of facility and safety feature, such as warning signs, marking buoys and nets.

EOT Beaches   The beaches cared for by the Greek National Tourist Organization EOT (▶ Information) are excellently equipped with features such as changing cubicles, snack bars and playgrounds, as well as restaurants and discos and a wide selection of sports facilities.

Hotel beaches   The hotel beaches are well cared for and their services are quite good because they are subject to state inspection, though lifeguards and first-aid stations are not the rule everywhere.

Popular Beaches   The popular beaches on the Adriatic Riviera are in Glýfada (most popular and well-equipped beach), Kavouri, Vouliagmeni, Varkiza, Lagonissi (exclusive beach recreational park) and Sounion. There are also well-frequented beaches at Vravrona, Loutsa, Marathon, Nea Makir and Rhamnous. Another favourite is the beach in Kinetta, between Athens and Corinth, where some luxury hotel complexes have been built. It is still possible to find pretty little uncrowded coves and beaches for bathing on the islands of Aegina, Póros, Ýdra and Spétses. There are bathing spots that can be recommended on the Chalkidikí peninsula, the island of Kos, near Líndos on Rhodes, on Elounda Beach in Crete, in Perama and Benitses on Corfu and on Kefalloniá (Cephalonia).

> **? DID YOU KNOW …?**
>
> ■ … that the umbrella-pine-lined Koukounariés beach in the southeast of the island of Skíathos is regularly listed among the three most beautiful beaches in the world?

Water quality

The quality of water almost everywhere on the Greek coasts is once again either good or very good. Some beaches have even been awarded the blue flag, a seal of quality for water, cleanliness and security. The isle of Crete has garnered most of the flags. High concentrations of harmful chemicals have been measured on only a very few beaches, mostly in the greater Athens area, but also on the islands of Corfu and Zákynthos. Besides environmental harm, it is also important to be aware of the dangerous currents that can occur on the Adriatic coast.

Tingaki's up to 100 m/110 yd wide sandy beach on Kos is a place one could stay a while

Nudity Going »topless« is normal on many beaches and nudity is allowed on a number of beaches. It is generally best, though, to remain at least minimally »clothed«.

Children in Greece

Whoever travels to Greece with children will very quickly realize that the little tykes are warmly welcomed everywhere in this country. The Greeks deal with children in a totally uncomplicated way. The children's TV programme, the Sandman, for example, is shown late at night – a logical consequence of the hot climate. The main attraction for children, as well as grown-ups, is the **beaches**, especially those with sand, where playing is even more fun. Do not forget to take along fins and snorkel equipment because there are a lot of interesting things to discover underwater! And bear in mind that youthful skin needs special sun protection. The strong rays of the sun demand a sun cream (waterproof!) with a high sunscreen factor. Protect the skin of the youngest ones on the beach with a T-shirt and shield their heads with a hat. Beach sandals should also be included when packing. For one thing, the sand can get very hot in the noon-day sun and for another, they protect against broken glass that might possibly be lying around. Another thing not to forget when packing is a children's first aid kit that includes mosquito repellent and medi-

Greece's beaches are ideal for sand castles, a perennial favourite with children.

cine for diarrhoea and sunstroke. By the way, because of the hot climate, the summer months are not recommended as a time to travel with babies and small children. Most restaurants do not offer special children's menus. Children are provided with their own plates and cutlery and simply eat the various dishes along with the parents. A small bed is placed in the room for travellers **overnighting** on their own with children. Larger hotels and apartment complexes usually offer their young guests a variety of supervised activities.

> ! *Baedeker* TIP
>
> **Swimming, splashing about, sliding ...**
> The giant water slide in »Aegina's Water Park« is fantastic fun – and not only for children. The park is located on the island of Aegina in the Saronic Gulf.

Electricity

As a rule, the power mains supply is 220 Volt a/c; onboard ship, it is often 110 Volt a/c. Standard Continental plugs are usually the norm, adaptors can be obtained from most electrical supply stores.

Emergency

 USEFUL TELEPHONE NUMBERS

IN GREECE

▶ **Tourist Police**
Tel. 1 71
The most important contact point for tourists is the tourist police, who provide general information and tips for accommodation in English.

▶ **Police**
Tel. 1 12

▶ **Road Assistance Service**
Tel. 1 04

▶ **First Aid**
Tel. 1 12

▶ **Red Cross**
Tel. 1 50

▶ **Pharmacy**
Tel. 1 07

▶ **Road Traffic Police**
Tel. 21 05 23 01 11

▶ **Fire Department**
Tel. 1 12

▶ **Coast Guard**
Tel. 1 12

Etiquette and Customs

Clothing What is acceptable in Greece and what is not? Whoever not only lives largely from, but frequently also together with tourists, will often find his tolerance sorely tested. And so it is with the Greeks. They turn a blind eye, sometimes even both of them, when guests exceed the boundaries of good behaviour. But one should know these boundaries. Whether it is appropriate to enter a restaurant scantily clothed is something everyone should recognize for themselves. It is against common decency, even in holiday resorts. The **dress code** in **churches and monasteries** is far, far stricter. When women stroll into a house of God with bare shoulders, trousers or a short skirt, the older women sitting at the entrance will emphatically call out after them. They will offer the women scarves or cloths to cover themselves. With men, the rules are not so clearly formulated, but muscle shirts and shorts are definitely not appropriate for a visit to a church. But even when the tourists use the scarves offered them, it is still considered inappropriate to show up half naked at a monastery gate and rely on such a stopgap solution.

Religious customs In matters of religion, you are always on the safe side when you do what the natives do. If, for example, a **funeral procession** passes a restaurant and all the guests rise, do the same. It is not expected of tourists, though, to cross themselves every time they pass a church as the natives do.

Taking photos As a rule, taking photos presents no problems. If you have chosen a local inhabitant as the main subject of a shot, it is a good idea to gain permission through a couple of gestures first. It is forbidden to take photographs of military facilities.

Gestures A word about gestures. Forming **a circle with the thumb and index finger** does not mean everything is O.K. In Greece it is an **insult**. And don't forget, **nodding your head means NO**; shaking the head expresses agreement.

In restaurants About the same rules apply in restaurants as in the English-speaking world, although non-smokers in Greece have to grit their teeth. **Smoking at the table** is a matter of course, even when others are still eating. Service charges are included in the bill in hotels, restaurants and cafés. An additional gratuity, for example, rounding off the bill, is still always welcome.

Tips ►

Philosophy of life As they always say, pack a lot of **patience**. Always consider any specific time named as a very rough estimate and every agreement, as well. Even the opening times of smaller museums or timetables of overland coaches can suffer if the gatekeeper happens to be having a family celebration or the coach driver has run into an old acquaint-ance. It's no help moaning about it and pointing to the officially posted times. Things just have to be taken as or when they come.

Festivals, Holidays and Events

⏵ CALENDAR OF EVENTS

LEGAL HOLIDAYS

▶ **1 January**
New Year's Day

▶ **6 January**
Epiphany

▶ **25 March**
Greek Independence Day

▶ **1 May**
Labour Day

▶ **28 October**
Ochi Day, commemorating Meta-xa's »no« (»ochi«) to Italy's ulti-matum

▶ **25 December / 26**
Christmas

RELIGIOUS HOLIDAYS

▶ **Katharí Deftéra**
the Monday before Lent

▶ **Easter**
later than in the Western Church

▶ **the Feast of the Dormition (corresponding to the Western Feast of the Assumption)**
15 August

JANUARY

▶ **New Year's Day**
Feast of St Basil; children's pro-cession (with adults participating) with house-to-house singing: (also 24 and 31 December).

▶ **Epiphany**
6 January; blessing of the waters with a cross being thrown into a lake, river or sea, particularly spectacular in Piraeus.

▶ **8 January: day of »female domination« (gynaecocracy)**
Women spend this day in the kafenions, usually reserved for men; widespread in Kilkis, Ko-motiní and Monoklissia.

FEBRUARY

▶ **Carnival**
In many places, particularly in

---

i **Easter on Kefalloniá**

■ A truly impressive resurrection mass can be experience on the night of Easter Eve in the monastery of Theotokos of Sission, located on the south coast. The joy of Easter is expressed in a completely differ-ent manner on Platía Vallianou, the main square in Argostóli, with the din of exploding firecrackers increasing to an inferno by midnight. And there is a great festival with music and folk dancing on Easter morning in the Theotókou Them-áton monastery near the village of Drakopouláta.

Pátras, Athens, Thessaloníki, Kozáni, Véria, Zákynthos, Xánthi, Lamia / Kefalloniá, Vólos, Ámfissa, Réthymnon and Iráklion / Crete, Kárpathos, Messini, Serres, Galaxidi, Thiva, Sparta, Poligiros / Chalkidikí, Kalambaka, Skyros, Ágia Ánna / Euboea, Agiassos / Lésbos; Mesta, Olimbi, Thimiana (all of Chíos).

Carnival Sunday (last before Lent): carnival parade through Athens.

Katharí Deftéra (Monday before Lent): kites are flown everywhere; setting the mood for Lent with unleavened bread, fish, seafood, salad and wine.

MARCH

► **Phanos Festival of Lights**
A Pontian folklore carnival is held in Kozáni at the beginning of the month.

► **Military Parades**
25 March; military parades on the national holiday.

APRIL / MAI

► **Feast of Saint Spyridon**
15 and 21 April; festival of the patron saint of Corfu.

► **Passion Week**
Candlelit processions everywhere on Good Friday and midnight mass on Holy Saturday

► **Easter**
The most important religious festival in Greece is celebrated on the first Sunday after the first full moon after the vernal equinox (March 21), which usually results in a later date than in the Western churches. The Easter celebrations in Oía on Santorini, Trípolis, Livadiá, Trapeza near Pátras and

Ochi Day is celebrated with parades in the whole of the country, as here in Rhodes Town.

Olympos on Kárpathos, an island steeped in tradition, are especially picturesque. Easter dates: 2009: 19 April; 2010: 4 April

► St George's Day
23 April; festivals in many places; special celebrations on Límnos and Kos (horseracing; singing and dancing), in Assi Gonia on Crete (sheep-shearing contest) and in Arachova.

APRIL – OCTOBER

► Son et Lumière (Sound and Light) Show
Regular evening sound and light show at the Acropolis in Athens and in the Park of the Grand Master's Palace in Rhodes

MAY

► Labour Day
1 May; parades everywhere, flower festivals and excursions into the countryside; special celebrations in Nea Filadelfia, Nea Chalkidona, Nea Smyrni, Kifissia and Karches near Florina.

► Ionian Day
21 May; anniversary of the re-uniting of the Ionian Islands and Corfu with Greece.

► Dance Festival
27 – 29 May; in memory of the Battle of Crete in Chaniá.

► Paleological Festival
29 May; in Mistrá.

► Kariaskaki Festival
End of May; in Karditsa.

► Church Festival
in Kolindro

An abundant amount of celebrating with family and friends is part of the Greek way of life.

MAY / JUNE

▶ **Acropolis Rally**
The WRC Rally will be making a stop-over in Greece.

MAY – SEPTEMBER

▶ **Sound and Light Show**
in the old fortress of Corfu Town

▶ **Folk Dance Performances**
in Filopappos Theater in Athens and Rhodes

JUNE

▶ **Papastratia Festival of Cultural and Sporting Events**
in Agrinio

▶ **Midsummer Night Fire Festival in Katakolo**
21 June; on Rhodes.

▶ **Feast of the Klidona**
End of June; in Piskokefalo and Krousta on Crete.

▶ **Sardine Festival**
in Nea Mudania / Chalkidikí

JUNI / JULI

▶ **Navy Week**
Every 2 years, inquire about exact dates in the individual venues; re-enactment of the tale of Jason and the Argonauts in Vólos.

JUNE – SEPTEMBER

▶ **Athenian Festival**
Performances of Classical dramas, operas, music and dance in the Odeon of Herodes Atticus Festival.

JULY

▶ **Papacharalambia Festival**
Arts, sports, and nautical events in Náfpaktos.

▶ **Fair**
Beginning of July; in Lefkimi / Corfu; with folklore.

▶ **Wine Festival**
Mid-July; in Dafnes and Réthymnon on Crete.

▶ **Sultana Raisin Festival**
in Sitia / Crete

The Hippocratic Oath is »re-enacted« annually during the »Hippokratia« festival staged in August in the Asclepieion on Kos.

► **St Paraskevi Feast Day**
26 July; folk music competition in Langadia.

JULY / AUGUST

► **Nikopolia Festival**
in Préveza

► **Festivals**
e.g. »Festival of Olympus« in the castle of Platamonas, in Katerini, Litochoro, Dion and Makrigialo; music and theatre festival in Itháki and Lefkadas; Epidaurus Festival, performances of ancient dramas; literature and art festival in Ioánnina.

JULY – SEPTEMBER

► **Wine Festivals**
At the Dafní monastery near Athens, in Alexandroupolis (until August) and in Rhodini, Rhodes; wine sampling, music and dance are all a part of it.

AUGUST

► **»Hippokratia«**
Cultural events (plays and concerts as well as flower shows and folk art) on Kos

► **Concerts, performances of plays and folk dances**
in Vólos

► **Fair**
6 August; with folklore in Anogia, Crete.

► **International Meeting of Medieval and Popular Theatre**
Mid-August; in Zákynthos.

► **Performances of Ancient Tragedies**
in Gýthio

► **The Feast of the Dormition of the Panagia (Virgin Mary)**
15 August; widely observed with festivals, particularly passionately in Tínos City, on Corfu and Lésbos, in Nepolis, Crete and Kyme, on Páros (fish and wine festival), Siatista (horsemanship games) and in Vlastis.

► **Pelioritic Wedding**
2nd half of August; in Portaria.

► **Theatre Festival**
in Itháki

► **Cretan Wedding**
in Kritsá, Crete.

► **Feast Day of St Dionysios**
24 August; in Zákynthos.

AUGUST / SEPTEMBER

► **»Aeschylus«**
Ancient dramas performed on archaeological sites in Eleusis

SEPTEMBER

► **Art Festival**
in Zákynthos

► **Vyronia, the Byron Festival of Literature and Art**
in Mesolóngi

► **Wine Festivals**
1 – 15 September: in Anchialos, Thessaly.
1 – 20 September: in Pátras.

► **Navy Festival**
8 / 9 September; in Spétses commemorating the victory over the Turks.

► **Folklore Festival**
Mid-September; in Nikiti, Chalkidikí.

OCTOBER

► **Demetria Festival**
in Thessaloníki: theatre and ballet performances, as well as concerts honouring Demetrius.

► **Ochi Day**
28 October; national holiday with military parades.

NOVEMBER

► **Celebration honouring St Spyridon**
4 November; on Corfu.

► **Commemoration of the Arkadi monastery**
8 November; commemoration of the holocaust at the Arkadi monastery, the Cretan national shrine, in Rethymnon on Crete.

DECEMBER

► **Christmas / New Year**
24 December: children's processions on Christmas Eve
31 December: children's processions;
parade of fishermen from the island of Chíos.

Food and Drink

Restaurants

Greece offers a wide range of from deluxe restaurants to simple tavernas and grill snack bars. International cuisine can be found in the larger towns in hotel restaurants. Tavernas are the traditional Greek restaurant with simple furnishings. Ouzerias are similar to tavernas, but naturally offering ouzo accompanied by a variety of appetizers. There are an increasing number of restaurants in the tourist centres along western European lines. Athens is the dominant centre of the New Greek Cuisine, a refinement of traditional Greek cooking. Menus are usually in Greek, English and German. Greeks eat their meals lukewarm. Also note that it is customary in Greece for only one bill to be made out per table.

Kafenion — Kafenions (► Baedeker Special p. 29) play an important role in the daily life of the Greeks. It is not only where drinks are served, but it is also a gathering place to have a conversation, play games and do business.

Mealtimes — **Breakfast** in the hotels usually corresponds to western European standards and is normally eaten between 8am and 10am. **Lunch** is served as a rule from noon to 3pm and the **evening meal** generally after 8pm. Many tavernas serve cooked meals from mid-day through to midnight.

Restaurants are normally open from noon to 4pm and from 8pm until midnight; some are open the whole night.

Greek Cooking

Greek cooking, in its basics, is rather plain and offers – so say the critics – not much variety. It is dominated by a few basic ingredients – olive oil, tomatoes, garlic, onions, lamb, goat and chicken meat, sheep's and goat's cheese and whatever vegetables are in season. Bread is always served with the meal. Bear in mind that no one in Greece attaches any great importance to getting the meal to the table hot. International cuisine is becoming available more and more, above all in Athens.

> ! **Baedeker TIP**
>
> **Simply delicious!**
> Greek yogurt (yaourti) is a special delicacy available in various forms; »natural« in the breakfast buffets in the larger hotels; served with fruit in bars and cafés or as a typical Greek dessert with honey and nuts.

The typical Greek **breakfast** is quite modest. A cup of coffee or a glass of milk is usually accompanied by a couple of slices of white bread with butter or margarine and jam (usually either apricot or strawberry). A really varied breakfast buffet can only be found in the upper grade hotels. **Lunch** is also of minor importance. The natives make do with small meals or snacks. Many restaurants serve only a

Eating habits

Instead of sweating in the sun, a relaxing afternoon break in a beach taverna

limited menu for lunch. The chances of getting properly served are best in tourist centres. The **evening meal** is the main meal and is rarely eaten before 9pm in restaurants, usually even later. Most restaurants serve cooked food all day from noon until late in the night anyway. The Greeks never order separate set meals individually. Starters, salad, fish and meat dishes all arrive on the table at the same time and everyone helps themselves.

Appetizers There is a wide range of things to start a meal, including tzaziki (a yogurt dip with garlic and cucumber), a thick garlic sauce (skordalia), fish roe purée (taramosalata), vine leaves stuffed with rice (dolmades) and fried smelts (marides) eaten whole. Added to that are baked aubergines and courgettes. Also very popular is a farmer's salad (choriatiki) made of cucumber, tomatoes, olives and sheep cheese, often advertised as »Greek salad«.

Soups When soups are offered, they are very hearty. A favourite is fasolada, a traditional Greek white bean soup. Fish soups (psarosoupa) are usually seasoned to taste with lemon juice.

Meat Very popular with tourist are meats grilled on an upright rotisserie (gýros) and skewered meat (souvlaki). Otherwise lamb (arnaki) is served, arriving at the table usually roasted or grilled. In addition there are pork chops (brisoles), chicken (katapoulo), ground meatballs (keftedes) and goulash (stifado), usually with beef.

Fish and seafood play a major role in Greek cooking. As the catch in the waters around Greece is no longer very plentiful and more and more fish is having to be imported, expect high prices. Fish is sold by weight. The most prevalent fish offered are bream (tsipoura), red mullet (barbouni), squid (kalamarakia), octopus (oktapodi) and shrimp (garides).

Bakes Bakes like pastitsio (macaroni and ground meat) and moussaka (potatoes and aubergines) are widespread.

Vegetables Typical garden vegetables are artichokes (anginares), aubergines (melitsanes), courgettes (kolokithakia) and Greek bell peppers (piperies) that are often cooked with ground meat or in oil. Horta, a wild vegetable similar to spinach, is very popular.

The choice of desserts in tavernas is very limited, Along with ice cream (pagoto), there are local fruits that vary according to the season, such as watermelons (karpusi), honey-dew melons (peponi), peaches (rodakino), pears (achladi), apples (milo), oranges (portokali), grapes (stafili) and figs (sika). Baklává is a well-known dessert made of puff pastry, nuts and honey.

Drinks

The most widespread drink is wine. Winegrowing has a long tradition in Greece. There are extensive winegrowing areas in the Peloponnese. Grapes for red wine (mavro krassi) and white wine (aspro krassi) are cultivated. Both dry and sweet wines are made. Inexpensive retsina wines are resinated so they will keep longer, thus gaining their characteristic tangy taste. They stimulate the appetite and are very easily digestible. Even the ancient Greeks had a fondness for **resinated wine**, as is attested to by the residue of resin (»retsina«) discovered by archaeologists in the oldest amphorae in Greece. Resinated red wine is called kokkineli. As open wines are less expensive, it is best to order wine »ap to bareli« (»from the barrel«). In addition, there are a number of unresinated red and white wines that comply with EU standards and are identified by the letters »V.Q.P. R.D.«.

After a wine tasting, most customers are sold on the quality offered.

Winegrowing areas ► Attica: The area around Athens is the home of retsina. Peloponnese: about a third of all Greek wine is grown on the Peloponnese; the specialty here are sweet wines and the top wine is Mavrodafni, a sweet, dark and heavy red wine. Islands: while the dry white wines are normally not worth the mention, the wines of Crete, Kefalloniá (Robola), Zákynthos (Verdea), Rhodes (Lindos) and Santorini are deserving of recognition. The white Muscat from Sámos is excellent.

Beer Greece's first modern-day king, Otto I, brought along to Greece the art of brewing from Bavaria. Recently, Greek beer has been able to establish itself on the market alongside German and Dutch brands. Popular Greek beer labels are Mythos and Alpha.

More alcoholic drinks The best-known aperitif is **ouzo**, an anise-flavoured liqueur drunk with ice cubes or diluted with a bit of water. Metaxa is a brandy that comes with 3, 5 and 7 stars. The most inexpensive Metaxa is the one with 3 stars, but it is best to take one with 5 or 7 stars. Raki or tsipouro is made from the skins of pressed grapes.

Non-alcoholic beverages The non-alcoholic drinks available everywhere include water and the usual soft drinks known world-wide. Fresh-pressed juices are worth recommending.

Coffee, tea **Greek coffee** (ellinikós kafés), drunk from small coffee cups, is prepared in a whole gamut of ways according to strength and sweetness; glikí vrastó (with a lot of sugar), varí glikó (strong and sweet), elafró (light). métrio (medium strength, medium sweet) is very popular. About the only »cosmopolitan« type of coffee available is Nescafé, called néss (»with milk« = me gála). The cold version – a frappé with thick foam and ice cubes – is something akin to Greece's national drink. Italian-style coffee like espresso and cappuccino with whipped milk can be found in the tourist centres. Tea (mávro tsái) is brewed from tea bags, but tisanes such as peppermint tea (tsái ménda) or camomile tea (chamoumíli) are also available.

Health

Health insurance UK and Irish residents are covered by reciprocal EU schemes. The **European Health Insurance Card (EHIC)** has been in use in the EU since 2005. But even with this card, a portion of the doctor's fees and costs for medicine often have to be paid by the patient. In such cases, request detailed receipts (apodíxi) of the costs incurred. Enquire about possible reimbursement procedure when obtaining the card.

Pharmacies As a rule, pharmacies are open Monday to Friday from 8am until 2pm.

⏵ USEFUL TELEPHONE NUMBERS

EMERGENCY CALLS

► **First Aid**
Tel. 1 12

► **Hospital (on call)**
Tel. 1 06

► **Physician on call**
Tel. 1 05

► **Pharmacy**
Tel. 1 07

Information

IN UK

► **Greek National Tourism Organization**
4 Conduit St, London, W1S 2DJ
Tel. +44 207 4959300
E-mail: info@gntoco.uk

IN USA

Olympic Tower 645 Fifth Avenue,
Suite 903 – New York, NY 10022
Tel : (001212) 4215777
E-mail: info@greektourism.com

DIPLOMATIC MISSIONS

► **Greek Embassy in the UK**
1a Holland Park
London W11 3TP
Tel. (0 20) 7229 3850
www.greekembassy.org.uk

► **Greek Embassy in USA**
2221 Massachusetts Ave NW
Washington DC 20008
Tel. 202 939 1300
www.greekembassy.org.

► **Greek Embassy in Canada**
76–80 Maclaren St
Ottawa, Ontario K2P 0K6
Tel. (0 01) 613 238 6271

► **Greek Embassy in Ireland**
1 Upper Pembroke St
Dublin 2
Tel. (0 1) 676 7254

► **Greek Embassy in Australia**
9 Turrana St
Yarralumba ACT 2600
Tel. (0 2) 6273 3211

► **Greek Embassy in New Zealand**
5–7 Willeston St
Wellington
Tel. (0 4) 473 7775

► **British Embassy in Greece**
Ploutarhou 1 3
GR-10675 Athens
Tel. 21 07 23 62 11
www.british-embassy.gr

► **US Embassy in Greece**
Leoforos Vass. Sofias 91
GR-11521 Athens
Tel. 21 07 21 29 51
athens.usembassy.gov

μπ	mb	mb (in middle of word)
ντ	d	d (begins word, seldom in middle)
ντ	nt	nd (in middle of word)
οι	i	ee
ου	ou	oo

SHORT LANGUAGE GUIDE

Useful Phrases

Yes / No	ne / 'óchi	Ναί / Όχι
Maybe	'issos	Ίσως
Please	paraka'ló	Παρακαλώ
Thank you (very much)	efchari'stó (pol'i)	Ευχαριστώ (πολύ)
Sorry!	sig'nómi!	Συγγνώμη!
Pardon? What do you want?	o'ríste?	Ορίστε;
I don't understand you.	ðe sass katala'véno.	Δε σας καταλαβαίνω.
Please repeat that.	na to ksana'péete, paraka'ló.	Νά το ξαναπείτε, παρακαλώ.
Do you speak English?	mi'late anggli'ká?	Μιλάτε αγγλικά;
I only speak a little Greek.	mi'ló 'móno ligo elliniká.	Μιλώ μόνο λίγο ελληνικά.
Could you please help me?	bo'ríte na me voi'θísete, paraka'ló?	Μπορείτε να με βοηθήσετε, παρακαλώ;
I would like …	'θelo …	Θέλω …
Do you have … ?	'échete … ?	Έχετε …?
How much is it?	'posso 'kostisi?	Πόσο κοστίζει;
What time is it?	ti 'ora 'ine?	Τι ώρα είναι
Today / Tomorrow	si'mera / 'ówrio	Σήμερα / Αύριο

Greetings an Meetings

Good morning!	kali'mera (soo / sas)!	Καλημέρα (σου / σας) !
Good afternoon!	kali'mera! / 'cherete!	Καλημέρα / Χαίρετε !
Good evening!	kali'spera!	Καλησπέρα!
Good night!	kali'nichta!	Καληνύχτα !
(general greeting)	'yassas!	Γειά σας !
Hello!	'yassu!	Γειά σου !
Goodbye!	a'dio!	Αντίο !
Cheerio!	'yassu!	Γειά σου !

On the Road

| left / right | ariste'ra / ðek'sya | αριστερά / δεξιά |

»Now if only one of us knew how to ask where the beach is...«

straight ahead	ef'θia	ευθεία
near / far	ko'nda / makri'a	κοντά / μακριά
How far is it to … ?	'posso ma'kria 'ine ya … ?	Πόσο μακριά είναι γιά…?
I would like to hire …	'θelo na ni'kyasso …	Θέλω να νοικιάσω …
… a car	'ena afto'kinito	ένα αυτοκίνητο
… a bicycle	'ena po'ðilato	ένα ποδήλατο
… a boat	'mia 'varka	μία βάρκα
Excuse me, where is … ?	Paraka'ló, pú 'íne … ?	Παρακαλώ, πού είναι …

At the Petrol Station

Where is the next petrol station, please?	'pu 'ine, paraka'lo, to e'pomeno vensi'naðiko?	Πού είναι, παρακαλώ, το επομένο βενζιναδικό;
I would like … litres …	'θelo … 'litra …	Θέλω … λίτρα …
… regular petrol.	… ven'sini.	… βενζινη.
… diesel.	… 'dizel.	… ντίζελ.
… unleaded	… a'molivði	… αμόλυβδη
Fill up, please.	ye'miste paraka'lo.	Γεμίστε παρακαλώ.
Check the oil, please.	ekse'taste, paraka'lo, ti 'staθmi tu lað'yoo.	Εξέταστε, παρακαλώ, τη στάθμη του λαδιού.

Breakdown

My car has broken down.	'epaθa zim'ya.	Έπαθα ζημειά.
Could you please send me a tow truck?	θa bo'russate na mu 'stilete 'ena 'ochima ri'mulkissis?	Θα μπορούσατε να μου στείλατε ένα όχημα ρυμούλκησης;

| Where is the next garage? | 'pu i'parchi e'ðo kon'da 'ena siner'yio? | Πού υπάρχει εδώ κοντά ένασυνεργείο; |

Accident

Help!	vo'iθya!	Βοήθεια!
Look out! Careful!	proso'chi!	Προσοχή!
Please, call quickly	ka'leste, paraka'lo, 'grigora	Καλέστε, παρακαλώ, γρήγορα …
… an ambulance.	… 'ena asθeno'foro.	… ένα ασθενόφορο.
… the police.	… tin astino'mia.	… την αστυνομία.
… the fire department.	… tin pirosvesti'ki ipire'sia.	… την πυροσβεστική υπηρεσία.
Please give me your name and address.	'peste mu to 'onoma ke ti ðieffiin'si sas, paraka'lo.	Πέστε μου το όνομα και τη διεύθυνσή σας, παρακαλώ.

Eating Out

Where is a good restaurant?	pu i'parchi e'ðo 'ena ka'lo estia'torio?	Πού υπάρχει εδώ ένα καλό εστιατόριο;
Is there a cosy taverna around here?	i'parchi e'ðo ta'verna me 'aneti at'mosfera?	Υπάρχει εδώ μια ταβέρνα με άνετι ατμόσφαιρα;
Please reserve a table for 4 for this evening.	kra'tiste mas ya 'simera to 'vraði 'ena tra'pesi ya 'tessera'atoma, paraka'lo.	Κρατήστε μας για σήμερα το βράδυ ένα τραπέζι για 4 άτομα, παρακαλώ.
May I have the bill please?	'θelo na pli'rosso, paraka'lo.	Θέλω να πληρώσω, παρακαλώ.
knife /fork	ma'cheri / pi'run	μαχαίρι / πηρούνι
spoon	ku'tali	κουτάλι

Shopping

| Where do I find …? | pu θa vro …? | Πού θα βρω …; |

a pharmacy	'ena farma'kio	ένα φαρμακείο
a bakery	'ena artopo'lio	ένα αρτοπολείο
a food store	'ena ka'tastima tro'fimon	ένα κατάστημα τροφίμων
the market	tin ayo'ra	την αγορά

Accommodation

Could you please recommend ...?	bo'rite na mu si'stissete ..., paraka'lo?	Μπορείτε να μου συστήσετε ..., παρακαλώ;
... a hotel	... 'ena ksenoðo'chio	... ένα ξενοδοχείο
... a guesthouse	... 'mia pan'syon	... μία πανσιόν
I booked a room with you.	'eðo se sas 'eklissa 'ena ðo'matyo.	Εδώ σε σας έκλεισα ένα δομάτιο.
Do you still have a room free ...	'echete a'komi 'ena ðo'matyo e'lefθero ...	Έχετε ακόμη ένα δομάτιο ελεύθερο ...
... for one night? ?	... ya mya 'nichta ?	... γιά μια νύχτα;
... for two days? ?	... ya 'ðio 'meres ?	... γιά δύο μέρες;
... for a week? ?	... ya mya vðo'maða ?	... γιά μια βδομάδα;
How much does the room cost with ...	'posso ko'stisi to ðo'matyo me ...	Πόσο κοστίζει το δομάτιο με ...
... breakfast?	... proi'no?	... πρωινό;
... half board?	... 'mena 'yevma?	... μένα γεύμα.

Doctor

| Could you recommend me a good doctor? | bo'rite na mu sis'tissete 'enan ka'lo ya'tro? | Μπορείτε να μου συστήσετε έναν καλό ιατρό; |
| I have a pain here. | 'echo 'ponnus e'ðo. | Έχω πόνους εδώ. |

Bank

| Where is a bank? | 'pu 'ine e'ðo mya 'trapeza? | Πού είναι εδώ μια τράπεζα; |
| I would like to exchange British pounds for euros. | 'θelo na a'lakso ... li'ra ang'glias se evró. | Θέλω να αλλάξω ... ελβετικά φραγκα σε ευρώ. |

Post

What is the cost of ...	'posso ko'stisi ...	Πόσο κοστίζει ...
... a postcard ...	... mya 'karta	... μια κάρτα
... to England / America / Ireland/Canada?	... ya ti ang'glia / ameri'ki / irlan'dia / kana'das?	

one / two stamps, please. ... 'ena / 'ðio grammat'osimo / ... Ένα / δύο γραμματόσημο /
grammat'osima, γραμματόσημα,
paraka'lo. παρακαλώ.

Signs

ΑΝΔΡΩΝ .... Gentlemen   ΓΥΝΑΙΚΩΝ .... Ladies
ΕΙΣΟΔΟΣ .... Entrance   ΕΞΟΔΟΣ .... Exit

Numbers

0	mi'ðen	μηδέν	19	ðekae'nea	δεκαεννέα	
1	'ena	ένα	20	'ikossi	είκοσι	
2	'ðio	δύο	21	'ikossi 'ena	είκοσι ένα	
3	'tria	τρία	22	'ikossi 'ðio	είκοσι δύο	
4	'tessera	τέσσερα	30	tri'anda	τριάντα	
5	'pende	πέντε	40	sa'randa	σαράντα	
6	'eksi	έξι	50	pe'ninda	πενήντα	
7	e'fta	εφτά	60	e'ksinda	εξήντα	
8	o'chto	οχτώ	70	ewðo'minda	εβδο-μήντα	
9	e'nea	εννέα	80	og'ðonda	ογδόντα	
10	'ðeka	δέκα	90	ene'ninda	ενενήντα	
11	'endeka	ένδεκα	100	eka'to	εκατό	
12	'ðoðeka	δώδεκα	200	ðia'kosya	διακόσια	
13	ðeka'tria	δεκατρία	1000	'chilia	χίλια	
14	ðeka'tessera	δεκατέσσ-ερα	2000	'ðio chi'lyaðes	δύο χιλιάδες	
15	ðeka'pende	δεκαπέντε	10 000	'ðeka chi'lyaðes	δέκα χιλιάδες	
16	ðeka'eksi	δεκαέξι	1/2	to/'ena	το / ένα	
17	ðekae'fta	δεκαεφτά		'ðeftero	δεύτερο	
18	ðekao'chto	δεκαοχτώ	1/4	to/'ena ' tetarto	το / ένα τέταρτο	

Κατάλογος φαγητών · Menu

προινώ	proin'o	**breakfast**
καφές (σκέτο)	ka'fes ('sketo)	(unsweetened) coffee
καφές με γάλα	ka'fes me 'yala	coffee with milk
καφές φίλτρου	ka'fes 'filtru	filter coffee
τσάι με λεμόνι	'tsai me le'moni	tea with lemon
τσάι από βότανα	'tsai a'po 'votana	herbal tea

σοκολάτα	soko'lata	chocolate
χυμό φρούτου	chi'mo 'frutu	fruit juice
αυγό μελάτο	ow'yo me'lato	soft-boiled egg
ομελέτα	ome'leta	omelette
αυγά μάτια	ow'ya 'matya	fried eggs
αυγά με μπέικον	ow'ya me 'beiken	egg with bacon
ψωμί / ψωμάκι	pso'mi / pso'maki	bread / rolls
τοστ	'tost	toast
κρουασάν	krua'san	croissant
φρυγανιές	frigan'yes	zwieback / rusk
βούτυρο	'vutiro	butter
τυρί	ti'ri	cheese
λουκανικό	lu'kaniko	sausage
ζαμβόν	sam'bon	ham
μέλι	'meli	honey
μαρμελάδα	marme'laða	yam
γιαούρτι (με καρύδια)	ya'urti (me ka'riðya)	yogurt (with walnuts)

ορεκτικά / σούπες	orektik'a / 'supes	**Hors d'œuvre / Soups**
ποικιλίαελιές	e'lyes	olives
φέτα	'feta	white sheep's cheese
μελιτζάνα σαλάτα	meli'dsana sa'lata	aubergine salad
ντολμαδάκια	dolma'ðakya	stuffed wine leaves (cold)
γαρίδες	ga'rides	shrimps
γίγαντες	'yigandes	large white beans
σαγανάκι	saga'naki	baked cheese
σκορδαλιά	skorðal'ya	purée of potato, garlic and oil
σπανακόπιτα	spana'kopita	spinach pockets
ταραμοσαλάτα	taramosa'lata	purée of roe
τζατζίκι	tza'tziki	yogurt cream dip with cucumber and garlic
τυρόπιτα	ti'ropita	cheese pockets
κοτόσουπα	ko'tosupa	chicken soup
κοτόσουπα αυγολέμονο	ko'tosupa owgo'lemono	chicken soup with lemon and egg
ψαρόσουπα	psa'rosupa	fish soup
λαχανόσουπα	lacha'nosupa	vegetable soup
φασολάδα	faso'lada	bean soup
μαγειρίτσα	mayi'ritsa	traditional Easter soup

σαλάτες	sa'lates	**Salads**
(ν)τοματοσαλάτα	tomatosa'lata	tomato salad
αγγούρι	an'guri	cucumber

χοριάτικι (σαλάτα)	chor'yatiki (sa'lata)	village salad
μαρούλι σαλάτα	ma'ruli sa'lata	iceberg lettuce
λαχανοσαλάτα	lachanosa'lata	coleslaw
πατατοσαλάτα	patatosa'lata	potato salad
άγρια χόρτα	'agria 'chorta	wild herbs salad
λαδολέμονο	laðo'lemono	lemon-oil sauce

ψάρια	ps'arya	**Fish Dishes**
αστακός	asta'kos	lobster
γαρίδες	ga'rides	shrimp
χταπόδι	chta'poði	octopus
μπαρμπούνι σχάρας	bar'buni 'scharas	grilled red mullet
γλώσσα τηγανητά	'glossa tiyani'ta	fried sole
μύδια	'miðia	mussels
καλαμαράκια	kalama'rakya	small squids
μπακαλιάρος φούρνου	bakal'yaros 'furnu	stockfish from the oven
σολομός	solo'mos	salmon
κακαβιά	kakav'ya	bouillabaisse
καραβίδες	kara'viðes	large scampi
χριστόψαρο	chris'topsaro	Zeus faber
σκουμπρί	skum'bri	mackerel
τσιπούρα	tsi'pura	gilthead seabream
φαγκρί	fan'gri	dentex
τόνος	'tonnos	tuna
ξιφίας	ksi'fias	swordfish

φαγητά με κρέας	fayit'a me kr'eas	**Meat Dishes**
άρνι ψητό	ar'ni psi'to	lamb roast
άρνι στο φούρνο	ar'ni sto 'furno	lamb from the oven
βοδινό φιλέτο	voði'no fi'leto	filet of beef
γαλοπούλα ψητή	galo'pula psi'ti	roast turkey
γύρος	'yiros	meat from the rotisserie
κατσίκι	kat'siki	kid
κεφτέδες	kef'tedes	ground meatballs
κοτόπουλο ψητό	ko'topulo psi'to	roast chicken
κουνέλι	ku'neli	rabbit
μιξτ γκριλ	'mikst 'gril	mixed grilled meat
μοσχάρι κοκκινιστό	mos'chari kokkini'sto	braised veal
μοσχάρι ψητό	mos'chari psi'to	roast of veal
μπόν φιλέ	bon fi'le	filet
μπριζόλες χοιρινές	bri'soles chiri'nes	pork chops
μπιφτέκι	bi'fteki	grilled ground meat
παιδάκια αρνίσια	pai'ðakya ar'nisia	lamb chops

παστίτσιο	pa'stitsyo	macaroni soufflé with meat filling
σουτζουκάκια	sudsu'kakya	rolls of ground meat
σουβλάκι(α)	su'vlaki (a)	skewered meat(a)

λαχανικά	lachanik'a	**Vegetable Dishes**
ντολμάδες	dol'maðes	stuffed wine leaves
λάχανο	'lachano	white cabbage
αγγινάρες	angi'nares	artichokes
μελιτζάνες γεμιστές	meli'dsanes yemi'stes	stuffed aubergines
ντομάτες γεμιστές	to'mates yemi'stes	stuffed tomatoes
πιπεριές γεμιστές	piper'yes yemi'stes	stuffed bell peppers
τουρλού	tur'lu	mixed vegetable stew
φασολάκια	faso'lakya	green beans
μουσακάς	mussa'kas	aubergine, mince and potato bake
πιπεριές τηγανητές	piper'yes tigani'tes	fried bell peppers
κολοκυθάκια	koloki'θakya	zucchini
φασόλια	fa'solya	white beans
πατάτες τηγανητές	pa'tates tigani'tes	chips / french fries

επιδόρπια	epid'orpia	**Desserts**
φρούτα	'fruta	fruit
παγωτό	pago'to	ice cream
μπακλαβάς	bakla'vas	puff pastry in syrup with nut filling
μπουγάτσα	bu'gatsa	puff pastry pocket filled with vanilla cream
κρέμα	'krema	semolina pudding
ρυζόγαλο	ri'sogalo	rice pudding
σταφύλια	sta'filia	grapes
καρπούζι	kar'puzi	watermelon
πεπόνι	pe'poni	honeydew melon
ροδάκινο	ro'ðakino	peaches
μήλο	'milo	apples
αχλάδι	ach'laði	pears

Αλκοολούχα ποτά	alkoo'lucha pot'a	**Alcoholic Beverages**
άσπρο κρασί	'aspro kra'si	white wine
κόκκινο κρασί	'kokkino kra'si	red wine
ρετσίνα	re'tsina	resinated wine
χύμα	'chima	wine from the barrel
ξερό	kse'ro	dry
ημίγλυκο	i'migliko	semi-sweet

ούζο	'uso	anise-flavoured liqueur
τσίπουρο	'tsipuro	marc liqueur
(μια) μπύρα	(mya) 'bira	(a) beer

μη αλκοολούχα ποτά	mi alkoo'lucha pot'a	**Non-Alcoholic Beverages**
φραππέ	frap'pe	cold Nescafé with thick foam
ελληνικος καφές	elini'kos ka'fes	Greek mocca
τσάι	tsai	tea
πορτοκαλάδα	portoka'laða	orange lemonade
λεμονάδα	lemo'naða	lemonade
(μια καράφα) νερό	(mya ka'rafa) ne'ro	(a jug of) water
μεταλλικό νερό	metalli'ko ne'ro	non-carbonated mineral water
σόδα	'soda	soda water

Literature

The Classics **Homer:** The Odyssey
The »Odyssey« is available in a number of translations; one is by E.V.Rieu (Penguin Classics, 2003).

Robert Graves wrote the classic retelling of the Greek myths in English. QPD 1991.

Fiction **Nikos Kazantzakis:** *Zorba the Greek*, Faber, 2000.
A novel about a friendship between two men, an intellectual writer and a dynamic working man, made popular by the film of the same name with Anthony Quinn in the title role.

Tom Stone: *The Summer of My Greek Taverna: A Memoir*, Simon & Schuster 2003. Very entertaining holiday reading set on the island of Patmos, where the author lived for over 20 years.

Odysseas Elytis: *The Axion Esti*. Anvil Poetry, 1980.
The Nobel Prizewinner Elytis tells of the fate of his country in the »Bible of the Greek nation«, as Mikis Theodorakis termed the work.

Tim Severin is a sailor who specializes in reconstructing ancient voyages and writing about them, for example *The Jason Voyage* (Arrow Books 1986) attempts to follow in the footsteps of the Argonauts, while *The Ulysses Voyage* does the same for Odysseus (Arrow Books 1988).

Lawrence Durrell: *Prospero's Cell: A guide to the landscape and manners of the island of Corcyra*, Faber & Faber 2000.

Durrell very poetically describes the landscape and takes a look at the inhabitants, their everyday lives, religion and festivals, with a great deal of empathy.

There is a huge selection of Greek **cookbooks** to choose from in English.

! | *Baedeker* TIP

»Captain Corelli's Mandolin«
Kefalloniá (Cephalonia) garnered a certain amount of notoriety through this novel by Louis de Bernières that was published in 1994. It is a love story with the massacre committed by the German wehrmacht in 1943 as its backdrop. The film shot on Kefalloniá with Nicolas Cage and Penélope Cruz was a flop, but the book, a thrilling epic, is a good read to take along on holidays.

Media

Radio and Television

The state radio and television company, Elliniki Radiophonia Tileorassi (ERT), comprises Hellenic radio (Elliniki Radiophonia, ERA) and Hellenic television; three channels: ET1, NET and ET3.

Take your choice, English-language newspapers and periodicals are available here too.

Television There are a number of private television stations besides ERT, like ANT 1, Mega, Alpha, Alter and Star. The foreign TV stations that can be received with a terrestrial antenna are CNN, TV5, Euronews and RAI. BBC World and Sky News are available free-to-air on the Astra satellite, as is Deutsche Welle TV, which has an extensive English-language service.

Newspapers and Periodicals

Foreign periodicals The major English-language newspapers and magazines are available usually only a day late in the main towns on the islands and in tourist centres.

Greek foreign-language newspapers »Athens News« (daily), published in Athens, provides information about what's going on in Greece and abroad and includes information of interest to tourists. Keeping up with the news on Corfu is »The Corfiot« (monthly) and, on Lefkáda, the English-language monthly »Planet Lefkas«.

Money

Euro The euro has been the currency of Greece since 2002.

Cash machines The simplest way to obtain money is from ATMs, which are also usually found in rural areas. Money can be withdrawn from them by using a usual debit or credit card – together with the secret PIN.

The usual international **credit/debit cards** are accepted by banks, major hotels, and upscale shops and restaurants. In case of loss, contact the credit card company or bank immediately.

ℹ️ Lost or stolen card?

■ If a credit or debit card or mobile phone gets lost or stolen, it is essential to have them blocked immediately. Make sure in advance that you know which telephone number to call for your particular card(s).

Post and Communications

Post Greek post offices are run by the Hellenic Post, Elliniká Tachidromía (ELTA). It is not possible to make telephone calls in a post office. Greek post-boxes are yellow.

Opening Hours Post offices are generally open Monday to Friday from 8am to 2pm and Fri until 1.30pm. In major cities the opening hours last till evening.

● USEFUL TELEPHONE NUMBERS

COUNTRY CODES

► **to Greece**
Tel. 00 30

► **from Greece**
to Britain: tel. 00 44
to Ireland: tel. 00 353
to USA and Canada: tel. 00 1

INFORMATION

► **Domestic**
Tel. 1 51

► **Foreign**
Tel. 1 61

A picture postcard or a normal letter to Europe costs 0.65 €. It is best   Stamps
to purchase stamps from the post office because they cost more in
other places, such as kiosks, hotel receptions and souvenir shops.

The Hellenic Telecommunications Organization (OTE) is responsible   Telephoning
for the telephone system in Greece. Phone calls can be made from
kiosks, tavernas and hotels, but it is expensive. Card payphones have
been introduced and cards are available from OTE and from kiosks.
There are no coin-operated phones.

North American visitors will have problems with their cellphones   Mobile
unless they have a dual or tri-band system handset. European mobile   telephones
phones will work in Greece if roaming is activated. Arrange with
your provider.

Prices and Discounts

The euro has definitely had an impact on the level of prices in   Price level
Greece, even more so because it is so easy to raise prices on a massive scale in restaurants and the tourist trades. So reckon on about
the same prices as in the UK. The lower limit for a daily budget – in
high season, not counting travel costs and with two persons sharing
a room – is about 50 € per person. Persons travelling alone wishing

● HOW MUCH DOES IT COST?

**Simple
double room**
from €35

Simple meal
from €4

3-course menu
from €12

0.5l beer
€2 – 3.50

Boredom is a foreign word on Greece's beaches.

Chartering boats   Within the Greek territorial zone only boats that fly the Greek flag and are officially licensed for chartering may be chartered. A copy of the rental agreement is to be left with the harbour authorities at the port of departure and a second copy must be in the possession of the ship's master at all times. The same holds true for the passengers and crew lists. A prerequisite for hiring a boat without a crew is that both the person hiring and a second person on board have an appropriate certificate of competency (e.g. in the UK, Yachtmaster).

Diving   Scuba diving is prohibited in Greece's seas, lakes and rivers – with few exceptions – to protect archaeological treasures not yet uncovered there. A list of the excepted regions and their current regulations, as well as information about underwater fishing, is available at the Greek Tourist Board (►Information). In any case, it is advisable to first enquire about the local regulations at the proper harbour authorities. The Hellenic Federation for Underwater Activities and Sportfishing can provide information about diving courses in recognized schools.

Golf   The game of golf has been relatively late in gaining much attention in Greece, so there are to date only a few golf courses. There are golf courses around Athens, in Sithonía on the Chalkidikí Peninsula, as well as on the islands of Corfu, Crete and Rhodes.

Hiking   Hiking in Greece is growing in popularity. The six-hour hike through Samariá Gorge, for example, is one of the most fantastic ex-

● ADDRESSES

ANGLING

► **Greek Fishing Association**
Moutsopoulou
Piraeus
Tel. 21 04 51 57 31
Piraeus Port Authority
Tel. 21 04 51 14 11

DIVING

► **Greek Diving Association**
Athens
Tel. 21 09 81 99 61

GOLF

► **Hellenic Golf Federation**
P.O. box 70003
GR-16610 Glyfada
Tel. 21 08 94 19 33
Fax 21 08 94 51 62

HIKING

► **Hellenic Federation of Mountaineering and Climbing,**
5 Milioni Street
106 73 Athens
Tel. 21 03 64 59 04

HORSEBACK RIDING

► **Hellenic Riding Club**
Paradisou 18, Maroussi
Athens
Tel. 21 06 81 25 06

► **Faliro Ippodromo Racetrack**
Tel. 21 09 41 77 61

MOUNTAIN CLIMBING

► **Greek Alpine Club**
Ellinikos Orivatikos (EOS)
Mihalikopoulou 39, Athens
Tel. 21 07 29 54 73
Fax 21 07 21 27 66
E-mail: alpinclub@internet.gr

ROWING

► **Hellenic Rowing Club**
Voukourestiou 34, Athens
Tel. 21 03 61 21 09

TENNIS

► **Tennis Federation**
Patission 89, Athens
Tel. 21 08 21 04 78

WATER SKI

► **Greek Waterski Association**
Thrakis 60, Chlioupoli
Tel. 21 09 94 43 34
Fax 21 09 94 05 21

WINDSURFING

► **Greek Windsurfing Association**
Filellinon 7
Athens
Tel. 21 03 23 36 96
Fax 21 03 22 32 51
www.ghiolman.com

WINTER SPORTS

► **Hellenic Ski Federation**
Karageorgi Servias 7, Athens
Tel. 21 03 23 44 12
Fax 2 10 32 30 12

YACHTING ASSOCIATIONS

► **Hellenic Sailing Federation (E I O)**
Possidonos 51
GR-18344 Moschato
Tel. 21 09 30 48 25

► **Hellenic Yachting Federation (H. Y. F.)**
Kountourioti 7
GR-18534 Piraeus
Tel. 21 04 13 73 51
Fax 21 09 30 48 29

Transport

By Car

Road network The Greek road network has been expanded according to plan during the last decades and effort is being made to improve and expand it further. A major part of it is surfaced. The asphalted roads are for the most part on the mainland, but in out of the way places they are often narrow and winding. In general, it is best not to drive at night because the shoulders of the roads are usually not marked and are very irregular and even very good roads can have large and deep potholes. There are still gravel roads, particularly on the smaller islands. Expect animals and cars without headlights on country roads at night.

Traffic regulations For the most part, international traffic regulations are in force in Greece. Offenders face drastic fines even with parking violations. Multi-lingual police officers wear an armband with the inscription **Tourist Police**. Sounding a horn in the city is prohibited. Seatbelts are mandatory when driving. Driving at night in brightly-lit towns with sidelights only is permitted. The sign »priority road« means no parking. The alcohol limit is 50 mg per 100 ml (0.5 per mille).

»Funcars« and »quads« provide the transport to the secluded coves and beaches.

TRANSPORT INFORMATION

AUTOMOBILE CLUBS

► **ELPA**
Messogion 2
Tel. 21 07 79 16 15
They also provide road condition reports.

Tel. 174
Use this number for information about hotels, events and sights worth seeing, etc.

Tel. 1 04
Emergency call

CAR HIRE

► **Making reservations from home**
Avis:
production.rent-at-avis.com
Europcar: www.europcar.co.uk
Hertz: www.hertz.co
Sixt: www.sixt.com
(for USA: www.sixtusa.com)

Speed limits

Speed limits for personal vehicles, also with trailers, (and motorcycles over 100 cc): in town 19 mph/30 kph – 31 mph/50 kph (25 mph/40 kmh), outside of towns 56 mph/90 kph (44 mph/70 kph), on national roads 68 mph/110 kph and on motorways 75 mph/120 kph. Driving too fast can result in heavy fines and possible loss of the driving licence. In some cases, the licence plates are removed from the car.

Petrol

Diesel and the usual grades of unleaded petrol, as well as motor oil (normal and super) are found almost everywhere and, infrequently, liquefied petroleum gas (LPG). Carrying canisters of fuel in the car is prohibited.

Breakdown services

The Automobile and Touring Club ELPA maintains a patrol service (OVELPA) with yellow vehicles with the sign **Assistance Routière**) along the more important tourist roads. In case of a breakdown, wave a yellow cloth or open the bonnet (hood) to attract attention. There is a fee for the service. On the spot service and towing to the next garage are without charge for those with AA (www.theaa.com/breakdown-cover/european-breakdown-cover.jsp) or RAC (www.rac.co.uk/web/breakdowncover/european) European breakdown cover.

Taxis

The charge for a trip in a taxi is cheaper than, for example, in the UK. There are large numbers of taxis available in the larger cities and, especially in Athens, they can be found in all places heavily frequented by the public (airports, train stations, Piraeus Harbour, Syntagma Square, Omonia Square, bus stations, etc.), as well as in front of large hotels and museums. They cruise about town practically all the time, night and day. Taxis will stop at the side of the road when called or waved at. It is customary to share the taxi with other passengers; this means no reduction in price, though. The taxis with the yellow taxi sign on the roof have meters. Additional fees are charged for entering the taxi at bus and train stations, harbours and airports; also for each piece of luggage and trips between midnight and 5am.

Car Hire

Besides the international car rental firms, whose reservation systems are dependable, there are local services – especially in Athens, Piraeus, Thessaloníki and in the larger tourist centres (on the islands, as well) – that offer cars for hire. Their rates are usually lower, but the vehicles are not always of the accustomed quality. Car rental firms are represented at the international airports; hotel receptions also arrange car rentals. It is frequently less expensive to book a rental car from home.

Hiring conditions The pre-condition for hiring a vehicle is possession of an international driving licence. A national driving licence is sufficient if issued in an EU country. In addition, a credit card is indispensable to avoid a high deposit.

Travellers with Disabilities

The Hellenic Chamber of Hotels' official guide contains listings of disability-friendly accommodation. It is available at the offices of the Greek National Tourist Organization EOT (▶Information). The gogreece website
http://gogreece.about.com/od/disabledtravel/Disabled_and_Handicapped_Travel_Greece.htm
also provides useful information

When to Go

Spring is the best time Considering its Mediterranean climate, the best time to travel to Greece is in spring, from about the second half of March to the end of May or start of June, as well as in autumn, during the months of September and October, sometimes even until the beginning of November. The summer months (mid-June to the start of September) are very hot. From mid-November until the end of March, the weather is very rainy. The months of March, April and May are mild and nature is blossoming forth. It is the ideal time for a hiking holiday. Summertime in Greece is perfect for a beach holiday. It is very hot at this time, particularly in the large cities, but the dry air and the north winds blowing constantly across the Aegean, the Meltemi, make it quite bearable. Although the winds provide pleasant cooling relief, they also cause one to underestimate the danger of the sun's rays. So adequate protection is necessary even when the temperature appears to be »pleasant« and it is wise to seek out a spot in the shade and not in the blazing sun, especially around noontime. It is recommended, even in summer, to take along warm clothing because it can become quite cool in the evenings on the sea and in the mountains. The temperature becomes mild once again beginning in October, with the fine weather often lasting into November, but count on the first rainfall.

Climate

There are basically really only three seasons in Greece – a relatively short spring from March to mid-May, when the vegetation explodes, a long, hot and very dry summer from the middle of May until October and a cool, wintry rainy season from November to March. Because of the way the countryside is divided up in small sections by the mountains, running mostly in an east-west direction, and its relative proximity or distance from the sea, Greece has been able to develop a wide range of regional climatic features.

Greece offers its guests up to 3,000 hours of sunshine a year.

Tours

YOU WANT TO EXPLORE GREECE
BUT YOU DON'T KNOW HOW TO
GO ABOUT IT? OUR TOURS WILL
TAKE YOU TO THE MOST IMPORTANT
SIGHTS AND MOST IMPRESSING NATURAL BEAUTY
SPOTS IN THE COUNTRY.

Travelling in Greece

When Zeus and his family of gods were looking for a place worthy to make their home, it was not by chance that they chose Greece. They recognized that there were no landscapes more varied, no islands more beautiful nor people more friendly anywhere else one earth. It is even said that the ocean is nowhere as blue as it is in Greece.

So merrily jump right into that blue water, discover millennia-old witnesses to the turbulent history of this country or just drift from island to island taking all the time in the world. Get ready to enjoy a bit of a one-of-a-kind Mediterranean lifestyle. Delight in the good food, the excellent wine and above all the heart-felt hospitality encountered every step of the way. Naturally, getting to know Greece is not such a simple undertaking because it is famously quite large, and silent witnesses to this nation's more than 5,000 years of history are lurking everywhere just waiting to be discovered. Where to begin? Perhaps with the legendary mountains, or with the world-famous sites of Antiquity or with the fabulously beautiful, endlessly long sandy beaches or with the lively, modern cities? Or with one of the following tours. They were especially designed for discovering the

For those who would rather not walk, there is always the traditional method of transport.

country and the people. The routes put together here – a mix of recommended, important cultural highlights in history, experiencing nature's own landscapes and practical tips for tourists off the beaten – will help you get quickly acquainted and familiar with the land. Depending on the time available, the tours can also, of course, be lengthened, shortened or combined.

Tour 1 From Thessaloníki to Athen

Start: Thessaloníki   **Length of the Tour:** 650 km/404 mi
Destination: Athens

To a great extent, this tour follows the route along the east coast that connects Thessaloníki and Athens, the main axis of the Greek road network. It includes both of Greece's largest and most important cities, with an abundance of sights worth seeing. Allow for a couple of days to tour each of them.

From ❶ ✱ **Thessaloníki**, the capital of Macedonia, the route leads to the southwest through the monotonous Kampania plain, the Axios river delta, Loudias and Alia km ón. Past Katerini along the foothills of Pieria Mountain (there are beaches and sand dunes at Makry-gialós) and 6 km /3.7 mi off the road is ✱ **Dion**, with the archaeological site of the city sacred to the Macedonians. The foot of the 2,917 m/9,570 ft mountain of the gods, ✱ **Olympus**, Greece's highest elevation, has now already been reached. The expressway passes the mighty crusader castle of Platamónas before entering the beautiful Témbi Valley (Vale of Témbe) between Olympus and the Ossa massif. At the exit of the valley there is an opportunity for an interesting detour to the picturesque village of ❷ ✱ **Ambelákia** (5 km/3 mi). Pinios Valley now opens up to the East Thessalian plain with ❸ **Lárisa**, the capital of Thessaly, which was the granary of Greece even in ancient times. Forget the port city of ❹ **Vólos**, if you do not want to go to ✱ **Pílion** with its picturesque mountain villages and wonderful beaches – which would be a shame. The road makes a wide curve around the 1,726 m/5,663 ft Othrys Mountains and later – with a view of Évia – along the Gulf of Lamía to ❺ **Lamía**, the chief town in the Fthiotis region. Southwest of the city lies the famous Thermopylae, though today it is no longer a bottleneck pass but rather just historically interesting.

Now head in a southerly direction to ❻ ✱✱ **Dephí**. Take time to look at the Gorgopotamos railway bridge before driving over Sperchios Valley – look back for a fantastic view – and the winding mountain passes to Bralos. Then cross through the Kifissos Plain over to Ámfissa in the olive-tree-rich region of Fokis and the site of

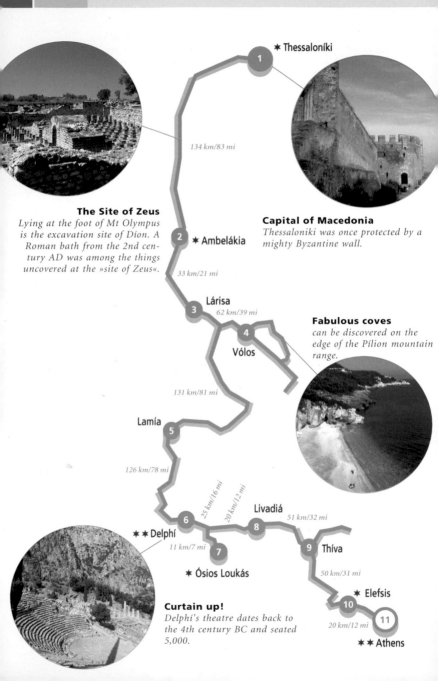

* Thessaloníki

1

134 km/83 mi

The Site of Zeus
Lying at the foot of Mt Olympus is the excavation site of Díon. A Roman bath from the 2nd century AD was among the things uncovered at the »site of Zeus«.

Capital of Macedonia
Thessaloniki was once protected by a mighty Byzantine wall.

2 * Ambelákia

33 km/21 mi

3 Lárisa
62 km/39 mi

4

Vólos

Fabulous coves
can be discovered on the edge of the Pílion mountain range.

131 km/81 mi

Lamía **5**

126 km/78 mi

25 km/16 mi   20 km/12 mi

Livadiá

6   **8**   51 km/32 mi

** * Delphí

11 km/7 mi   **7**   **9** Thíva

* Ósios Loukás

50 km/31 mi

Curtain up!
Delphí's theatre dates back to the 4th century BC and seated 5,000.

* Elefsis

10

11

20 km/12 mi

** * Athens

the famous ancient oracle of ✶✶ **Delphi**, set in a magnificent land-scape. Whoever has a craving for the sea can take a detour to Galaxí-di. After leaving ✶✶ **Delphí**, it's back to the east again. The mountains of ✶ **Parnassus** can be reached from Arachova, a village in a picturesque setting. A cul-de-sac 13 km/8 mi to the east branches off to the monastery of ❼ ✶ **Ósios Loukás**, which is world-famous for its 11th century mosaics. Along the way is Dístomo, which German occupation forces destroyed in 1944. 45 km/28 mi east of Delphí lies ❽ **Livadiá**, the capital of Boeotia. A Minoan vaulted grave can be seen

13 km/8 mi to the east in Orchomenós. From there, drive to the east to the motorway access at Kastro, where the mighty Mycenaean fortress, Gla, still stands. It is easiest to take the motorway to ❾ **Thíva**, the important city of Thebes in ancient mythology. There is a view out over the whole plain of Thíva from the Sagmata Monastery (12 km/7.5 mi to the northeast). If not planning on heading to the isle of Euboea (Évia), then choose the road from Thíva (E 926) going south through the scenic and historical Boeotian-Attic border area. The road beyond Erithres cuts across Gyphtokastro Pass. A nice side trip from the Attic fortress of ancient Eleutherai is to ✶ **Pórto Gérmeno**, beautifully situated on the Gulf of Corinth 23 km/14 mi to the west. It is only 21 km/13 mi from Inoi to the Saronic Gulf and the site of the Eleusinian Mysteries, an ancient cult centre in ❿ ✶ **Eleusis**, which today is surrounded by the industrial city of Elefsina. Finally, the motorway then leads to the Greek capital of ⓫ ✶✶ **Athens**.

Tour 2 The North of Greece

Start: Igoumenítsa   **Length of the Tour:** 450 km/280 mi
Destination: Igoumenítsa

This tour leads through the varied landscape of northwest Greece, an area of the country that has remained less frequented by tourists until now.

Starting in ❶ **Igoumenítsa**, the route first goes south-eastwards through the mountainous landscape of Thesprotia. A road branches off 5 km/3 mi past Margariti for a »swimming detour« to ❷ ✶ **Párga**, a resort situated in a pretty cove. The ancient oracle of the dead, the Nekromanteíon of Ephýra, can be seen a bit further south at

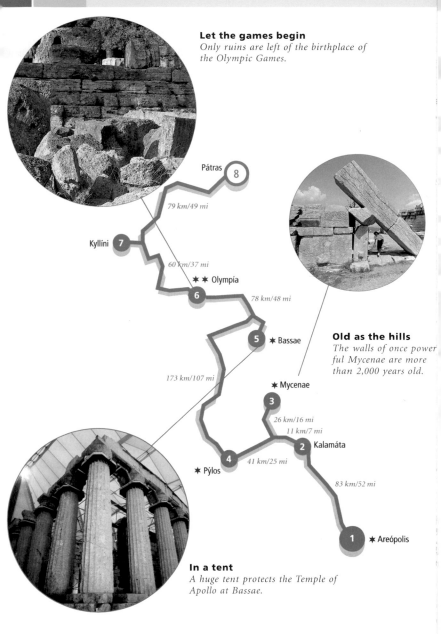

Let the games begin
Only ruins are left of the birthplace of the Olympic Games.

Pátras **8**

79 km/49 mi

Kyllíni **7**

60 km/37 mi

✶✶ Olympía

6

78 km/48 mi

5 ✶ Bassae

173 km/107 mi

Old as the hills
The walls of once power ful Mycenae are more than 2,000 years old.

✶ Mycenae

3

26 km/16 mi

11 km/7 mi

2 Kalamáta

4 *41 km/25 mi*

✶ Pýlos

83 km/52 mi

1 ✶ Areópolis

In a tent
A huge tent protects the Temple of Apollo at Bassae.

The Bay of Koroni near Kalamáta is located in a fabulous setting. →

Sights from A to Z

WORLD-FAMOUS ANTIQUITIES AND
AN EXUBERANT CAPITAL,
INCREDIBLE LANDSCAPES,
HEAVENLY BEACHES AND AN
ENTHRALLING WORLD OF ISLANDS –
THERE IS A LOT TO DISCOVER IN
GREECE.

★★ Aegina · Αίγινα

J / K 9

Island Group: Saronic Islands
Altitude: 0 – 532 m/1,745 ft
Capital: Aegina

Area: 83 sq km/32 sq mi
Population: 12,000

The mild climate and low precipitation make the hilly, fertile island in the Saronic Gulf – renowned for its excellent pistachios – one of the favourite destinations of the Athenians for a daytrip or holiday – no wonder, after all the island is right at their doorstep.

Mythology and history

According to mythology, **Aeacus**, the son of Zeus and Aegina and father of Peleus and Telamon, was made a judge of the Underworld together with Minos and Rhadamanthys because of his wise and just rule and is considered to be the ancestral father of the Aeacidae. As

 VISITING AEGINA

INFORMATION

Tourist Police
Leonárdou Ladá
Aegina Town
Tel. 22 97 02 77 77

GETTING THERE

Connections by ship with Piraeus and Galatas on the mainland and with the islands of Ankístri, Póros, Spétses and Ýdra.

WHERE TO EAT

► Moderate

Agorá
Aegina Town
Behind the fish market hall, street parallel to the harbour
Excellent fish dishes at acceptable price

► Inexpensive

Taverna Lekkas
Aegina Town
Beautifully situated on the promenade in the direction of Kolóna Hill; Greek cooking that even the locals enjoy.

WHERE TO STAY

► Mid-range

Eginitikó Archontikó
Ag. Nikoláou & Thomaídos 1
Aegina Town
Tel. 22 97 02 49 68
E-mail: fotisd@aig.forthnet.gr
13 rooms
The hotel is in a 19th-century manor house and has a roof garden with bar.

► Budget

Artemis
Kanari 20
Aegina Town
Tel. 22 97 02 51 95
www.artemishotel-aegina.com
24 rooms.
Pleasant house; all rooms feature a balcony.

Plaza
N. Kazantzaki 3
Aegina Town
Tel. 22 97 02 56 00
8 rooms
Popular, small hotel on the shore road with good rooms facing the sea.

Vegetable dealers on Aegina use boats as their market stall.

early as the second millennium BC, the island was an important trading hub for pottery. Aegina was first mentioned as a colony of Doric Epidaurus, with which it came under the rule of King **Pheidon of Argos** in the 7th century BC. After separating from the mother city in the 6th century BC, Aegina began to flourish, with trading posts on the Black Sea and elsewhere, which brought the island state into competition with Corinth. The maritime state was at the height of its power at the start of the Persian Wars. Clashes occurred with Athens, who saw the strong island as a hindrance to the expansion of its sea power. The Athenians forced the city to surrender in 456 BC. At the beginning of the Peloponnesian War (431 BC), the Aeacidae were finally driven from their island and the land was divided up among Attic citizens. Although the overthrow of Athens in 404 BC made it possible for many to return, the island's golden years were past. Repeated military campaigns brought it anew under the rapidly growing Attic power, whose fate they shared from then on. Aegina, the main town on the island, was the capital of Greece in 1828.

What to see on Aegina

The **main town on the island**, Aegina (pop. 6,000), spreads gently up around a wide bay on the northern west coast. It is a pleasant little bustling town with some Neo-classical buildings still adding to its image. The centre of life here can be found mainly around the harbour jetty with its numerous pavement cafés and restaurants. On

Aegina town

Aphaia-Temple Plan

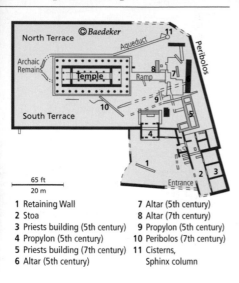

1 Retaining Wall
2 Stoa
3 Priests building (5th century)
4 Propylon (5th century)
5 Priests building (7th century)
6 Altar (5th century)
7 Altar (5th century)
8 Altar (7th century)
9 Propylon (5th century)
10 Peribolos (7th century)
11 Cisterns,
    Sphinx column

Kolóna Hill, jutting up in the north of the city, is an 8 m/26 ft high Doric column from the **Temple of Apollo** by the harbour (460 BC). Traces of pre-Mycenaean and Mycenaean settlements were found under the temple and, to the west, two smaller temples though to have been dedicated to Artemis and Dionysus. Archaeological finds from the 3rd millennium up to Roman times, particularly those from the temples of Aphaia and Apollo, are displayed in the interesting **archaeological museum**.

The drive to the Temple of Aphaia on the east coast of the island, about 3 km/2 mi north of the resort Agía Marína, leads through wooded and cultivated hill country. Some 2 km/1.2 mi along the way is the church of **Ágii Theódori**. It was erected in 1289 using materials from an ancient temple and has some Byzantine frescoes very much worth seeing.

Ágios Nektários

Just a few kilometres further on, the large modern church of the Nektarios Monastery comes into view visible in the distance. The monastery, named after Archbishop Nektarios, who died in 1920 and was canonized in 1961, is an important pilgrimage site.

Palaiochóra

Right close by is Palaiochóra, the **medieval capital of the island** abandoned around 1800, with the remains of a Venetian castle. Between the ruins of the city scattered over the hill are twenty churches from the 13th and 14th centuries, some decorated with frescoes.

★ ★
Temple of Aphaia

The 5th century BC temple of **Aphaia**, dedicated to a deity regarded as a **protectress of women**, rests on the foundation of a shrine from the 6th century BC and is arranged as a peripteros with 6 : 12 columns. The pronaos and opisthodomos – here there is a stone altar – were enclosed by antae walls with two columns between. The roof of the cella is supported by two rows of columns. 23 columns of yellowish limestone with parts of their original plaster covering have survived. The sacrificial altar was in front of the whole width of the east front and connected to it by a ramp, while south of the east front is the small propylaea with octagonal columns. The whole of the sacred site was levelled with earth and buttressed in part by natu-

Aphaia, the daughter of Zeus, was venerated as a protector of women in the over 2,500-year-old temple on the east coast of Aegina.

ral rocks and in part by walls of blocks of stone. Remains of Late Neolithic (4th / 3rd millennium BC) settlements were discovered in the area. There is a magnificent view from the temple grounds over a large part of the Saronic Gulf all the way to the mainland coastline from Athens to Cape Soúnion. To gain an overview of the construction history of the Aphaia Temple, visit the **archaeological museum** right next to the way leading up (open: April–Oct daily 8am– 7.30pm). ⏲

Agía Marína

About 3 km/2 mi south of Aphaia Temple, the island's **tourist centre**, Agía Marína, stretches out on a beautiful bay with sandy beaches, modern hotels and many cafés, tavernas and souvenir shops.

Ankistri

Some 5 km/3 mi southwest of Aegina lies the wooded island of Ankístri; at only 12 sq km/ 4.6 sq mi, it is the smallest inhabited island in the Saronic Gulf. Its 700 or so inhabitants are descendants of Albanians who immigrated here in the 16th century. Good bathing beaches can be found at Skála and Megalochóri.

✳ Amorgós · Αμοργός

Island Group: Cyclades
Altitude: 0 – 826 m/2,710 ft
Principal city: Amorgós Chóra

Area: 120 sq km/46 sq mi
Population: 1,800

For people who enjoy hiking and spending their holidays far from the madding crowd, the mountainous Cycladic island of Amorgós is the ideal place to go.

Eastern Cycladic island

Theof Amorgós, 33 km/20.5 mi long and 2 to 6 km /1.2 to 3.7 mi wide, lies to the southeast of Náxos. The rock cliff face on the southeast coast rises spectacularly up to 800 m/2,625 ft above the ocean; the northwest coast is more gentle and has two deep bays: Aegiáli Bay and Katápola Bay with the island's most important port. Tourism is concentrated primarily in Katápola.

The monastery of Panagiá Chozoviótissa clings like a bright hornets' nest to the rock face.

▶ VISITING AMORGÓS

INFORMATION
www.amorgos.gr

Tourist Information
In the tourist offices in Katápola

GETTING THERE
Ship connections to Piraeus on the mainland as well as to the other Cycladic islands.

WHERE TO EAT
▶ Moderate
Mouragio
Katápola
Tel. 22 85 07 10 11
This restaurant, close to the platía, serves good Greek cooking.

▶ Inexpensive
Bitzéntos
Katápola

Good Greek dishes are served directly on the waterfront in »Bitzéntos«.

WHERE TO STAY
▶ Luxury
Aegiális
Aegiáli
Tel. 22 85 07 33 93
www.aegialis-amorgos.com
32 rooms
Just outside Aegiáli, the hotel, situated between two sandy bays, offers nicely decorated rooms with a magnificent ocean view.

▶ Mid-range
Amorgos
Katápola
Tel. 22 85 07 10 13
10 rooms
Quite comfortable guesthouse located by the harbour.

What to See on Amorgós

Katápola, situated on a deep bay, is the main port and **tourist centre of the island**. The monastery of Panagía Katapolianis, built on the foundation of an early Christian basilica, is worth seeing. The remains of the city of **Minóa**, assumed to have been built by Cretans in the 2nd millennium BC, lie on a rise in a green valley that opens up to the south of the bay.

Katápola

The island's chief town, Amorgós-Chóra, is located 5 km/3 mi above Katápola. Its white Cycladic houses, over 40 family chapels and the remains of a 13th century Venetian castle are nestled around strikingly distinctive rocks. The **archaeological museum** next to Zoodóchos Pigí church provides an insight into the island's early history. Outstanding examples of Cycladic art have been uncovered on Amorgós, some of which can be seen in the Cycladic museum in Athens.

Amorgós-Chóra

The famous Byzantine Panagía Chozoviótissa monastery, daringly built on a steep cliff face, is very impressive. The monastery can be

★
Panagía Chozoviótissa

reached by foot in about 40 minutes from Amorgós Chóra on a stepped path that begins on the eastern end of the town. The legend of its founding tells of a woman in Palestine who placed an icon in a boat to save it from the iconoclasts. The picture was driven to the coast here and the locals erected a church on a spot marked for them by an iron nail. The fortified monastery building was founded by **Emperor Alexios Komnenos** in 1088 and contains valuable icons. There is an impressive view across the sea from the terrace (opening hours: daily 8am–1pm, additionally in the summer 5pm–7pm).

! *Baedeker* TIP

Up on Kríkelo

A hike up Kríkelo (826 m/2710 ft) is wonderful, especially in spring when everything is turning green and in blossom. Plan on four to five hours for a roundtrip hike totalling 18 km/11.2 mi.

In the southwest of the island near the pretty little village of Arkesíni lie the ruins of a city called **Kastrí** that was occupied from Mycenaean to Roman times. The archaeological site, situated in a captivating location, can be reached with a 2 km/1.2 mi long walk from Vroutsi.

✴ Ándros · Άνδρος

M 9

Island Group: Cyclades	**Area:** 380 sq km/147 sq mi
Altitude: 0 – 994 m/3,261 ft	**Population:** 10,000
Principal city: Ándros-Chóra	

Luxuriantly green Ándros, the northernmost and, after Náxos, the second largest of the Cycladic islands, is still pretty much undiscovered as a holiday destination. The relatively modest tourist trade activities are mostly concentrated on the beaches around Batsí and Gávrio on the west coast.

What to See on Ándros

Ándros Chóra

Ándros Chóra, the chief town, is spread out over a rocky ridge between two bays on the east coast. A picturesque stepped path leads up from the harbour to Platía Kaíris between the old and new towns, where there is a remarkable archaeological museum. The highlight of the museum, which offers a comprehensive look into the island's history, is the Classical marble statue of **Hermes of Ándros** (opening hours: Tue – Sun 8am – 2.30pm).

✴
Archaeological Museum ►
🕐

✴
Museum of Modern Art ►

The Museum of Modern Art nearby is one of the few of its kind in Greece. Important modern Greek artists are presented, along with the sculptor, **Michael Tombros**, a native of Ándros. The collection al-

VISITING ÁNDROS

INFORMATION

Tourist Information
Gávrio
information kiosk at the harbour
Tel. 22 82 02 51 62
www.androsweb.gr

GETTING THERE

Ship connections with Rafína on the
mainland as well as with the islands
Amorgós, Donoussa, Iráklia, Kéa,
Koufónissa, Kýthnos, Mýkonos,
Náxos, Páros, Sýros and Tínos.

WHERE TO EAT

► **Inexpensive**
Parea
Platía Kaíris

Ándros Chóra
The taverna at the entrance to the old
town offers Greek dishes along with a
beautiful view of the beach.

WHERE TO STAY

► **Luxury**
Paradise
Ándros-Chorá
Tel. 22 82 02 21 87
www.paradiseandros.gr
38 rooms, 3 suites
The hotel located at the southwest
entrance to the town offers spacious,
well-appointed rooms; there is a
magnificent view that opens up from
the dining room; a shuttle bus drives
regularly to the beach.

---

so includes some works by Picasso, Klee, Matisse and Chagall (opening hours: Oct–June Mon–Sat 10am–12 noon, July–Sept also
6pm–8pm). The beautiful old town kástro (castle) can be entered
from Platía Kaíris through Kamara Gate. The old town is surprisingly impressive with its Neo-classical townhouses. The **Panagía Pa-
latianís** church, furnished with a valuable carved templon, dates back
to the 13th century. Ship models are on display in the small **maritime museum** that can be found at
the end of the kástro at Platiá Afaní
Nafti. A single-arch bridge leads to
Castle Island, where there are some
scant remains of a Venetian fortress.

Steniés, 4 km/2.5 mi north of the
main town on the island, is surrounded by fruit and almond trees.
Below it stretches a sandy beach
with the name **Giália**. Situated in a beautiful site 6 km/3.7 mi northwest of Ándros Chóra is Apikía, the source of Sáriza, Greece's well-
known mineral water. The spring is open to the public in a pump-
room. From here a one-hour hike will take you to the **Ágios Nikólaos** monastery, where there is a famous icon of St Nicholas, fashioned of gold and silver strands and human hair.

> ! **Baedeker TIP**
>
> **A specialty ...**
>
> ... of the island is »froutália«, an omelette with
> potatoes and sausage to be found primarily in
> the hinterland, in the village of Katákilos, for
> example, located 5 km/3 mi from Batsí.

Messariá Valley   The fertile Messariá Valley spreading out across the island from Ándros Chóra is cultivated with citrus fruits and vineyards. Standing in the pretty town of **Messariá** is the Taxiarchis Church from 1158. **Panagía Panachrántou**, founded in 961, is the oldest and largest monastery on the island. The fortress-like complex lies at an altitude of 800 m/2,625 ft and 4 km/2.5 mi south of Messariá. **Zagorá**, the only well-preserved settlement from the Geometric Period (900 – 700 BC) in Greece, is located 2 km/1.2 mi south of the Stavropéda intersection, but is not open to the public.

West coast   **Paleópolis**, the former capital of the island that flourished down to Byzantine times, was once located where today there is a village of the same name. There are scattered remains of the acropolis and the harbour. The new archaeological museum of Paleópolis has displays

The beautiful beach of Batsí is quiet and relaxing.

of vessels, tools, jewellery, coins, sculptures and inscriptions that were found in the old capital. Pretty **Batsi**, the island's tourist centre, has a number of beautiful sandy beaches. North of Batsí, at an elevation of 300 m/984 ft, is the convent of **Zoodóchos Pigí** (»Life-giving Source«). It was founded in 1325 and has valuable icons dating from the 14th to the 16th centuries. The small museum displays liturgical vestments and sacred art. The Bay of **Gávrio** served as a sheltered anchorage even in Antiquity. Today the fishing village is the **island's main port**. Some 2 km/1.2 mi to the northwest, at Ágios Pétros, stands the massive Hellenistic round tower of the same name (4th / 3rd centuries BC).

✳ Argolis · Αργολίδα

H /J 9 /10

Argolis occupies the northeast of the Peloponnese. It was settled as early as the Neolithic period and over 3000 years ago during the Mycenaean period it was the most densely populated of all the Greek regions with its centres of trade and power: Mycenae, Tiryns and Argos.

What to See in Argolis

Argolis, one of Greece's most important cultural landscapes, was occupied around 2000 BC by the Achaeans, who were early Greeks. In the Doric period, Argos became the most powerful city in the region, and the Heraion of Argos was the central shrine. Rising up on a hill a little further to the northeast are the formidable walls of the fortress of ►Mycenae and to the northwest is the shrine dedicated to Zeus at Neméa and in the east of Argolis is ►Epidauros with its famous theatre. During Venetian times, ►Náfplion on the Argolic Gulf was built into a massive stronghold. Today, Náfplion and the bathing resorts further east, Toló, Ermióni and Porto Chéli as well as the offshore islands of Spétses and Ýdra, are tourist centres.

Significant cultural landscape

▶ **ARGOLIS**

INFORMATION
Tourist Information
25. Martiou
Náfplion
Tel. 27 52 02 44 44

Argos, **chief city**, transportation hub and economic centre **of Argolis**, is spread out on a fertile plain at the foot of the 289 m/948 ft Lárissa Hill with a castle perched on it. The pretty Platía in the city centre, dominated by Ágios Pétros Church built in 1859 and lined by cafés and shops, is always bustling. Well worth seeing is the nearby **archaeological museum** in the pedestrian zone, with displays of stat-

Argos

A sweeping view across the plains of Argos unfolds from the ruins of the Sanctuary of Hera near Néa Iréo.

⊙ ues, grave steles, pottery and mosaics from Lerna and ancient Argos (opening hours: Tue–Sun 8am–3pm). The remains of the ancient city were unearthed on the road to Trípolis. The ruins of 2nd-century Roman baths were uncovered first. The theatre (c. 400 BC) alongside has seating for 20,000, making it one of the largest in Greece. Also preserved are parts of the Roman odeon, the shrine to Aphrodite and the agorá. **Lárissa Hill** can be reached on foot from the excavation site in 45 minutes. The summit is crowned by a mighty castle that dates back to the Byzantine period. A splendid view can be enjoyed there.

Heraion 11 km/7 mi northeast of Argos, near the village of Néo Iréo, lies one of the most important Hera shrines of ancient Greece, the Heraion (Iraion). Although only little remains to be seen of the shrine, its fantastic location is stunning. Since Mycenaean times, the Heraion was the **principal shrine of the Argives**. It was laid out on terraces on the slopes of a hill from the 8th to the 5th century BC. A broad, ancient stairway leads up to the first terrace with the remnants of a stoa and the foundation of the 5th-century BC Hera temple for which **Polykleitos**, a native of Argos, created a chryselephantine statue of Hera.

✳ **Neméa** Some 25 km/15.5 mi north of Argos, by the wine village of Archéa Neméa, lies ancient Neméa, with its **Zeus shrine**, surrounded by vineyards, olive trees and cypresses. In 1251 BC, the seer Amphiaraus founded the Pan-Hellenic **Nemean Games** in honour of Zeus. The Nemean Games were held every two years beginning in 573 BC until they were moved in the 2nd century BC to Argo. The Nemean Games were revived in 1996, and now include sports and cultural events. A Doric peripteros temple with 6 : 12 very slender columns was built on the site of an ancient temple, of which a crypt has survived. Recognizable on the east side is the tuffstone foundation of the altar. There was an elongated guesthouse south of the temple upon which a basilica was erected in the 5th / 6th centuries; in addition, a palaestra, the oldest surviving Hellenic bath in Greece, and a relatively well-preserved stadium. The museum has coins, pottery and Mycenaean artefacts from the area as well presenting as a history of the excavation. (opening hours: Tue–Sun 8.30am – 3pm).   🕐

The Stymphalian Lake lies some 30 km/18.6 mi northwest of Neméa and is noted for its interesting bird and plant life. It is where Heracles killed the man-eating Stymphalian birds in mythology.

★
Stymphalian Lake

On the southern edge of **Míli**, 12 km/7.5 mi south of Argos, is the covered excavation site of Lerna, which was settled as far back as the Neolithic period. The centre of the complex is occupied by an **Early Helladic palace** built around 2200 BC and, measuring 24×11 m/ 79×36 ft, it is the largest structure in the pre-Greek period in Greece. Two Mycenaean shaft tombs are an indication that the Mycenaeans had occupied the site around 1600 BC. Directly to the north lies the Hydra spring, where, according to legend, Heracles killed the nine-headed »Lernaean serpent«, the Hydra.

Lerna

Islands off Argolis

The 33 sq km/13 sq mi island of Póros lies in the Saronic Gulf and is separated from the north coast of Argolis by a narrow sound. Ferries and ships sailing for the island close to the mainland leave from the harbour of Galatás. The inhabitants live off the agricultural yield from the fertile stretch of coast on the mainland belonging to Póros as well as from the tourist trade.

Póros

The chief town (pop. 3,900) on the island is also called Póros and is beautifully situated on a small hill on the sea. The **archaeological museum** on Platía Korýzi has displays of artefacts found on the island dating from Mycenaean up to early Christian times, including grave steles and vases.

◄ Póros (town)

Some 5 km/3 mi northeast of the city are traces of a Poseidon shrine dating from the 6th century BC, which was the centre of the Kalaureian Amphictyony (cult community) formed of maritime cities on the Saronic and Argolian Gulfs. The numerous remains of buildings in the vicinity suggest that this was the site of the **ancient city of Kalaureia**.

◄ Temple of Poseidon

About 4 km/2.5 mi east of the town of Póros stands the 18th-century monastery of Zoodóchos Pigí, which is decorated with a beautiful gilt iconostasis from Asia Minor. Some small remains of the **ancient city of Troizén** have survived at the village of Damalás, some 10 km/ 6.2 mi west of the monastery,

◄ Zoodóchos Pigí monastery

Mules waiting for their next load in the harbour of Ýdra Town.

Ýdra
Ýdra is a bare, 12 km/7.5 mi long and up to 5 km/3 mi wide island off the southeast coast of Argolis. Ferries cast off from Piraeus and Ermióni on the mainland and the islands of Aegina und Spétses for this charming island, whose inhabitants live primarily from tourism and crafts – jewellery, pottery, embroidery, weaving and leatherworking.

Ýdra (town) ▶
The chief town of the island, Ýdra (pop. 2,500), built up picturesquely on the hills about a small, sheltered harbour cove on the north coast, is the gathering place of numerous artists and intellectuals who give the island its character. Standing on the quay is the church of the former 17th-century monastery of Panagía with an interesting cloister and a small **Byzantine museum**. The **maritime museum** near to where the ships dock concentrates mainly on the Greek battle for freedom of 1821. The harbour basin is lined with the early-19th-century villas of rich shipowning and merchant families. Behind, simple Cycladic-looking townhouses can be seen ascending the hills. Towering above the city are the ruins of a medieval castle and below it a fortress from the War of Greek Independence.

Kamínia, Vlychós ▶
20 minutes on foot along the shore to the west of Ýdra town lies the peaceful fishing village of Kamínia, offering a gravel beach. A little further west at Vlychós are the remains of the **ancient city of Chorisa**; in addition, there are nice tavernas and a less frequented gravel beach.

Mandráki ▶
Mandráki, with its popular sandy beach, is 30 minutes west of the harbour of Ýdra town past the navy school. The 19th-century con-

vent of **Agía Matróna** across the bay from Mandráki can be reached in about 45 minutes. The remains of the 15th-century **Profítis Ilías** convent are set charmingly in the mountains, and can be reached with a 75-minute hike. Directly below the convent ruins lies the convent of **Agía Efpraxía**, from where

! *Baedeker* TIP

Island Delicacy
Do not pass up the chance to try a delicacy of the island of Ýdra – almond biscuits known as »amygdalota«.

there is a superb view of town, mainland and island. The hike to the 16th century **Zourvás** monastery on the eastern tip of the island takes 2 to 3 hours.

Spétses, **known as Pityousa in ancient times**, is a 22 sq km/8.5 sq mi hilly, densely wooded island off the southwest coast of Argolis, which has, because of its beautiful beaches, developed into a popular tourist attraction. Favoured by a mild climate, the tourist trade represents the most important source of revenue for the inhabitants of the traffic-free island. Laskarina Pinotzis, known as Bouboulina (►Famous People), one of the most colourful characters of the War of Greek Independence, lived on the island. Spétses was the first island to join in the battle for freedom in 1821. A celebration is held on the first Sunday after 8 September at the old harbour in commemoration.
Spétses

The island's main town, Spétses (pop. 3,600), draws back from the broad harbour bay up the gentle slopes of the hills. The way the town looks today, with its stately townhouses and three interesting churches in Kastélli, the upper part of the town, dates from the 19th century.
◄ Spétses (town)

Spétses' museum is in the beautiful **Chatzigianni Mezi**, a mansion built in 1795. The oldest exhibits date from Hellenic and Roman times. In addition, sacred objects such as icons and liturgical implements as well as a collection of pottery from the 18th century are on display. Furthermore, the role that the Spetsiotes played in the battle for freedom in 1821 is explained, the exhibits including a display of the shrine with the mortal remains of Bouboulina. The freedom fighter also has a museum dedicated to her in a house near the harbour.
◄ Museums

A 12 km/7.5 mi island hike leads from the main town of Spétses south-eastward past the monastery of Ágios Nikólaos to **Agia Marína**, where minor traces of a pre-historic settlement are to be found. From there it is on to Cape Kouzouna, where the remains of an early-5th-century Christian basilica have survived. **Bekiri cave**, a former hideout of the freedom fighters, has a beach on the inside and is located at the **bathing cove of Ágii Anárgiri**. The hike continues from here through Ágia Paraskeví to Brélou in a densely wooded area. The trail back leads over the island's highest point, the 244 m/ 800 ft Profítis Ilías, past the monastery of Ágii Pántes and back to Agía Marína.
◄ Island Hike

★ Árta · Άρτα

D 6

Prefecture: Epiros
Population: 30,000
Altitude: 30 m/98 ft

The pretty little town of Árta, lying on the banks of the Árachthos, is the busiest market centre of the region.

History The city was founded in 645 BC as a Corinthian colony. Its ancient name, **Ambracia**, has been retained in the name of the Ambracian Gulf situated to the south and almost completely sealed off from the Ionian Sea. In the 13th and 14th centuries, Árta was the capital of the Despotate of Epiros, a Byzantine Greek state independent of Byzantium. The fortress and a number of churches and monasteries in the vicinity are reminders of the despotate's princes.

What to See in Árta

★ **Panagía Parigorítissa** The central Platía Skoufas is dominated by the four-storeyed palatial church of Panagía Parigorítissa (»Mother of God the Swiftly Consoling«), erected about 1290 by Anne, the wife of the despot Nikephoros Palaiologos. The church has an unusual construction with three rows of columns placed on top of each other supporting a 24 m/79 ft high dome. The dome is decorated with a Pantocrator mosaic and the iconostasis has a picture of the patron saint of the church, the Virgin Mary. (Opening hours: Tue – Sun 8.30am – 3pm).

City Tour The Parigorítissa Church is a good place to start a short tour through the city. Opposite the church is the small **archaeological museum**, with displays from various eras. Walk a ways up Konstantinou street,

VISITING ÁRTA

INFORMATION

Tourist Information
Platía Kristálli
Tel. / Fax 26 81 07 85 51
E-mail: eotartas@otenet.gr

WHERE TO EAT

► **Inexpensive**

Protomastoras
The cosy taverna by the historic Árachthos Bridge serves good regional dishes.

WHERE TO STAY

► **Mid-range**

Xenia
Dodonis 33
Tel. 26 81 02 74 13
22 rooms
Xenia Hotel is centrally located and peacefully set in a medieval castle in a park. It has a restaurant and a fine café.

A look at its dome clearly reveals the daring construction of the church of Panagía Parigoritissa.

then down the stairway left to the pedestrian zone and across Platía Ethnikís Antistáseos and turn into Perivólou street, which leads to a market hall. The 13th-century church of **Ágios Vassílios** stands nearby, whose multi-patterned exterior walls are decorated with faience. The originals can be seen in the Byzantine Museum in Ioánnina. It is not much further from there to the medieval **fortress** built during the reign of Michael II on the site of an ancient acropolis. The small café in the inner courtyard is just the place to take a break. On the way back, take Pyrrou street from the market hall. A small side street leads to the 13th century church of **Agía Theodóra**, which was extended by the mother of the despot Nikephoros, Theodora, who was later canonized. The front of her sarcophagus in the narthex shows Theodora together with her son. Besides the modern bridge on the road leaving the city for ►Ioánnina, the beautiful 17th-century bridge across the Árachthos can be seen: one of the oldest stone bridges in the country.

◄ Árachthos Bridge

Around Árta

There are a number of interesting Byzantine churches and monasteries round Árta; for example, the 13th-century monastery church, Káto Panagía, (1 km/0.6 mi to the south) and, in Vlácherna (6 km/ 3.7 mi to the northeast), the 13th-century Vlacherna monastery. Parts of the marble frames of the church doors are from the original interior furnishings.

Káto Panagía, Vlácherna

Árachthos and Loúros form a large delta on the Ambracian Gulf south of Árta; a protected wetlands with many species of rare plants and birds like Dalmatian pelicans and waders. Good places for bird watching are the karst hill at **Strongýli**, Mavrovouni Hill northwest of **Vígla** and the causeway to **Koronissia**. Dolphins can be seen now and then in the gulf itself.

Ambracian Gulf

! Baedeker TIP

Coastal serenity
The deserted coast south of Préveza that stretch between the small villages of Páleros und Astakós is incomparably beautiful. The villages have hardly been touched by tourism and there is only scant macchia vegetation, white limestone rocks and ocean, small coves and a stunning view of the Ionian Islands from Lefkáda to Itháki and Kefallónia.

The port of **Préveza** (pop. 15,000) lies some 40 km/25 mi southwest of Árta on the barely 350 m/1,148 ft wide entrance to the Ambracian Gulf. The many places to shop in the city, the yacht harbour and kilometres of beach that stretch along the Ionian Sea up to Loutsa, have drawn tourists to the region. Worth seeing are the **Venetian clock tower** dating from 1756 and a carved, gilt iconostasis from 1828 in the **cathedral**. The late medieval Venetian castle offers a broad view of the gulf landscape.

Mighty fortifications with gateways and towers still surround Nikópolis, the »City of Victory«, founded by Emperor Augustus.

About 6 km/3.7 mi north of Préveza, on the isthmus between the Ionian Sea and the Ambracian Gulf, are the excavation grounds of Nikópolis. Octavian – later Emperor Augustus – founded the »City of Victory« following his victory in the **Battle of Actium** against the Egyptian and Roman fleet of Antony and Cleopatra in 31 BC, which made him the sole ruler of the Roman Empire.

The ancient site is today dominated by buildings of Late Antiquity (2nd – 6th centuries AD), including a large theatre, where the holes for the supports for the awnings can still be seen, an odeon, a stadium and a defensive wall with towers and a gateway (opening hours: Mon 10.30am – 5pm, Tue – Sun 8.30am – 5pm).

✶✶ Athens · Αθήνα

K 8/9

Prefecture: Attica
Population: 745,000
(Greater Athens: 4 million)

Altitude: 40 – 150 m/131 – 492 ft

The capital of Greece, the cradle of Western culture, greets its visitors as an exuberant metropolis, where the past and present seem to blend into each other.

Athens with its world famous Acropolis and important museums is a must for every visitor to Greece – as a stop-off during a tour of the mainland or on the way from Piraeus to the Greek islands. Since gearing up for the Olympic Games of 2004, Athens, sprawling out on a broad coastal plain on the Saronic Gulf, has been radiating a new lustre. The transportation infrastructure was extended, repaired and improved. Many places in the city were redesigned and planted with greenery. Areas with reduced traffic were created with new footpaths, especially in the inner city, that harmoniously connect together the important attractions like the Acropolis, Theatre of Dionysus, Kerameikós Necropolis and the old city quarter, the Pláka.

History

The development of Athens began with the union of various settlements (synoikismos) in the Attic region under King **Theseus** in the 10th century BC. **Solon** was only able to temporarily ease the social tension in the 7th century BC through his reforms. After his death, the tensions soon broke out again, making possible the tyrannies of **Peisistratos** and his sons (560 – 510 BC). The power of the aristocracy was weakened during their rule – an important pre-requisite for the development of Attic democracy. Under the leadership of **Themistocles**, Athens eventually emerged victorious from the Persian Wars (500 – 479 BC) in which the polis supported the cities of Asian

VISITING ATHENS

INFORMATION

Tourist Information
Amalias 26
Tel. 21 03 31 03 92
Fax 21 03 31 06 40
www.gnto.gr

airport office:
arrival level
Tel. 21 03 53 04 45

GETTING AROUND IN ATHENS

Although Athens sprawls over an area of more than 400 sq km/154 sq mi, the places of interest to tourists are confined to quite a small section with most of them well within walking distance of each other. Express bus lines and the Metro line 3 connect Eleftherios Venizelos Airport, 27 km/ 16.8 mi east of the city centre, with the city. Serving the inner city are the Metro, with 3 lines, a tram, minibuses and the yellow trolley-buses. Blue and white buses travel from the centre to the suburbs. The sightseeing bus drives to 30 sights, where one can get off or on the bus at will.

SHOPPING

The quarter with the most elegant shops and the trendiest clubs is Kolonáki on the southern slope of Lykavittus Hill. Fashions from inter-national and Greek designers, jewel-lery and antique shops, as well as a number of art galleries can all be found here. Ermoú street, which has

Great shopping in the Odós Ermoú shopping street

largely been converted into a pedestrian zone, is recommended for the more modest budget. One of the most pleasant places to walk around is Pláka, the traffic-reduced old part of town, with its picturesque narrow lanes. Souvenir shops and leather goods and jewellery stores are lined up here one after the other. Craftwork is to be found at Monastiráki Square and Avissinias Square. The flea market is also held there on Sundays. Athínas Street is the »stomach« of Athens; almost all the foodstuffs to be had in Greece can be found in the large market hall.

GOING OUT

There are a vast number of pubs, bars, clubs and discos in Athens with music programmes to suit every taste: from rock to Greek folk music. Holiday tourists are usually drawn to the traditional music tavernas in the Pláka. In the clubs and discos, where appropriate dress is usually required for entry, things don't really get moving until after midnight, which is why they stay open until sun-up, particularly at weekends.

WHERE TO EAT

► **Expensive**

① *Symposio*
Erechthiou 46, Makrigianni
Tel. 21 09 22 53 21
Modern Greek cuisine using regional organic-farm products; garden restaurant with a view of the Acropolis.

② *Daphne's*
Lysikratous 4
Tel. 21 03 22 79 71
Small restaurant in a Neo-classical building from 1840 with wall and ceiling paintings; frequented by celebrities; beautiful inner courtyard with remains of an Antique wall; light

Greek and international cuisine with regional dishes; reservations recommended.

► **Moderate**

③ *Tou Psara*
Erechtheou 16
Tel. 21 03 21 87 33
Best fish taverna in the Pláka in an historic building with shady courtyard; the house wine is from the barrel.

④ *Thespidos*
Thespidos 18
Popular taverna directly below the Acropolis with outside seating on different levels.

► **Inexpensive**

⑤ *Platanos*
Diogenous 4
Tel. 21 03 22 06 66
Romantic taverna with traditional cooking on the small, idyllic Palea Agorá Square; popular with locals and tourists.

⑥ *Xynos*
Geronda 4
Tel. 21 03 22 10 65
One of the oldest garden tavernas in Athens; typical of the Pláka, very popular with the locals.

WHERE TO STAY

► **Hotel Prices in Athens**
Luxury: over 180 €
Mid-range: 100 – 180 €
Budget: up to 100 €

► **Luxury**

① *Grande Bretagne*
Platía Syntagma
Tel. 21 03 33 00 00
www.grandebretagne.gr
262 rooms, 59 suites
Athens' most tradition-rich luxury

The rich and the beautiful and the powerful meet in Grand Bretagne.

Tel. 21 05 23 11 11
www.grecotel.info
167 rooms
The hotel on noisy Omonia Square offers well-appointed rooms along with a restaurant, a bar, fitness centre and a panorama terrace.

⑤ *Omiros*
Apollonos 15
Tel. 21 03 23 54 86
Fax 21 03 22 80 59, 37 rooms
Peacefully located, small hotel in the midst of the Pláka. The rooms are functionally furnished. The roof garden has a superb view of the Acropolis.

hotel stands directly opposite the Parliament building. The grandiose hotel is furnished with antiques and has, among other things, a fin-de-siècle ballroom and a winter garden.

② *St George Lycabettus*
Kleomenous 2, Kolonaki
Tel. 21 07 29 07 11
www.sglycabettus.gr
157 rooms and suites
The idyllic hotel stands serenely on the slope of Lykavittus in the exclusive Kolonáki district. Many of the rooms and the swimming pool on the roof have a marvellous view of the city.

► **Mid-range**
③ *Athens Acropol*
Pireos 1

► **Budget**
④ *Arethusa*
Metropoleos 6 – 8
Tel. 21 03 22 94 31
www.arethusahotel.gr
87 rooms
the hotel is centrally located close to Syntagma Square. Large rooms, some with terraces offering a view of the Acropolis; restaurant on the roof terrace.

⑥ *Adonis*
Kodrou 3
Tel. 21 03 24 97 37, 26 rooms
Small hotel, quietly situated in a park; rooms with balcony; a view of the Acropolis and the Lykavittós can be enjoyed already with breakfast in the roof garden.

Minor. The rise of Athens to a leading economic and cultural power in Greece was made possible by the system of **Attic democracy** (from 461 BC) The city-state experienced its golden age under **Pericles** (443 – 429 BC). The turning point was the Peloponnesian War (431 – 404 BC), in which Athens lost the struggle for supremacy in Greece to its rival Sparta. **Sulla** led the Romans in their conquest of the city in 86 BC. The Roman emperors, above all Hadrian, erected further monumental buildings in Athens. A sudden end was put to

Athens' greatness, however, with the invasion of the East Germanic Heruli (AD 267). Sacked several times during the Barbarian invasions, Athens finally was reduced to an inconsequential provincial town of the East Roman or Byzantine Empire and did not experience a flourishing again until it came under Frankish rule in the 13th century. After a short Venetian interlude from 1394 to 1402, the **Ottoman Turks** took Athens in 1458 and the city remained Turkish up until the 19th century. Athens was hotly contested during the wars of liberation (1821–1833). In 1834, King **Otto I**, a Bavarian, elevated Athens to the capital of the modern Kingdom of Greece and had it developed with the help of German and Danish architects. The first Olympic Games of the modern age were held in Athens in 1896. The city was once again the venue for the Olympic Games in 2004. Vast new districts were created after the Greco-Turkish War of 1923 when some 300,000 refugees from Asia Minor fled to Athens, whose integration remained a problem for decades. Today, Athens and Piraeus have long since grown together into a megalopolis whose modern development takes in the historic substance only in the most central area.

A view of the one-time centre of power in the ancient world, the Acropolis

Athens Map

Platia Omonia
National Archaeological Museum

German
Archaeological
Institute

City Hall

Platia Kotzia

Piraeus

Platia
Koumoundourou

Market Hall

Ministry of
the Interior

Agios
Athanasios

Kyriaki

Agii Theodori
Platia

Klafth-
monos

Agia
Chrisospiliotissa

Athens
Municipal
Museum

KERAMEIKOS

Agii Asomati

Agios
Georgios

Agia
Irini

Platia
Ag. Irinis

Kapnikarea

Keramaikos Cemetery, Iera Odos

Pl. Monastiraki

Stoa of
Zeus

Pantanassa
Church

Tsisdarakis
Mosque

Temple of Hephaestus
Temple of Ares

Stoa of
Attalos

Library of
Hadrian

Grand
Mitropolis

Métroon

Platia
Mitropoleos

Platia Palea
Agorá

Odeon

Little
Mitropolis

Bouleterion

Roman
Agorá

Agios
Andreas

Agora

Agii Apostoli

Tower of
the Winds

P L A K A

Hill of the
Nymphs

Kanellopoulos
Museum

University
Museum

Metamorfosis
tou Kottaki

ANAFIOTIKA

Centre of
Folk Art and
Tradition

A r e o p a g

Metamorfosis
tou Sotiros

Erechtheion

Beulé Gate   Propylaea

Acropolis

Filopappos Hill
Pnyx

Nike-Temple

Museum

Parthenon

Agia Ekaterini

Odeon of
Herodes
Atticus

Lysikrates
Monument

Theatre of
Dionysos

Hadrian's
Arch

Where to eat

= = = Presumed course of
the ancient city wall

① Symposio
② Daphne's

③ Tou Psara
④ Thespidos

⑤ Platanos
⑥ Xynos

Where to stay

① Grande Bretagne
② St George Lycabettus
③ Athens Acropol
④ Arethusa
⑤ Omiros
⑥ Adonis

Highlights Athens

Acropolis
The most famous structure of the country was once, at the same time, the centre of political power and a religious cult site.
► page 180

Temple of Hephaestus
The Hephaestion on the Agorá hill is one of the best preserved temples of Greek Antiquity.
► page 195

Lycabettus
A superb view of the metropolitan sea of lights comes along free with the meal when dining in the Orizontes restaurant on »Wolf Mountain«.
► page 208

Archaeological National Museum
The Archaeological National Museum presents the largest collection of ancient Greek works of art in the world.
► page 205

Benaki Museum
The museum provides an insight into the 4,500-year history of Greek culture.
► page 208

Cape Soúnion
Enjoy a fantastic sunset at the famous Temple of Poseidon on the southern tip of Attica, only a few kilometres from Athens.
► page 218

✳ ✳ Acropolis

🕐 Opening hours:
April – Oct
daily 8am – 7.30pm
Nov – March
daily 8am – 5pm

The Acropolis, the quintessence of the Classical heritage monument, is the **most famous structure in Greece** and the main attraction of Athens. The »high city« erected on a 156 m/512 ft limestone outcrop – which falls steeply down to the north, south and east – was at first a fortress of the kings of Athens and at the same time a time-honoured cult site. Later it was reserved as the seat of the patron deities of the city. This religious centre of ancient Athens was given its Classical form during the time of **Pericles**. In spite of the destruction wrought over the centuries – not least the devastating explosion in 1687 when a Venetian grenade blew up a Turkish powder magazine in the Parthenon and made a ruin of this famous temple which was by then already more than 2,100 years old – the buildings still radiate something of the splendour of the age of Pericles. During the 19th and early 20th centuries, the removal of post-Classical structures and restoration work once more revealed as much as possible of its state in the 5th century BC. On the other hand, it was left to the 20th century to be more destructive than the preceding millennia. The exhaust fumes of households and traffic, plus the three million or so visitors that year after year climb up to the Acropolis, have resulted in the surface of the rock and the marble facing being worn down, the Pentelic marble gradually turning into gypsum and the still surviving Classical sculptures crumbling. When the destruction had reached frightening proportions, UNESCO, which had declared the

Towering above the Agorá is the »upper city« of ancient Athens.

Acropolis to be a World Heritage Site in 1987, created an aid programme to save it. Since then, restoration and reconstruction work are permanently under way on the rock of the Acropolis.

In the Mycenaean period, the »cyclopean« fortress walls closely followed the contours of the rock. In the north wall were two small gates leading down to the Klepsydra spring that supplied the Acropolis with water and to the caves on the north slope. Standing on the site of the later old Temple of Athena was a royal palace. Surviving from the Archaic period, 7th / 6th centuries BC, are the remains of several buildings as well as parts of two temples. All buildings of the Archaic period were destroyed in 480 BC by the Persians. During the reconstruction, which was begun immediately after the destruction, **Themistocles** used column drums and pieces of beams still visible in the north wall. After 467 BC, **Cimon**, who built the straight length of wall still existing today, altered the southern perimeter of the Acropolis. Within the fortified area by Cimon **Pericles** went on to develop the site with the Classical buildings whose ruins we see today. The Parthenon, the Propylaea, the Temple of Athena Nike and the Erechtheion were all built between 447 and 406 BC. The only ruins dating from a later period are those of a circular temple in front of the east end of the Parthenon dedicated to Roma and Augustus dating from the early imperial Roman period.

Development up to the Classical period

Beulé Gate Today, the entrance to the Acropolis is south of Beulé Gate, located to the west below the Propylaea. The gate named after its discoverer, the French archaeologist **Ernest Beulé**, was erected in AD 267. It lies with its two flanking towers on the axis of symmetry of the Propylaea and was connected to it by a broad marble stairway built during the reign of Emperor **Septimius Severus**, parts of which have survived.

Agrippa Monument Standing directly below the Pinacotheca on the way up from Beulé Gate to the Propylaea is a high, two-coloured marble plinth of a monument that was built for a benefactor of Athens in the 2nd century BC. It is named after **Marcus Vipsanius Agrippa**, son-in-law of Augustus, whose quadriga was set on it in 27 BC.

> ## ! *Baedeker* TIP
>
> ### The most beautiful view ...
>
> ... of the Acropolis is from Filopáppos Hill. Here also is the monument to Filopáppos, a prince from Commagene in southern Anatolia who was banished to Athens by the Romans and died here in AD 116. Filopáppos was a great benefactor of the city and, in gratitude, the Athenians granted him a privileged spot for his elaborate tomb.

The towering **Propylaea**, the **gateway to the temple**, conceived by **Mnesikles** as a monumental tripartite structure, was built from 437 to 432 BC, replacing a 6th-century BC propylon, traces of which are still evident. On the natural rock is a staircase, whose lowest step is of grey Eleusinian marble, while lighter-coloured Pentelic marble was used for the rest. The central part of the structure is a gate wall with five doorways, which increase in width and height from the sides to the centre. To the west is a deep portico, whose central doorway is bordered by 2 x 3 Ionic columns. The front of this portico, on the other hand, consists of six Doric columns, which supported the pediment.

Adjoining the west portico are side wings, including the Pinacotheca, which contained a collection of panel paintings. In front of it is the marble plinth of the Agrippa Monument erected in the second century BC.

From the 13th century onwards, the Propylaea served as the residence of princes and military commanders and, as such, was completely disfigured. The holes for the beams to support intermediate ceilings, for example, can still be seen. Its use as an ammunition dump in the mid-17th century resulted in the destruction of the central structure.

★ Temple of Athena Nike A shrine dedicated to Athena, the bringer of victory (Nike), was on the projecting rock, the **Nikepyrgos**, south of the Propylaea. The temple was built from 432 to 421 BC. with four Ionic columns at the front and four at the back. The form of the column bases and capitals was already old-fashioned at the time it was built, suggesting that after the rule of Pericles the earlier design by **Kallikrates** was used. In

The way is steep that leads up to the monumental temple portico, the Propylaea.

Turkish times the temple was incorporated into a bastion, from which **Ludwig Ross** isolated it in 1836. Rebuilt at that time and again from 1936 to 1940, the temple presents itself to the visitor today as the most delicate and elegant building on the Acropolis.

Among the many shrines located behind the Propylaea was also a cult site dedicated to Athena Hygieia. A semicircular base at the southern column of the east hall of the Propylaea once supported a bronze statue of the goddess.

Sanctuary of Athena Hygieia

The bronze statue of Athena Promachos, **Athena who fights in the front line**, was placed exactly on the axis of the centre passage of the Propylaea. The famous work by **Phidias**, which was about 9 m/30 ft high and first set up in 454 BC, later ended up in Constantinople and was lost during the siege by the crusaders in 1203.

Statue of Athena Promachos

The Acropolis rock gradually rises behind the Propylaea. Standing beyond the shrine of **Artemis Brauronia** and the **Chalkothek**, in which bronze offerings and weapons were stored, is the Parthenon. The temple of **Athena Parthenos**, the Virgin Athena, constructed from 447 to 439 BC – the pediment figures were completed in 432 BC – is the masterpiece of the architects **Iktinos** and **Phidias**, whom

★ ★ Parthenon

The Parthenon, an architectural masterpiece, was the symbol of the power and wealth of the ancient city-state of Athens.

Pericles entrusted with the overall supervision of the Acropolis building programme. This temple which was based on an earlier, narrower building. The older foundation, which can be seen projecting further out to the east, is on the south side. The temple was given eight columns on the ends instead of the previous six, and 17 instead of 16 columns on its sides. The roof was covered with marble tiles, while the lion heads in the sima were not bored through and therefore could not have served as waterspouts as was usual. There were gutters for rainwater at the four corners of the temple. The holes on the architrave of the east end mark the position of the pegs used for hanging the shields captured in 334 BC by **Alexander the Great** at the battle of the Granikos (334 BC) and dedicated to Athena.

Cult image of Athena Parthenos ▶

The state treasure was probably stored in the first of the two temple chambers – whose ceiling was supported by four Ionic columns. In the other stood the chryselephantine statue of Athena, armed with lance and shield. Only known through descriptions and later copies, it was one of the famous works by Phidias and was completed in 438 BC. The gold plating used for the garments was said to have weighed more than a ton, and Phidias used ivory for the face and hands. Like Athena Promachos, the work was later taken to Constantinople, where it was lost.

Sculptural Decorations ▶

The sculptural decorations of the Parthenon were equally famous: the two pediments, the Doric metopes and the Ionic frieze running around the upper part of the cella wall. Parts of them are held in the Acropolis Museum, some in the Louvre in Paris, but most of them (»the Elgin Marbles«) are in the British Museum in London. The pediments were finished in 432 BC; the eastern one depicted the birth of Athena out of the head of Zeus, while the western one showed the contest for the land of Attica between Athena and Pos-

Acropolis Plan

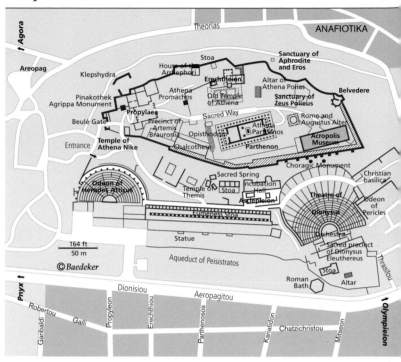

eidon. The 92 metopes of the Doric frieze also depicted mythological scenes. The Ionic frieze on the outer wall of the cella shows the procession that took place during the great Panathenaic Festival, which was held every four years, making its way from the Gymnasium, past the Agorá to the Acropolis to present a new »peplos« (garment) to the goddess Athena.

The Erechtheion was erected from 421 to 406 BC, making it the youngest building on the Classical Acropolis. It incorporated several very ancient shrines and the new building was designed to accommodate these, which explains its complicated ground plan. The eastern part was occupied by the temple for the wooden cult figure of the patron of the city, **Athena Polias**. In the western part of the building was the tomb of King **Erechtheus**, who gave his name to the whole structure, as well as the tomb of **Cecrops**, the legendary first king of Athens. It lay beneath the **caryatid porch** projecting out to the south of the Erechtheion, its entablature supported by six figures of maidens (caryatids or »kore«) instead of columns. The originals are in the Acropolis Museum.

★★
Erechtheion

Six figures of young girls support the entablature of the Caryatid Porch that was added to the Erechtheion, the youngest of the Classical buildings on the Acropolis

Another cult monument is on the north side. Seen through an opening in the floor is a rock on which the ancient Athenians saw the marks resulting from a blow by Poseidon's trident during his dispute with Athena over Attica. The north and east porticos each have six columns. On the exterior of the cella wall, above delicate palmette ornamentation, is a frieze of grey Eleusinian marble on which white marble figures were set; the originals can also be seen in the Acropolis Museum.

The Old Temple of Athena — In 525 BC, the tyrants **Hippias** and **Hipparch** erected a temple with a peristasis with 6 : 12 columns, whose foundations can be recognized immediately south of the Erechtheion. The large pediment of »poros« limestone which can be seen in the Acropolis Museum was once part of the old Temple of Athena. In the centre are bulls being attacked by lions, on the left Heracles and Triton, to the right the »three-bodied demon«. The temple was destroyed by the Persians in 480 BC along with all the other buildings of the Archaic period. The ruins were levelled in 406 BC and the cult image was placed in the new Temple of Athena.

The House of Arrhephoroi — Four girls between the ages of seven and eleven from the noblest families in Athens lived in the House of Arrhephoroi built against the north wall of the Acropolis. They assisted the priestess of Athena in serving the goddess by making a new peplos every four years for the Panathenaic festival. A flight of steps led through a gate in the outer wall of the Acropolis and down a passage tunnelled in the rock to the shrine of Eros and the Cave of Aglauros. From there, the Arrhephoroi – the **bearers of secrets** – were sent to fetch cult objects.

In 27 BC, the Romans built a circular temple, whose roof was borne by nine Ionic columns, in front of the east end of the Parthenon and on its central axis. The ornamentation of the capitals was modelled on those of the Erechtheion. The temple was dedicated to Roma and Augustus and their statues as divinities stood in it.

Temple of Roma and Augustus

The Acropolis rises to its highest point north of the Temple of Roma and Augustus. This was the site of the sanctuary of Zeus Polieus, an open cult precinct. The only evidence remaining of this sanctuary precinct is the cutting away of the rock.

Sanctuary of Zeus Polieus

The square was laid out on the north-eastern corner of the Acropolis for the royal family in the 19th century and offers a fantastic view of the city.

Belvedere

The **new Acropolis Museum** has been in the process of construction for a number of years south of the Dionysus Theatre in Makrigiani Street. It was designed by the Swiss architect, Bernhard Tschumi. There have been some delays during the course of the work, not least because an early Christian settlement was discovered during the excavation of the foundation. Future visitors to the museum will be able to see it through a glass floor. The museum began opening in stages in 2008. The museum's holdings are one of the world's most valuable collections of Greek art which, until the opening of the new museum, could only be displayed in a representative selection. The figures from the marble pediment of the Old Temple of Athena are interesting. The **kore**, figures of women in peplos and later in richer chitons, over which they usually wear a garment known as a himation (5th – 7th century BC), are masterworks. Originally, the mostly life-sized sculptures were painted; remains of the paint have survived, particularly on the garments. The Peplos Kore, fashioned by the sculptor Phaidimos around 530 BC and named after its Doric clothing, is outstanding. The monumental korai of the Erechtheion are part of the collection. Among the famous sculptures of the Classical Period (5th century BC) are the »Fair-Headed Youth« (before 480 BC) and the relief of the Mourning Athena (460 / 450 BC).

✱ ✱
Acropolis Museum (closed)

Theatre of Dionysus · Stoa of Eumenes · Asclepieion

Standing on the south slope of the Acropolis are the Odeon of Herodes Atticus, the Stoa of Eumenes and the Theatre of Dionysus, regarded as the birthplace of European theatre. The south wall of the Acropolis offers a superb view over the theatre.

✱
Theatre of Dionysus

In the 6th century BC, **Peisistratos** brought the cult of Dionysus from Eleutherai in the Kithairon mountain range to Athens and had a temple built for the ancient cult image of Dionysus, the god of intoxication, metamorphosis and ecstasy. The Theatre of Dionysus was built in a natural hollow on the slopes in association with the **Dionysus cult**. Nine building phases have been distinguished. The theatre and the temple precinct were separated about 420 BC, when a columned hall opening to the south was built that required the old limestone temple to be moved.

Around 330 BC. the theatre was given stone tiers that can still be seen today, providing seating for some 17,000 spectators. There are inscribed seats of honour in the first row and one in the middle for the priest of Dionysus Eleuthereus with fine reliefs and post holes in the floor, suggesting there was once a canopy. Diagonally behind it was the seat of honour for Emperor **Hadrian**. The spectator gallery included an orchestra paved with slabs and a stone barrier to separate it from the animals used in the games in Roman times.

The stage building joining to the south was remodelled repeatedly, as was the whole theatre. The reliefs depicting scenes from the Diony-

The Dionysus Theatre below the Acropolis is regarded as the cradle of European drama.

sus legend dating from Roman times on the partially surviving bema, the orator's platform, are striking. The significance of the Theatre of Dionysus is that it was built when tragedy was first being introduced, and indeed being created. The first drama was presented in 534 BC, probably still in the Agorá, by **Thespis**, who travelled through the country with his theatre troupe in »Thespian carts«. This was an early form in which a single actor appeared opposite the chorus, and the beginning of a development that led to the perfection of the tragedy in the 5th century BC. It was in this theatre that the works of the three Attic tragedians, **Aeschylus**, **Sophocles** and **Euripides** were first performed as part of the Dionysus cult celebrations. The Theatre of Dionysus thus became the nucleus of European theatre (opening ☺ hours: daily 8am – 6pm).

The square Odeon built by **Pericles** stood east of the theatre. The building, once famous as the most beautiful concert hall in Greece, was completed in 443 BC, and after being destroyed by Sulla (86 BC) was rebuilt from 62 to 52 BC.

Odeon

Standing west of the Theatre of Dionysus is the Stoa of Eumenes, built by King **Eumenes II** of Pergamon (197 – 160 BC). The building simply served visitors to the Dionysus sanctuary and Theatre of Dionysus as a spacious hall to stroll about. The hall had two floors with Doric capitals outside, Ionic capitals inside on the ground floor and Pergamene capitals on the upper floor. As the Stoa is propped against the slope, a retaining wall reinforced by pillars and round arches was built to stand against it, whose arcade, still visible today, was originally covered with marble slabs.

Stoa of Eumenes

Located on a narrow terrace above the Stoa of Eumenes is the Asclepieion. The cult of the healing god **Asclepius**, originally from Epidaurus, had its shrine here from 418 BC. It was erected on the initiative of Sophocles.
The complex centres on two springs. The first part to be built was that in the west, of which the foundation of a hall and a small temple have survived. To be seen at the west end is a cistern composed of polygonal walls dating from the same period; a later one is located to the south. The east end of the Asclepius precinct was erected around 50 BC. Directly at the Acropolis rock stood a 50 m/164 ft long, two storied hall for the sick to lie in. Belonging to it was a cave with a spring that is still regarded as having curative powers. For this reason, the cave is used today as a Christian chapel.

✷
Asclepieion

Adjacent to the Stoa of Eumenes in the west is the Odeon built in 161 BC by **Herodes Atticus** (101 – 177 BC) after the death of his wife Regilla. Herodes Atticus was one of the great patrons of Antiquity and rose to high office during the reigns of the emperors **Hadrian** and **Antoninus Pius**. He was recognized for his rhetoric but, as a

✷
Odeon of Herodes Atticus

Library of Pantainos	Immediately south of the Stoa of Attalos, the remains of a library have survived, which was built by **Flavius Pantainos** in AD 100 and destroyed in AD 267 by the Herulians. Still well recognizable to the south of the library is the **Wall of Valerian**, erected following the attack by the Herulians.
Nymphaion	A semi-circular fountain house, the Nymphaion, was constructed in the 2nd century AD in the southeast of the Agorá. Bordering directly to the southwest is the Enneakrounos fountain house (6th century BC). The building next to it (5th century) is believed to have served as a mint.
Ágii Apóstoli	Standing above the Nymphaion is the 11th century church of Ágii Apóstoli. It was the only edifice to be preserved when the city district was razed to allow for the excavating of the Agorá. The exterior is notable for its blocks decorated with Kufic characters. The dome is supported by four columns, the apse and the arms of the transept are semi-circular conches. The painting in the portico (c. 1700) came from the Spyridon Church.
Stoae	There were several buildings in the southern section of the Agorá that served public functions. Between 425 and 400 BC, the **South Stoa I** was built. It has a two-aisle hall, behind which are 15 small rooms furnished with couches for dining. The building was partially built over in the 2nd century BC by the **South Stoa II**, a single-aisled hall with 30 Doric columns. The **Middle Stoa** was built between 175 and 150 BC. The 146 m/479 ft long structure was divided into two aisles by Ionic columns. The **East Stoa** was constructed around 150 BC. It was destroyed along with all the other stoa buildings by the Romans in 86 BC
Heliaia	The **court** set up by Solon in the 6th century BC was held on the south side of the Agorá. It was named after the sun god Helios, because its sessions took place before sunrise.
Odeon of Agrippa	The centre of the Agorá is occupied by the Odeon of Agrippa. Built around 20 BC by the Roman commander Agrippa, the son-in-law of Augustus, it contained a square room with a stage and 18 rows of seats for about 1,000 spectators. The entrance was on the south side. In the 2nd century AD, a new entrance was created in the north. Three Titans and three Giants – three of the figures are still standing – bore the roof of the portico. After the Odeon was destroyed by the Heruli, a gymnasium was built on the site around AD 400.
Tholos	Standing on the southwest side of the Agorá is the Tholos, a round building with a diameter of 18 m/60 ft. Erected about 465 BC, it served as the meeting place of the 50 **prytaneis**, the representatives of the individual ancestral tribes of the city-state. The east side of the

Tholos was given a new portico in the 3rd century BC. It was rebuilt after being destroyed by Sulla in 86 BC and was in use until about AD 450.

Agorá Hill is dominated by the temple of Hephaestus. The **Hephaistion** was located close to the blacksmith and craftsman district and dedicated to the deities of blacksmiths and the arts, Hephaestus and Athena. It is one of the best-preserved of the Greek temples because, being converted into a Christian church, it was able to avoid destruction.

★ ★
Temple of
Hephaestus

A Doric temple built at about the same time as the Parthenon on the Acropolis, it has a classical ground plan of 6 : 13 columns. The damaged pronaos frieze shows battle scenes being observed by the gods and the west frieze shows battles between Lapiths and centaurs. In the centre, the Lapith Caeneus, considered to be invulnerable, is being rammed into the ground by two centaurs. Despite the lack of space, the cult image of Hephaestus and Athena, created by **Alkamenes** and set up in the cella in 420 BC, was surrounded by columns.

The Haphaestus temple stands on Agora Hill and is one of the best preserved cultic structures in the country.

Symbols of the power and wealth of ancient Athens towering over the Agorá, the social and economic centre of the city

ART, CULT AND POLITICS

The Acropolis and the Agora – the cultural, economic and political centres of the ancient city-state of Athens – symbolize the power and wealth of the Greek polity even today.

Even as ruins, the two ancient centres, the Acropolis and the Agora, dominate the appearance of Athens.

The Acropolis became the primary cult site for the **patron of the city, Athena**, through a major temple-building project during the reign of the tyrant **Peisistratos**. It was her help, maintained the Athenians, which eventually led to their victory over the Persians; although they had to suffer through the destruction of their city in the process. In expression of their gratitude, the Athenians had the architects **Iktinos** and **Kallikrates** build the monumental temple between 448 / 447 and 438 / 437 BC. In addition, the magnificent sculptural decoration and the 92 metopes with the depiction of the great battle myths as well as some 50 pediment figures in the east pediment dealing with the birth of Athena and her dispute with Poseidon over Attica were fashioned between 438 and 433 BC in the workshop of the sculptor, **Phidias**.

This masterpiece, the temple of Athena Parthenos, was finished about 432 BC. It was not so much the Athenians themselves that had to pay for the immense costs for the reshaping of the Acropolis, but rather the other members of the Delian League. With the help of their fleet, which was decisive in the naval victory of 480 BC over the Persians, the Athenians had gained the dominant role in the Delian League and made their fellow members tributary. Those that no longer wanted to pay tribute found themselves engulfed in a war. The city building programme, primarily the redevelopment of the Acropolis, was financed by the revenues which thus accrued.

Its reshaping meant a huge job creation programme and, at the same time, served to glorify the Athenians.

No costs or effort were spared in the most famous item decorating the Parthenon, the 12 m/40 ft statue created by Phidias of the goddess Athena, whose visible body parts were of ivory, while her robe was fashioned of removable plates of gold.

The Goddess Athena

Athena wore a richly decorated helmet crowned by a sphinx flanked by two winged horses. The goddess held a winged Nike in her right hand and a lance with a golden tip in the crook of her arm. The left hand rested on a shield that had a serpent coiled around its inside rim, while the head of Gorgon decorated the inside surface and the outside was decorated with a gigantomachy, the battle between the Athenians and the Amazons. A 160 m/525 ft relief frieze ran around the cella of the temple. It had the effect of considerable depth and illustrated a **ceremonial procession** through the whole of Athens. This was when the citizenry of Athens ostentatiously paraded every four years in the procession celebrating the birth of city's patron from the Dipylon Gate across the Agora and up to the Acropolis to attend the presentation to the ancient cult image of the new peplos woven by the Attic virgins.

The Scene of Politics

Lying at the foot of the Acropolis was the Agora, with its monumental buildings, where the Athenian popular government conducted its business. The system of government only gradually evolved from a kingship to an aristocratic oligarchy and the era of the Tyrants was shaped into a democracy that reached its culmination in the 5th century BC under **Pericles**. The Athenians identified in large measure with their city-state in which they were able to live in accordance to their own laws, free of foreign domination.

Only »full citizens«, however, participated in political life, which was in the form of a direct democracy. They made up 13% of the city's population around 430 BC and were exclusively men, largely belonging to the upper class. A prerequisite for the full citizens' participation as jurymen in

Only a fraction of the works of art once on the Acropolis have remained in Athens; among them, the famous »Calf-Bearer« of marble, a votive offering dating from the 6th century BC.

the people's courts and in the assembly was a social policy that included daily expense allowances for the officials, judges and those taking part in the assemblies, caring for the city's lower classes, the »demos«, through service in the fleet and putting production and services in the hands of foreigners, the less-entitled and slaves. Social pressure brought on by a population explosion was alleviated by the founding of colonies. Sufficient food was procured through trade.

The Decline and Fall of Athens

The Acropolis and Agora deteriorated with the city's decline in the 5th / 6th centuries AD. The statue of Athena remained in the Parthenon down into the 5th century AD, until it was dismantled during the process of Christianization and probably taken to Constantinople, where it disappeared.

The Parthenon temple was converted into a Christian church in the 6th century and it served as a mosque during the Ottoman era after a major part of it was demolished when the gunpowder stored there exploded during the Venetian bombardment in 1687.

The Elgin Marbles

With the permission of the Turkish authorities, the British diplomat **Lord Elgin** procured a large number of metopes and sculptures from the Parthenon during the period of 1801 to 1803, the so-called »Elgin Marbles«. These works of art were purchased by the British government in 1816 and have since been on display in the British Museum in London. Although the Greek government has again and again demanded the return of the works, the British have refused, arguing that all the world's major museums would be empty if everything were to be given back to its country of origin.

Today, a full appreciation of the former greatness of Athens in the Classical era can only be gained by travelling throughout half of Europe. On the site itself, only fragments can be seen, which need to be supplemented by those in the museums of Europe's capitals.

When the temple was converted into a Christian church, probably in the 5th century, the wooden roof construction was replaced by the present barrel vault. When King **Otto I** entered the new capital in 1834, he was greeted with a mass in the church, which is dedicated to St George. This was the last liturgical act in the building, which served as a museum until the 20th century.

In the second half of the 2nd century BC, a shrine for the **mother goddess** (Méter Theón) was built on the west side of the Agorá. At the same time, a front portico was built on the east side to unify the façade facing the square. A Christian church was installed in the Metroon in the 5th century, to which the mosaic floor visible today was added.

Metroon

The Bouleuterion, the **seat of the council of Athens**, was built below the Temple of Hephaestus in 403 BC. The main hall was entered through an anteroom. The 500 members sat in ascending rows of seats arranged as in a semicircular theatre. The building was destroyed by the Herulians in AD 267, but rebuilt and used until about AD 400.

Bouleuterion

A narrow, elongated base can be seen opposite the Metroon on which stood the statues of those heroes that belonged to the individual phyla (»tribes«) of the Attic population, explaining the name »eponym«, i.e., name-giving.

◄ Monument of the Eponymous Heroes

A few paces east of the Monument of the Eponymous Heroes is an altar of Pentelic marble probably dedicated to Zeus as lord of the Agorá (Zeus Agoraios).

◄ Altar of Zeus Agoraios

A statue of Emperor Hadrian (117 – 138) was erected in the 2nd century AD on the west side of the Agorá in the midst of other monuments, whose bases have survived. The beautifully worked sculpture – the armour is especially richly decorated with figures – is well preserved.

Statue of Hadrian

Between the Metroon and the Stoa of Zeus lies the foundation of the Temple of Apollo Patroos built in the 4th century BC. The cult image has survived and is now in the Agorá Museum. Athens' oldest vital statistics register was found in an annex.

Temple of Apollo Patroos

The Stoa of Zeus Eleutherios, who guaranteed the city its freedom, occupies the northwest corner of the Agorá up to the Metro station. Originally 47 m/154 ft wide, the building was erected in the 5th century BC. Side wings projected from either side. A statue of Zeus Eleutherios stood in front of it.

Stoa of Zeus

The 18 m/60 ft long so-called Royal Stoa (Stoá Basileios), north of the Metro station, was built in the 6th century BC. It was rebuilt soon after the attack by the Persians (480 BC) and in the 4th century

Royal Stoa

BC was given two side wings like the larger neighbouring Stoa of Zeus. It was the **seat of the Archon Basileus**, the magistrate who had inherited all the cultic functions of the earlier kings. Among them was to try the crime of impiety. The trial of **Socrates**, who was sentenced to death by poisoning for impiety and corrupting the youth of Athens in 399 BC, was probably held here.

Altar of the Twelve Gods The Altar of the Twelve Gods was regarded as the **central point of Athens** and it was the point from which distances were measured. Its remains suffered damage during the construction of the underground so that today only a corner of the original building still exists.

Temple of Ares The Temple of Ares once rose up south of the altar. It was built on a different spot around 440 BC and moved to this site during the time of Augustus. The cult image of Ares, the god of war, fashioned by **Alcamenes**, has not survived. On the other hand, a statue of Athena and a number of reliefs from the interior frieze were discovered and are now displayed in the Agorá Museum.

Pláka

Pláka, »**plate or slab**«, is the name of the idyllic old neighbourhood of Athens spread out between the north slope of the Acropolis and Odós Ermoú, one of city's most important shopping streets, and stretching to the east almost to Leofóros Amaliás. The old part of town with its narrow, picturesque lanes dominated by mostly modest 19th century houses and nice little squares, pleasant tavernas and open-air cafés, is quite a charming contrast to the hectic activities of the business city of Athens.

On **Monastiráki Square**, named after the Pantánassa Church, which once was part of a monastery (»Monastíri«), it is possible to encompass all the eras of Athenian history with one look. In the middle of the square stands the church, on the south corner is one of the two surviving Turkish mosques, the Tzisdarakis from 1759. Right behind the mosque lies Hadrian's Library from Roman times. The square, with its Metro station and the adjacent streets and lanes, is one of the most colourful and chaotic in Athens. Countless little shops selling icons and small antiques along with souvenirs and jewellery have been established in Pandrosou Lane to the east.

! **Baedeker TIP**

Archaeology in the Metro

Numerous remnants dating back to Mycenaean, Classic and Byzantine periods were uncovered during the construction of the Metro between 1993 and 2000, and they are displayed at some Metro stations. When riding on the Metro, allow for time to view the valuable artefacts. Ancient sculptures, gravestones, jewellery and household articles can be marvelled at in the Akropoli, Evangelismos, Panepistimiou and Syntagma stations.

The best place to end the day is a cosy taverna on the pláka.

The Pantánassa Church in the centre of the square is the remains of a convent founded in the 10th century. The nave of the basilica, whose aisles are each separated by three columns, is arched over by an elliptical dome.

◄ Pantánassa Church

The Tzisdarákis Mosque, a few yards south of Pantánassa Church, today houses the **pottery collection of the Museum of Greek Folk Art**, which was collected from all over Greece. It includes pottery primarily of the first two decades of the 20th century (opening hours: daily except Tue 9am – 2.30pm).

Tzisdarákis Mosque

🕐

Visible behind the mosque are the Corinthian columns of the library founded by Emperor Hadrian at some time after AD 132 (not open to the public). The middle room in the east wing, which is to a large extent still standing, served as the library. There was a pool was in the courtyard surrounded by a garden. The columns standing on the grounds and the other building remains were part of the Megale Panagía Church from the 5th century.

Hadrian's Library

While the Greek Agorá grew gradually over time, the Roman Agorá was constructed according to a unified plan about the time of the birth of Christ. The square has two gates, the Doric gate in the west erected between 12 BC and AD 2, and the Ionic propylon, thought to date back to the time of Emperor Hadrian (2nd century), in the east. The Tower of the Winds is included today in the grounds of the Roman Agorá. The octagonal and excellently preserved tower, erected

Roman Agorá

◄ Tower of the Winds

Around the turn of the eras, the Romans laid out their own market place and centre of city life near the Greek agorá.

around 40 BC, contained a **water clock** that displayed the time according to the height of the water in a cylinder. The tower took its name from the eight wind gods depicted in reliefs. The structure next to the entrance to this excavation site is a marble **latrine** that could accommodate almost 70 persons (1st century A.D.). In the Turkish period, the **Fethiye Mosque** was built in the northern part of the market, and serves today as a finds depot. (opening hours: daily 8am – 7pm).

Ágii Anárgyri

Pritaníou Street leads in the east to a complex planted with cypresses that is subordinate to the Monastery of the Holy Sepulchre in Jerusalem. The **only church decorated in Baroque style in Athens** is primarily noteworthy for its carved, gilt iconostasis.

Lysikrates Monument

Tripodon Street leads in the southeast to the monument that Lysikrates erected in 334 BC following his victory in the tragedy competition, during which he had financed the chorus rehearsals. The walls of the round structure are divided by Corinthian columns. The narrow frieze running around below the roof shows Dionysus' battle with sea pirates and their transmutation into dolphins. In 1669, the monument was made part of a Capuchin monastery and used as a library.

Great Mitropolis

Platía Mitropoleos in the north of the Pláka is dominated by the **city's large, main church**. The Great Mitropolis or Cathedral was designed by **Eduard Schaubert** and built between 1842 and 1862. The mortal remains of Patriarch **Gregorios V**, who was executed by the Turks in 1821, are interred in a shrine at the second pillar to the right.

The Little Mitropolis next door, dedicated to **Panagía Gorgoepíkoos** (»Holy Mary, Swift Answerer of Prayer«) and **Ágios Eleftherios**, is a very beautifully proportioned 12th century four-columned cruciform church. Many ancient and medieval fragments were used in its walls, such as two sections (in the wrong order) of a 4th-century calendar frieze, framed by two pilaster capitals, above the entrance and below the sima. Some of the ancient fragments have been »Christianized« with crosses.

> ! **Baedeker** TIP
>
> **Take a break ...**
>
> ... while strolling through the old part of town at any of the many picturesque tavernas lining Palea Agorá Square by Hadrian's Library.

Modern Athens

Modern Athens was born in the reign of King Otto I (1834 – 1862) of the Bavarian House of Wittelsbach. The plan behind the re-design of the city and public buildings, which was intended to transform it an insignificant provincial town into a capital and royal residence, was in the hands of a group of architects composed of Germans, Danes, a Frenchman and a Greek. **Eduard Schaubert** and his friend **Stamatios Kleanthis** created the plan for the city north of the old town in 1832 / 1833. Essentially it covered the area between Omónia, Sýntagma and Monastiráki squares. | History and overview

Ermoú and Stadíou Streets lead into the large square called Platía Syntágmatos, **»Constitution Square«** since the revolution of 1843. The palace for King Otto I was built here from 1834 to 1838; it has served as the **Parliament** building since 1935. Built by **Friedrich von Gaertner** on the highest spot on the square, it dominates the ministries, hotels, office buildings and banks lining the square. The Evzones keep watch at the **Tomb of the Unknown Soldier** in front of Parliament. There is a changing of the guard every hour and the grand ceremonial **parading of the guard** takes place Sundays around 10.30am. | Sýntagma Square

A walk from Sýntagma Square down Venizélou- / Panepistimíou Streets can give an impression of modern Athens and at the same time of the efforts made by Otto I and George I to give the city an urbane character.
Heinrich Schliemann lived with his Greek wife Sophia in the palatial Schliemann House built by Ernst Ziller from 1870 to 1881 in the style of the Italian Renaissance. Today the numismatic collection of the Archaeological National Museum is housed here and, with | Venizélou, Panepistimiou

★
◄ Numismatic Museum of Athens

*Evzones in traditional uniforms during the changing of the guard on
Sýntagma Square in front of the Parliament building*

600,000 coins, it is one of the most important museums of its kind
in the world (Venizélou 12; opening hours: Tue – Sun 8am – 2pm).

**University
Academy, Natio-
nal Library**

The main focus of the urban planning was the elegant, yet quite academic appearing so-called **Athenian trilogy**, which, while elegant,
comes across as rather academic: the university, built from 1837 to
1852 by the Dane, Christian Hansen, flanked by two elaborate buildings by his brother, Theophil, who was ten years older, the Academy
of Sciences (1859 – 1885) and the National Library (1887 – 1902).
The frescoes at the University and Academy were by the Bavarian
Karl Rahl. In front of the Academy are two columns with statues of
Athena and Apollo and on either side of the staircase are statues of
Plato and Socrates sitting. Standing in front of the entrance to the
University are sculptures of **Kapodistrias**, governor of Greece from
1827 to 1831, as well as of the poet and scholar **Adamantios Korais**.
The initiator of the building of the university, King Otto I, is por-
trayed surrounded by muses in a painting above the door.

**Platiá
Klafthmónos**

Standing on Platiá Klafthmónos is **Ágii Theodóri** church, a distinctive
building erected around 1050 in cloisonné masonry with a bell-tower
and remarkable portals built on.

City Museum ▶

King Otto I and his wife Amalia lived from 1836 until 1842 in
Vouros House built in 1834 on the east side of the square. Today, the
Museum of the City of Athens is housed here. The old kitchen and

models of Athens in the year 1842 can be seen on the ground floor; on the upper floor are the chambers of the royal couple with Empire and Biedermeier period furniture as well as a large number of mementoes.

The Neo-classical building in Stadíou Street, designed by the French architect, François Boulanger and built in 1858, was the **seat of Parliament until 1934**. The National Historical Museum today housed here presents the history of Greece from the conquest of Constantinople by the Ottoman Turks in 1453 to the Italian invasion of Greece in 1940. The interesting collection of national costumes – one of the most extensive in Greece – and the jewellery from the different regions convey a vivid image of the wealth of forms in Greek customs. An imposing equestrian statue of **Theodóros Kolokotrónis**, a patriot of the War of Greek Independence, stands in front of the flight of steps (opening hours: Tue – Sun 9am – 2pm).

★ National Historical Museum

🕐

One of the highlights of a stay in Athens is a visit to the National Archaeological Museum, housed in a Neo-classical columned building erected in 1860 and designed by the German architect **Ludwig Lange**. It holds the largest collection of the art of Greek Antiquity in existence. The wealth of its collections only becomes clear with repeated visits, but even the first tour leaves an overwhelming impression of the immense diversity of art created in ancient times. The collections date from the Geometric period (9th / 8th centuries), from the Archaic (7th / 6th centuries.) and the Classical (5th / 4th centuries), the Hellenistic (3rd – 1st centuries BC) and the Roman periods.

★★ National Archaeological Museum

Artefacts (1600 – 1150 BC) discovered by Heinrich Schliemann in the mountains of Mycenae are in the Mycenaean section. Items on display include the gold mask of a king, the so-called **Mask of Agamemnon** (c. 1580 BC) with schematized facial features, stylized beard and large ornamental ears. The famous red-figure **Warrior Vase** (c. 1200 BC) displays Mycenaean warriors in full armour on the way to battle.

◄ Mycenaean Art

The finds from the Cyclades, linked at an early stage through sailing and trade (3rd / 2nd millennia BC), testify to the highly developed art in these islands during the transitional period between the Neolithic and the Bronze Ages with copper tools, other metal items and the peculiar stone **Cycladic idols**.

◄ Cycladic Art

In the 9th and 8th centuries BC, before any columned temples and large sculptures existed in Greece, potters were able to produce monumental vases up to 1.5 m/5 ft in height, not for everyday use but rather for burial rites. The geometric burial amphorae like the famous **Dipylon Vase** from the time of Homer (c. 750 BC) stand out not only because of their ornamentation of geometrically arranged lines but equally because of the memorably simple depictions of burial scenes with the funeral bier, the mourners and the cortège.

◄ Geometric Art

Néa Anáktora   On the east side of the National Garden, the architect Ernst Ziller created the palace for Crown Prince Constantine in the years 1890 to 1893. The palace of the crown prince later served as a royal residence (Néa Anáktora = New Palace) and since 1973 as the **official residence of the Greek prime minister**. Evzones are on guard in their traditional uniforms in front of the building.

✴
National Gallery

The National Gallery (Alexandros Soutzos Museum) is dedicated to Greek and West European art with the focus of the collection being on Greek art of the time after the War of Independence.

First floor ►

The museum's oldest works of art are **icons**, including three works by Domenikos Theotokopoulos, also known as **El Greco**. In addition, the gallery owns important icons of the Ionian Islands' Western-influenced school of painting, represented by Nikolaos and Pangioris Doxaras and Nikolaos Kantounis, among others.

The time of King Otto I is recalled with portraits, landscapes and historical paintings. The period up to the beginning of the 20th century is at first dominated by academic painting and the Munich School. Among the Gallery's best-known paintings are »The Children's Engagement« and »The Fortune Teller« by **Nikolaos Gyzis** as well as »The Homecoming from the Festival«, »Milkman Resting« and »The Kiss« by **Nikiforos Lytras**. In addition, there are works by the Impressionists Ioannis Altamouras, Iakovos Rizos and Georgios Iakovidis. Hanging in the small hall are works by West European masters, including Caravaggio, Tiepolo, Rembrandt and Breughel as well as Pablo Picasso and Georges Braque. A place of honour is reserved for El Greco, a native of Crete.

Second floor ►

The second floor is devoted to Greek art of the 20th century with works by Konstantinos Parthenis, Nikos Chatzikyriakos-Gikas and Giannis Moralis (Vas. Konstantinou 50; opening hours: Mon, Wed – Sat 9am – 3pm, Mon, Wed also 6pm – 9pm, Sun 10am – 2pm).

✴
Olympieion

When Odós Singrou was laid out from Piraeus to Athens in the 19th century, it was planned to lead to two massive columns. These are part of the Olympieion, which dominates the area east of the Acropolis. This, the largest of Athens' sacred structures, dates back to the Peisistratides (6th century BC). The Seleucid king **Antiochus IV** (175 – 164 BC) resumed its construction, but it was Emperor **Hadrian** who had it completed in AD 130.

As an expression of the tastes of the time of the tyrants, a Syrian king and a Roman emperor, the **Temple of Olympian Zeus** was and remains at odds with the Attic sense of dimension. The Olympieion still stands today in the shadow of the Acropolis, even though the quality of its construction is deserving of greater consideration. Gone is the cella that once held a statue of Hadrian along with the cult image of Zeus; gone too are most of its 104 columns that took 15,500 tons of marble to create. But the surviving group of 13 columns on the southeast corner are of imposing size. Added to that are the two

It took some 700 years, from 510 BC to AD 130, before the massive Temple of Zeus was finally completed.

columns still standing and the one on the south side that fell over in 1852. It is still unclear whether the 13 extant columns are from the Hellenistic period and the three southern columns from the Roman structure, or whether they are all from the Roman period. (Opening hours: summer daily 8am – 7pm, winter daily 8.30am – 3pm).

Hadrian's Gate

Standing next to busy Leoforos Amalias road to the west of the Olympieion is Hadrian's Gate (AD 131 / 132), marking the boundary between ancient Athens and the Roman extension of the city, between the »city of Theseus« and the »city of Hadrian«, as the inscriptions on the outside and inside of the gate formulate it.

★
Stadium

The Athenian stadium, nestled between two hills east of the Olympieion, is today called the **Panathinaikos**, the Panathenaic Stadium. The stadium of Pentelic marble with a seating capacity of 60,000 is modern, but it has the same form and is on the same spot as its ancient predecessor in which the Panathenaic Games were held. **Herodes Atticus**, whose grave is on the hill adjacent to the north, had the stadium rebuilt in marble in AD 140 – 144. The stadium was again rebuilt for the Olympic Games of 1896. Sports competitions are no longer held in it today, but rather rallies and concerts. An exception was made during the Olympic Games of 2004 when the archery competition was held here and the marathon ended here.

1,017 m/3,337 ft Mount Ymittós. The name of the monastery goes back to a spring at an ancient shrine of Aphrodite. Emperor Hadrian had an aqueduct built from the spring to Athens in the 2nd century and that is why it is called »kaisariane« or »imperial«. The spring's water, considered to have healing powers, still flows today out of an ancient ram's head in the forecourt.

Church ► The monastery surrounds a **domed-crossing church** erected around AD 1000. The dome is supported by four columns with Ionic capitals that imbue the church interior with an air of lightness. The decoration dates from the 16th century and was probably done by an Áthos monk. The portico, with a fine depiction of the Holy Trinity, was not built until the 17th century, when the bell-tower and the chapel on the right dedicated to St Anthony were also added.

Monastery ► There are still quite well preserved remains of the monastery buildings including a Roman-style bath, a two-storeyed wing of cells, a tower house belonging to the Venizelos family of Athens, who were among the benefactors of the monastery, a kitchen and a refectory (opening hours: Tue – Sun 8.30am – 3pm).

Piraeus Piraeus (pop. 180,000), forms a single metropolitan area together with Athens. It is Greece's largest port and the starting point for shipping routes to neighbouring countries as well as for most of the domestic lines. It was Themistocles who, in 482 BC, developed Piraeus into Athens' merchant and naval port. With its destruction by Sulla in 86 BC, Piraeus lost its importance. It began its recovery in the 19th century after the War of Independence, when Eduard Schaubert laid out a modern plan for the city. Today, in addition to the principal harbour of Kantharos, the smaller docks on the east side, Zéa and Mikrolímano, are also in use. The city presents itself with a mixture of busy harbours, bustling urban life and a special atmosphere that can be experienced, for example, around **Mikrolímano** harbour with its tavernas or on **Korais Square**. The **archaeological museum** exhibits artefacts discovered in Piraeus and on the Attic coast, funerary monuments and reliefs from the 4th and 5th centuries BC, Hellenistic and Roman sculpture with two colossal statues of Emperor Hadrian, as well as the famous **bronze statues of Apollo and Artemis** from the 4th century BC. (Chariláou Trikoúpi 31; opening hours: Tue – Sun 9am to 2pm, Sun until 1.30pm).

! Baedeker TIP

Harbour Trip

Do not even try to penetrate the confusion of one-way streets and narrow, steep lanes of Piraeus by car. On the other hand, it is worth taking a ride on the water from the central port to the ports of Zéa and Mikrolímano, crowded with innumerable yachts. Cafés and tavernas line the promenade along the shore; the good – and very expensive – fish restaurants in Mikrolímano are particularly famous.

Greek Maritime Museum ► The Greek Maritime Museum, housed in a modern, semi-circular building directly on the Zéa Marina, provides an insight into the de-

Fish restaurants line the Mikrolímano, the »little harbour«, of Piraeus.

velopment of Greek seafaring since Classical Antiquity, using ship models, flags and nautical instruments. The exhibit is augmented by an account of the Greek merchant marine and traditional shipbuilding. (opening hours: Tue – Sat 9am – 2pm).

⏲

★
Eleusis

A secret mystery cult based on the myth of the goddess Demeter held its celebrations in the shrine of Eleusis, located in what is now an in-dustrial estate 22 km/14 mi west of Athens. There is evidence of Eleusis being the site of a **Demeter shrine** from the 7th century BC. The Eleusinian mysteries were celebrated until the 4th century AD. The archaic shrine was fundamentally altered and enlarged under Pericles in the 5th century BC. The shrine experienced another hey-day during Roman times. The buildings that characterize the site were built between 60 BC and the 2nd century AD. The Visigoths destroyed Eleusis in AD 395. The core of the sanctuary is the **Teleste-rion**, a hall for celebrating the mysteries. The Solonic Telesterion was built around 600 BC on the site of a small Mycenaean temple with an inner sanctum, which remained the focal point of the structure until Roman times. The portico of Philo was added from 330 to 310 BC. The hall had steps around it with 3,000 seats; those hewn in the rock of the mountain slope have survived.

The Eleusian Mysteries were celebrated every year in Eleusis in honour of the fertility goddess Demeter.

Museum ▶ The museum on the excavation site primarily displays exhibits from the time of the Eleusinian mysteries in the 5th / 4th centuries BC, including a Demeter statue from the workshop of **Agoracritos**, a pupil ⏱ of Phidias (opening hours: summer Mon 12 noon – 7pm, Tue – Sun 8am – 7pm, winter Tue – Sun 8.30am – 3pm).

Salamís Salamís (Salamína), the largest island in the Saronic Gulf with a richly indented coastline, closes off the Bay of Eleusis to the south with its northern end. The hills, partially of karst, are sparsely wooded. The capital has been located since the 6th century BC at Ambeláki, where the remains of an acropolis and a harbour are visible under water. Salamís made history when, in 480 BC, the battle-weakened Athenians led by Themistocles inflicted a devastating defeat on the numerically far superior Persian fleet at the **Battle of Salamís**, once and for all destroying the Persian king Xerxes' plans for expansion. The battle took place in the waters south of Salamís between the islands of Ágios Geórgios in the north and Psyttaleía and the Kynosoúra Peninsula in the south.

Salamína town ▶ The not very attractive main town on the island, Salamína, lies in the deep bay of the same name. Around 3 km/2 mi to the east is the main port of Paloukia, the home port of the Greek Navy. The archaeological museum on Ágios Nikólaos beach, 4 km/2.5 mi from Paloúkia, displays mostly 4th-century funerary reliefs from the necropolis of the ancient city.

A very scenic road leads 6 km/4 mi west of Salamína to the monastery of Faneroméni, which has remarkable frescoes. It was built in 1661 using materials from an ancient shrine on the same site. Not far to the south are the remains of the small fortress of Boudorón (6th century BC).

◀ Faneroméni Monastery

In the village of Peanía, 7 km/4.5 mi east of Athens on the slopes of Mount Ymittós, are some interesting late-Byzantine churches with frescoes, predominantly from the 17th century. The attraction in the village is the very fine Vorres Museum of **Contemporary Art** and **Greek Folk Art**.

Peanía

✳

◀ Vorres Museum

The collection was installed in a very attractively designed series of old and new buildings with gardens and courtyards. On display are paintings and sculptures by notable Greek artists, mostly from the post-war period. The folk-art collection has its place in three old farm buildings. The oldest items on display are 5th-century BC burial objects from children's graves; the icon collection consists of exhibits from the 18th and 19th centuries and the folk-art collection includes folk paintings and antique furniture (Diadóchou Konstantínou 1; opening hours: Sat and Sun 10am – 2pm).

☉

Daphní monastery, 10 km/6 mi to the west, is famous for its magnificent 11th-century mosaics which, as one of the few **completely preserved mosaic cycles**, are among the most important treasures of Byzantine art in Greece. The name recalls the shrine of the god Apollo, to whom the laurel (»daphne«) was sacred. In 1205, after the Franks captured Athens, the monastery was given to Cistercians from Burgundy and served as the burial place of the later dukes of Athens. The battlement-crowned defensive walls and a number of sarcophagi date from this period. Daphní was damaged and abandoned during the Greek War of Independence. A thorough restoration in the mid-1950s saved the monastery from further deterioration. In 1990, Daphní monastery was included in the list of UNESCO World Heritage Sites. In 1999, the monastery was severely damaged by an earthquake and is not open to the public until the restoration work is complete.

✳ ✳
Daphní

The 1,109 m/3,628 ft Mount Pentéli borders the plain of Attica to the northeast. Ever since ancient times it has been the source of **Pentelic marble**, the material used not only for the buildings on the Acropolis in Athens but also by the great sculptors of that time.

Mount Pentéli

Drive from Athens on Leofóros Kifissías in a north-easterly direction to a square planted with poplar trees 8 km/5 mi past Chalándri where Pentéli monastery was built in 1578. Sacred scriptures are displayed on the lower floor, which can be entered from the outside. In

◀ Pentéli monastery

addition, a secret school from the time of the Turkish occupation can be seen. The church, built in 1233, has a Byzantine mural and beautiful paintings and icons dating back to the 16th and 17th centuries.

Mount Párnis 1,413 m/4,636 ft Mount Párnis, a national park 35 km/22 mi to the north, is a popular destination for hikers and nature lovers. Of interest on the southwest slope of Párnis are the Panagía ton Klistón monastery and the ancient border fortress of Fýle.

Panagía ton Klistón ► The isolated monastery can be reached via Anó Liossía and the village of Filí. It takes its name – »Mother of God of the Gorges« – from its spectacular location on a rock face over the Goula river gorge. The monastery is thought to have been founded in the 14th century, although the church and the cells date from a later time.

Fýle ► Some 7 km/4.5 mi from the monastery are the remains of the ancient fortress of Fýle, a **border fortress** built by Athens after the Peloponnesian War and intended to protect the country against attacks out of Megaris and Boeotia. Fýle lies on a 683 m/2,241 ft high plateau next to the pass over which the route from Athens to Tánagra in Boeotia ran. The 4th century castle's massive ashlar walls – with four towers and two gates – have survived to the height of the battlement parapet.

✱
Brauron (Vravróna) The village of Brauron (Vravróna), located 33 km/20 mi from Athens on Attica's east coast, gained importance in ancient times through its **shrine of Artemis**, where girls from Athens were educated. In Mycenaean times, the goddess Artemis had the additional name »Iphigeneia« in Brauron. According to **Euripides**, the daughter of King Agamemnon of Mycenae, **Iphigenia**, lived here as a priestess after her return from Tauris until her death. The remains of Middle Helladic buildings (2000 – 1600 BC) were found on the acropolis and there is evidence of dense settlement during the Mycenaean period (1600 – 1100 BC). Brauron experienced its highpoint in the 5th and 4th centuries but was abandoned after 300 BC because of the increasing flooding of the Eridanos River (opening hours: summer Tue – Sun 8.30am – 3pm).

✱
Cape Soúnion Cape Soúnion, 70 km/44 mi from Athens on the southern point of Attica is justly famous for its magnificent **Temple of Poseidon**, poised on a sheer cliff. It is also almost obligatory for holidaymakers in Greece because of its sunsets. Even in ancient times, the poet Homer spoke of Attica's southern point as »Soúnion's sacred cape«. It is no wonder that a shrine dedicated to Poseidon was erected on this spot, the entrance to the Saronic Gulf, for after all, seafaring depended on his good will. Beginning in 431 BC during the Peloponnesian War, the cape was fortified with walls and provided with a harbour.

Construction began around 500 BC on a temple that was still uncompleted when it was destroyed by the Persians in 480 BC. A Clas-

Magnificent sunset on Cape Sounion

sical marble temple was built on its foundation in 449 BC, a Doric peripteros with 6 : 13 extremely slender columns. It stands on an artificially extended terrace accessible through a propylon (opening hours: daily 10am until sunset).

On a hill northeast of the Temple of Poseidon lies a 6th-century shrine dedicated to Athena. Situated next to a small building, which still has, among other things, the base for its cult statue, is the foundation of a temple in the same form, but on a larger scale. The roof was supported by four columns, whose bases can still be seen.

Shrine of Athena

The **silver mining** region extending 10 km/6 mi to the north from theTemple of Poseidon to Thorikós was the basis of a good part of Athens' wealth and power. First traces date back to the 3rd millennium BC and the systematic mining of ore went on from the 5th until the 2nd century BC. A new ore-processing technique made mining profitable again from 1865 until 1981. The present appearance of Lávrio, dominated by Neo-classical buildings, dates from this era.

Lávrio

The ancient centre of mining, the Thorikós, is some 2 km/1.2 mi further north, in the vicinity of a power station. To be seen here are a mining tunnel and a reconstruction of an ore-washing system. Next to it is a theatre (5th / 4th century BC) belonging to a Dionysus shrine. Its orchestra is almost square and the rows of seating for 5,000 correspondingly deviate from the usual circle form. In addition, Archaic and Classical-era settlements have been excavated.

◀ Thorikós

The colourful monastery of Panteleímonos on the west coast of the Áthos Peninsula is inhabited by Russian monks.

tic villages and hermitages, mostly on the south coast that drops off steeply into the sea. Most of the monasteries are Greek, but the whole Orthodox world is also represented today on Áthos; Russians live in Panteleímonos, Bulgarians in Zográfou and Serbs in Chiliandaríou. An influx of young monks has once again been registered in recent years in some monasteries. The monks live according to the Julian calendar, which is 13 days behind the Gregorian.

✳ Chalcidice · Χαλκιδική

J-L 3-5

Population: 80,000

The charming mountain scenery and picturesque coastal landscape immediately outside the bustling city of Thessaloniki are attracting increasing numbers of holidaymakers.

Lying to the southeast of Thessaloniki is the 3,000 sq km/1,158 sq mi peninsula of Chalcidice with its distinctive form of a hand with three fingers – the peninsulas of Kassándra, Sithonía and ▶ Áthos. Its northern boundary is marked by Lakes Koróni and Vólvi. Its name is a reminder that the Euboean city of Chalcis founded 32 townships here. Thanks to the wide, sandy beaches, this less populated area of

Greece – the two western »fingers« to be exact – has gradually become developed for tourism. Monopolization by the tourist industry is still being kept within reasonable limits though and it is still possible to find many almost deserted beaches along the coast of Chalcidice even in the high season.

What to See in Chalcidice

The best impression of Chalcidice can be gained on a drive from Thessaloníki across the Kassándra and Sithonía peninsulas and through Polýgyros and Arnéa to Ouranoúpolis. The motorway from Thessaloníki heads south to Néa Sílata. A detour can be taken here to **Petrálona**, where a 700,000-year-old skull, a »preliminary stage« of Homo sapiens, was found in its limestone cave. The museum nearby exhibits the finds from the cave, including bones, tools and fossils. Drive further south past Néa Moudaniá to the Isthmus of Potídea. **Potídea**, was located here. It was founded about 600 BC and presumably in the 4th century a canal was dug and some of its walls are still visible. The remaining ruins date back to the 6th century. The road leads in the direction of Sithonía past Ágios Mámas with its stork colonies. The coast is an interesting wetland biotope with sand dunes and lagoons. Some 2 km/1.2 mi beyond Ágios Mámas is Néa Ólynthos and the burial grounds of the ancient city of **Ólynthos**. Macedonians settled in the already inhabited area around 800 BC After its destruction in the Persian Wars (480 BC), the city was resettled by the city of Chalcis and developed into the most important city on the Chalcidice peninsula. In 348 BC, Philip II of Macedonia had Ólynthos totally destroyed. Excavations have revealed streets arranged on a rectanular grid system, public buildings and private homes. The city's 5th-century pebble mosaics are well known.

> **? DID YOU KNOW ...?**
>
> ■ ... that the Greeks call Chalcidice's three peninsulas »feet« and not »fingers«?

The »point of entry« to the peninsula of Kassándra, the western »finger« of Chalcidice, is **Néa Potídea**, which offers an inviting beach and a pretty harbour. A turn-off to the west 9 km/5.6 mi to the south leads to **Sáni** with fantastic beaches and an extensive luxury resort. Further along the main road on the east coast is **Áfytos**, a charming place with a number of Neo-classical houses, followed 4 km/2.5 mi to the south by **Kallithéa**, the largest and most exuberant holiday spot on the peninsula.

Kassándra

A road runs around the peninsula of Sithonía between the turquoise-blue sea, fantastically beautiful beaches and verdant low mountain scenery. Dead-end roads lead off to innumerable secluded coves and on the west coast some stretches run directly beside the

Sithonía

► VISITING CHALCIDICE

INFORMATION

Tourist Information
Tsimiski 136
Thessaloniki
Tel. 23 10 22 11 00
Fax 23 10 22 13 80
E-mail: the_info_office@otenet.gr

Eagle's Palace – the fantastic view is free of charge.

WHERE TO EAT

► Expensive
Sousourada
Road to the beach,
Áfytos
Gourmet restaurant run by the well-known TV chef Nikolaos Katsanis with an excellent wine list.

► Moderate
Dionysos
Bus stop
Néos Marmarás
Offered here is a large selection of starters along with a superb view of the harbour.

► Inexpensive
Platanos
On the main square of Arnéa
The honey from the region can be sampled in this taverna, as well as the honey-sweetened Ouzo Moundovina.

WHERE TO STAY

► Luxury
Eagle's Palace
Ouranoúpolis
Tel. 23 77 03 10 47
www.eaglespalace.gr
153 rooms, 15 bungalows
The hotel complex located 4 km/2.5 mi from Ouranoúpolis has a private beach; the hotel offers, among other things, tours on its private luxury yacht.

Aristoteles Beach
Áfytos
Tel. 23 74 09 15 68
www.aristotelesbeach.gr
200 rooms
Aristoteles Beach consists of a main building and a number of bungalows beautifully situated above the coastal road, 2 km/1.2 mi distance from Áfytos. There is a lift from the hotel down to the beach.

► Mid-range
Gerakini Beach
Gerakini
Tel. 23 71 05 23 02
413 rooms, 39 suites
large hotel complex situated on an excellent beach with disco, children's club and a programme of activities.

Skites
Ouranoúpolis
Tel. 23 77 07 11 40
www.skites.gr
21 bungalows, 4 apartments
The tasteful bungalow complex peacefully set on the sea, app. 1 km/0.6 mi from Ouranoúpolis, fits well into the landscape.

Smart beach bar near Pórto Cárras on the Sithonia Peninsula

sea. The first stop on the tour is a lively vacation spot called **Néos Marmarás**, whose charm consists mainly of being situated on four tiny points of land framing three coves. It is worth taking a detour from here to the attractive mountain village of **Parthenónas**, a village that was recently abandoned and is now repopulated with some of the houses having been nicely restored. There is a superb view from the village.

Lying to the southeast of Néos Marmarás is **Pórto Cárras**. The Greek shipping magnate, John Carras, had huge hotels, a yacht harbour and a golf course built here in 1970 (entrance fee!). **Toróni**, a little further to the southeast, is a pretty little place with one of the most beautiful beaches on Chalcidice. The remains of a Byzantine castle have survived on a cape at the southern end of the bay. Not quite 2 km/1.2 mi further south lies **Pórto Koufó** on an almost landlocked, natural harbour.

Most of the beautiful coves on the southern point of the peninsula can only be reached from the sea. The bay of **Kalamítsi** is particularly attractive, revealing a dream of a vista. Pretty **Sykiá**, one of the few villages on the peninsula that developed naturally, lies with its bathing cove 3 km/2 mi from the coast, while the resort town of **Sárti** sits on a narrow, agriculturally cultivated coastal plain.

The 32 km/20 mi stretch to **Vourvouroú** is quite scenic with Áthos forming the backdrop when the weather is clear. A boat trip can be taken from the port of Órmos Panagías across to Ouranoúpolis, the border town to the Autonomous Monastic State and a popular tourist attraction.

League, but was able to maintain its independence. In 412 BC, Chíos broke away from Athens, and in 392 from Sparta, under which it had greatly suffered. The island belonged to Venice from 1204 to 1304, then Genoa and, after 1566, Turkey. The Chians, always regarded as excellent seamen and clever merchants, rose up against the Turks in 1822, who retaliated with a horrific massacre among the population in which 30,000 people lost their lives or were taken into slavery. An earthquake in 1881 left severe devastation in its wake. When a Greek squadron appeared off the island during the Balkan War in 1912, the island was turned over to the Greeks after brief resistance. After World War I Chíos had to accept the loss of its economic hinterland in nearby Turkey and take in many of the Greek refugees driven out from there.

Island Interior

Chíos Town
The island's **chief town and principal port**, Chíos (pop. 25,000), lies approximately on the site of the ancient city on the central east coast. Its houses are situated around the harbour, towered over by a 14th-

The capital of Chíos is spread around a sweeping harbour bay on the east coast.

Afternoon chat in a beach café in the resort of Karfás

century medieval Genoese castle and the minaret of a 19th-century mosque. Little remains of the old town. The houses that survived the massacre of 1822 were destroyed in the earthquake of 1881. And yet, the town possesses a pleasant oriental atmosphere. **Giustiniani House**, built in the 5th century, has a small collection of Byzantine and Post-Byzantine art. Further to the north is a Turkish cemetery. The **Korais Library**, housed in a Neo-classical building in the new part of town spreading out to the south, is based on the important collection of books of the Chian philologian, Adamantios Korais (1748 – 1833). A painting and folk art collection is also on display in the building. The **Chíos Maritime Museum** in Odós Tsouri Stefánou 20, presents watercolours and models of Greek ships of the 19th and 20th centuries. The **archaeological museum** in the south of the town has finds from Embório and Faná on display, including a collection of Hellenistic and Roman grave steles. A special exhibit is the stone from the year 332 BC with a »letter« from Alexander the Great to the Chians chiselled on it, in which he promises them more democracy. A small group of hotels has developed on **Karfás** beach, 6 km/4 mi to the south of Chíos Town.

Close to the shore at the north end of the village of Vrontádos, 6 km/4 mi north of the island's capital with a number of large villas, is

Vrontádos

Néa Moní monastery is one of the major Byzantine structures in Greece and is located in lush, green mountains.

a stone showing traces of having been worked in early times and that once presumably served as a **Kybele shrine**. Locally it is known as »Scholí Omírou«, »Homer's school«, and recalls the island's claim to being the homeland of the ancient poet.

★ ★
Néa Moní convent

A panoramic road leads 15 km/9.3 mi from Chíos Town through the colourful village of Karyés northwest to Néa Moní set in the midst of lush green mountain scenery, one of the few monastic sites inhabited by nuns. It was founded by Emperor **Constantine IX Monomachos** (reigned 1042 – 1055) on the spot where a miracle-working Madonna icon was found in a myrtle bush. The dome of the convent church rests on eight pillars and spans the full width of the church. The walls still retain their original facing of red marble. The convent's 11th century **mosaics grounded in gold**, partially destroyed in the earthquake of 1881, are most certainly the work of artists from Constantinople. The Late Byzantine frescoes in the outer portico are work dating from 14th century. The chapel to the left of the convent gate, dedicated to the dead of 1822, contains a **charnel-house**. To the right of the gate is a small **museum** with displays of religious art (opening hours: Mon – Sat 8am – 1pm, 4pm – 8pm).

Avgónyma

The main road continues to rise beyond Néa Moní and then leads downward to Avgónyma. New life has moved into the village, which was completely abandoned in the 1990s. Houses have been restored as holiday homes and tavernas have opened their doors.

The neighbouring village to the north, Anávatos , impressively nest- ◄ Anávatos
ling below a sheer rock with castle ruins, was already almost deserted
in 1822. Here, too, a few houses in the lower area of the village have
been restored as holiday accommodation.

North of the Island

Langáda, 18 km/11 mi north of Chíos Town, is a pretty village situ- Langáda
ated on a deep bay with cafés and tavernas waiting for guests; followed 12 km/7.5 mi further north by **Kardámyla**, whose pleasant
platía is the gathering place of the village and its harbour, **Mármaro**,
a popular holiday venue with some good beaches.
The 13th-century church of Panagía Agiogaloúsena in the small village of **Ágio Gála** in the northwest of the island stands directly at the
entrance to a limestone cave and is decorated with old icons.

South of the Island

Lying some 30 km/18.6 mi southwest of Chíos Town is the pictu- Pyrgí
resque little town of Pyrgí in the centre of the **Mastichochoría**, the
20 mastic-producing villages. The grey-and-white houses, whose
geometric patterns are created by a
technique known as sgraffito, are
particularly charming. Dominating
the town is the tower of a Genoese
castle. The **Ágii Apóstoli** church
(12th century), with frescoes dating from 1665, follows the example
of Néa Moní, as do other churches
on the island.
The archaeological site at **Káto Fá-
na**, with remains of a temple to
Apollo, lies 8 km/5 mi to the southwest of Pyrgí. Located a few kilometres northwest of Pyrgí is **Olýmbi**, a beautiful medieval village
with a castle, and **Mestá**, whose outer ring of fortified houses formed
the city wall.

! *Baedeker* TIP

Relaxing beach-life
There are many beautiful beaches that are
almost deserted during the off-season along the
central west coast approximately opposite the
Néa Moní convent.

Inoússes Islands

Lying to the northwest of the island of Chíos are the Inoússes Is- »Luxury Islands«
lands, some of the richest islands in Greece, comprising the main island of the same name and several more islands. The small island
has simply wonderful beaches and offers great places to hike. Despite
that, not too many tourists are seen here. It is said that the reason is
because of the many rich shipowners who want to remain undis-
turbed in their luxurious domiciles. The only attraction in Inoússes,
the town, is the **maritime museum** with an interesting collection of
historical ship models.

★★ Corfu · Kérkyra · Κέρκυρα

B / C 5 / 6

Island Group: Ionian Islands   **Area:** 592 sq km/228 sq mi
Altitude: 0 – 906 m/2,972 ft   **Population:** 110,000
Capital: Kérkyra

Corfu – or Kérkyra, as the Greeks call it – is one of the most popular islands in the Mediterranean. The gentle mountain countryside is really something special with its ancient, silvery-gleaming, light-green olive trees and slender, dark cypresses, its fabulous coves and, not least, its capital with its Italian flair.

The northernmost of the Ionian Islands is separated from the coast of Albania and the Greek region of Epiros by a 2 to 20 km/1.2 to 12 mi wide channel. Although Corfu is not the largest island in the archipelago, it's a good 60 km/37 mi long and up to 28 km/17 mi wide, and it does have the largest population. Even back in the late 19th century, the picturesque island with its lush green landscape, peaceful villages and magnificent bathing coves, was attracting holiday guests. The island's interior is the most delightful, particularly in the mountainous north, with its secluded towns and villages where time seems to stand still. The island's only »trade mark« is its ancient olive trees that reach up to 25 m/80 ft in height and have formed real forests. In fact, during Venetian times a premium was paid for every new olive tree planted. And a specialty of Corfu is **kumquats**, dwarf oranges, planted nowhere else in Greece.

> ! **Baedeker TIP**
>
> **Souvenir Hunt**
> Naturally, Corfu Town is flooded with all sorts of tourist rubbish. But time and again, between all the garish kitsch, quality mementoes can be found to take home, like traditional weaving and embroidery, hand-worked jewellery and pottery.

Mythology and history
Corfu is thought to be the Homeric **Scheria**, the land of the Phaeacians and their king Alkinoos. Odysseus, who was stranded on the shores of Scheria during his Odyssey, was brought to Alkinoos by Nausikaa, the beautiful daughter of the king. There he related his adventures and was finally able to continue his journey home in one of the Phaeacian king's ships. Colonized by Corinth in 734 BC, the island developed into a dangerous rival to Corinth itself. It became part of the Roman Empire in 229 BC. When the Roman Empire was divided in AD 395, it fell to Byzantium. The medieval name Corfu seems to have derived from the Greek word **Korýfi**, meaning »peak«. Corfu was under Venetian control from 1386 until 1797, when it became part of Napoleon's empire. After 1815, it and the rest of the Ionian Islands were British until 1864, when it went to Greece. Corfu was repeatedly devastated during the course of its history, so that evidence of its ancient and medieval past has largely been destroyed.

Highlights *Corfu*

Corfu Town
Its Italian »grandezza« and charming maze of lanes make the island's capital one of Greece's most appealing places.
▶ page 233

Vlachérna Monastery
A tour of Corfu's most famous picture postcard sites is a must.
▶ page 237

Achilleion
Empress Elisabeth of Austria-Hungary hoped to finally find her peace of mind here.
▶ page 237

Paleokastrítsa and Angelókastro
Scenic foothills on the wild and romantic west coast; one with an ancient monastery and beautiful beaches, the other with castle ruins.
▶ page 239

✶ ✶ In and Around Corfu Town

The appearance of the island's capital, situated on a promontory on the east coast, is dominated by two mighty fortresses with the wonderfully beautiful **old town** spread out between them. The old town has been added to the UNESCO's list of World Heritage sites. It is a maze of lanes spanned by buttress arches alternating with splendid palazzi and ornate wrought-iron balconies, the product of Venetian, French and British occupations.

Island capital

The harbour lies on the northern edge of town, towered over by the massive New Fortress (1546 – 1588). From the harbour, the main shopping street, Nikifórou Theotóki, leads to the Spianáda (»esplanade«), one of the most beautiful squares in all of Greece. The west side, with its arcades and cafés, is called **Listón**. Standing on the north side is the Neo-classical former **Governor's Palace**, built from 1818 to 1823 for the British Lord High Commissioner and later becoming the summer residence of

✶ Spianáda

> ### *i* All-in-One Museum Tour
>
> ■ There is a combination entrance pass for the Old Fortress, the Archaeological Museum, the Byzantine Museum and the Museum of Asiatic Art.

the Greek king in 1864. Housed here are the **Museum of Asiatic Art**, a very worthwhile museum that exhibits Chinese, Japanese and Korean art and crafts, and the **Municipal Pinacotheca**, which gives priority to presenting local artists from the 19th and early 20th centuries (opening hours: Museum of Asiatic Art Tue – Sun 8.30am – 3pm; Municipal Pinacotheca daily 9am – 9pm).

A bridge on the east side of the esplanade, where there is an equestrian statue commemorating Count **Johann Matthias von der Schulenburg**, who defended the city against the Ottoman Turks in 1716,

VISITING CORFU

INFORMATION

Tourist Information
Platia San Rocco
Corfu Town
www.corfu.gr
The branch in the airport is also open
from May to Oct.

The magazine »The Corfiot« (English,
monthly) contains much practical and
cultural information.

GETTING THERE

There are boat services to and from
Italy (Venice, Trieste, Ancona, Brindisi), with Igoumenítsa and Pátras on
the Greek mainland, and with the
island of Paxí.

TRAVELLING AROUND CORFU

Although the public bus network with
its centre in Corfu Town is well
developed, most of the interesting
places on the island can only be
reached by private car.

WHERE TO EAT

► Expensive
Nafsikaa
Odós Nafsíkas 11
Kanoni
Tel. 26 61 04 43 54
This restaurant on Kanoni Peninsula is
considered to be one of the best in the
surrounding area; it has a pretty
garden where its international and
Korfiot specialties are also served.

► Moderate
Bella Vista
Gastoúri
Near the Achilleion
The restaurant has its name from its
beautiful terrace and rightly so; the
view over the east coast of the island is
magnificent.

Estiatorio Rex
Kapodistriou 66
Corfu Town
Tel. 26 61 03 96 49
A restaurant steeped in tradition
behind the Liston Arcades with good
Korfiot cooking.

► Inexpensive
Il Pirata
Paleokastrítsa
In the centre of town
Large selection of Italian and Greek
dishes; terrace with a sea view.

Spyros
Benítses
In the town centre
Korfiot and international cuisine is
served here, the dishes from the
charcoal grill are especially tasty.

WHERE TO STAY

► Luxury
Arcadion
Vlasopoulou 2/Esplanade
Corfu Town
Tel. 26 61 03 01 04
www.arcadionhotel.com
32 rooms, 1 suite
The dignified hotel combines histor-
ical ambiance with modern comfort.

► Mid-range
Agios Gordis
Agios Gordis
Tel. 26 61 05 33 20
www.hotels-corfu.com
219 rooms
This hotel, with main building and
some chalets, is on one of the island's
most beautiful beaches; the roof garden with a bar greets its guests with a
superb panoramic view.

Grecotel Daphnila Bay

Dasia
Tel. 26 61 09 03 20
www.grecotel.gr, 260 rooms
Hotel complex situated in the midst of olive trees above a private beach; well-furnished terraced chalets are grouped below the main building; a broad range of sporting activities await the guests.

Konstantinoupolis

Odós Zavitsianou 1
Tel. 26 61 04 87 16
www.konstantinoupolis.com.gr
31 rooms
Early 19th century hotel located on the old harbour with a great deal of charm and a museum piece of a lift.

Corfu · Kérkyra *Map*

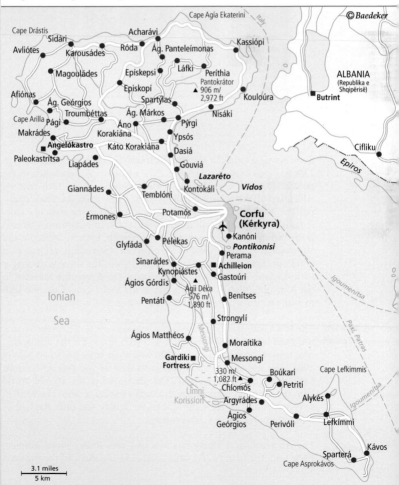

The cafés and restaurants in the Listón Arcade of Corfu Town are a popular place to meet for tourists and locals alike.

leads across a canal to the **Old Fortress**. The fortress dates back to 1386 and was expanded between 1572 and 1645. An explosion in the powder tower destroyed most of the buildings in the 18th century, which is why the present buildings date largely from the British period. The Anglican church of St George was built in the style of a Doric temple in 1840. Spreading out to the north of Nikifórou Theotóki is the picturesque old part of town, **Kambiello**, with its Italianate and Venetian-style houses and a number of interesting ecclesiastical buildings. Ágios Spyrídon church (1589) holds the silver sarcophagus with the body of the town's patron saint. The **Byzantine Museum** in the Antivouniotissa church displays in the main icons from the 15th to 19th centuries (opening hours: Tue – Sun 8.30 – 3pm).

G. Theotoki Square

The **town hall**, standing west of the Spianáda on G. Theotoki Square, was built between 1663 and 1691 as a club house for the aristocracy, was turned into a theatre in 1720 and then into the town hall in 1902. The east side of the square is flanked by the Roman Catholic **Cathedral**, which was built in 1658, destroyed in the Second World War and then reconstructed with a Neo-classical facade. The Bank of Greece building on the south side of the square was once the Catholic archbishop's palace (18th century).

Archaeological Museum

The Archaeological Museum, south of Corfu Palace Hotel, displays finds from the island's excavation sites. The highlight of the museum is the **Gorgo Medusa pediment** from the shrine to Artemis; fashioned in 585 BC, it is one of the best preserved works of Archaic sculpture in Greece. Also worth noting is a statue of a lion from the 7th century BC, thought to have stood on the tomb of Menecrates. The modest remains of the tomb of this »consul of Kérkyra« lie some 200 m/220 yd south of the Archaeological Museum (opening hours: Tue – Sun 8.30am – 3pm). ⊙

Standing in a spacious and beautiful park in the southern suburb of Anemómylos is the Neo-classical Monrepos Villa that the British governor, Sir Frederic Adam, built in 1828. HRH Prince Philip, Duke of Edinburgh was born here in 1921. It now contains a museum displaying a colourful mixture of archaeological, historical and botanicalexhibits (opening hours: June – Aug Tue – Sun 8.30am – 7pm, Sept – May Tue – Sun 8.30am – 3pm). To the north of the parks stands a superb Byzantine church dedicated to SS. Jason and Sosipater (11th / 12th centuries) with ancient stone blocks from Paleópolis and a remarkable iconostasis. Some 500 m/550 yd further to the southwest are the ruins of the 5th-century **Basilica of Paleópolis**. Lying below the villa is Corfu Town's beautiful old bathing beach.

✱
Monrepos Villa

⊙

There is a narrow lane that branches off the road to Kanóni shortly beyond the Basilica of Paleópolis, which leads to the meagre remains of a 6th-century BC shrine to Artemis.

Shrine of Artemis

There is a beautiful road that leads to the southern point of the promontory between the sea and Lake Chalikiópoulos, where the airport's runway has been built. The famous view of Corfu is the one from Rondell Kanóni. In the foreground, the little 17th-century monastery church, Vlachérna, and beyond, the little island of Pontikonísi, the »Mouse Island«. Vlachérna can be reached on foot across a causeway, and Pontikonísi by boats that set sail from this causeway. Mouse Island, on which a 16th-century Byzantine chapel stands, is considered to be the model Böcklin used for his painting »Island of the Dead«, although the artist was never here. The Greeks saw the island as the Phaeacian ship turned to stone that took Odysseus home to Itháca.

✱
Vlachérna, Pontikonísi

The South of the Island

One of Corfu's major attractions is the magnificent Villa Achilleion. It stands above the sea in a beautiful park south of Gastoúri, 9 km/ 5.6 mi from Corfu Town. It was built in 1890 / 1891 for the Empress **Elisabeth of Austria**, known as »Sisi«, in the Italian Renaissance style and was purchased in 1907 by **Kaiser Wilhelm II**. It has been state property since 1928. It contains many mementoes of »Sisi« and Wilhelm II. The park is fascinating, with its fabulous location and magnificent view. A large number of statues stand in the park; among

✱ ✱
Villa Achilleion

them, the »Dying Achilles«, commissioned by the Empress, and the »Victorious Achilles«, commissioned by the Kaiser (opening hours: June – Aug 9am – 7pm, otherwise 9am – 2.30pm).

Benítses The once charming fishing village of Benítses, 3 km/2 mi south of the Achilleion, now has the stamp of tourism on it, even though its pebble beach is tiny. The **Shell Museum** at the north end of the village has a rich collection of shells and corals. The scant remains of the bath from a 2nd-century Roman villa can be reached in a few minutes from the northern end of the carpark.

! *Baedeker* TIP

Oasis of Tranquillity

During the high season, boats cross over hourly from the old harbour to the small island of Vído, just offshore from Corfu Town – for free! On the island, you can lie around sunning yourself on the pebble beach (with a taverna) or tour the wild animal and bird protection centre. In all events, this is an oasis of tranquillity.

Korissía Lagoon has, spread out around it, a fantastic landscape that originally was dunes. The lake and the surrounding wetlands are home to a wide variety of birdlife. More than 120 species can be observed here. **Issos Beach** is very pretty and seldom visited.

The North of the Island

East coast The east coast in the north up to Pýrgi is firmly in the hands of tourists. The trip north passes the **Abramo Fortress**, and, further on, Lazarett Island can be recognized in the sea to the right.

✷
Mount Pantokrátor Outside Pýrgi a road branches off past Spartýlas and Strinýlas, through woods of olive trees and holly oak, and up Mount Pantokrátor – at 906 m/2,972 ft, the island's highest mountain. Besides a forest of antennae, there is a 17th-century monastery on the summit. The attraction in **Strinýlas** is a platía under the shade of a mighty elm tree and lined with tavernas.

Kalámi The winding coastal road on the other side of Pýrgi runs past several quiet villages and bathing coves. Lying on a beautiful bay is the little village of Kalámi that also has, along with a small fishing harbour, a few hotels and apartment complexes.

✷
Kassiópi Kassiópi differs from Corfu's other tourist centres in that its heart, centred on an idyllic harbour with the remains of a 13th-century Byzantine castle rising over it, is still seemingly quite original. Standing not far from the harbour is the peculiar church of Panagía Kassópitra (1590); the residence of the priest is above the nave. The best place for a swim in the area is **Kalamáki**, a family-friendly sandy beach 4 km/2.5 mi to the west, and the pebble beach, Avlaki, about 2 km/1.2 mi east of Kassiópi.

Café Kanóni has a wonderful view of the Vlachérna Monastery and tiny »Mouse Island«.

North and west coasts

The popular resorts on the north coast are **Róda** and **Sidári** on extensive sandy beaches punctuated by picturesque cliffs. The sandstone cliffs west of Sidári are cut by deep clefts and are known as »Canal d'Amour«. The beaches between Cape Drastis and Paleokastrítsa can be reached by car. The **Bay of Ágios Geórgios** at Afiónas is particularly pretty.

★
Paleokastrítsa

The heavily frequented town of Paleokastrítsa, the **tourist stronghold on the west coast** nestling in an exceptionally beautifully setting, can be reached over the scenic Troumbeta Pass. It takes 15 minutes to walk up to the monastery of Panagía Theotókos, built in 1228 on the peninsula on the outskirts of town. Adorned with luxuriant flowers, it presents a pretty picture with its campanile. The monastery church has an interesting depiction of the Last Judgement (17th century) above the entrance. A small museum belonging to the monastery exhibits valuable icons.

★
Angelokástro

The ruins of the 13th century fortress, Angelokástro, crowning the massive, projecting rock can be reached from the village of Makrádes. The view is even more impressive than the castle. In Venetian times, Angelokástro was repeatedly attacked by the Turks, but always managed to withstand the onslaught. The fortress was eventually razed under British rule.

Érmones, a few kilometres south of Paleokastrítsa, has a very fine beach-lined bay. Not far from there, in **Rópa Valley**, is an 18-hole golf course considered to be the best in the Mediterranean. Spreading out to the south are the beautiful sandy beaches of **Myrtiótissa** and **Glyfáda**, the island's most famous beach.

Neighbouring Islands

Paxí, located to the south of Corfu, is numbered among the most attractive destinations in the archipelago because of its exceptionally picturesque landscape, its beautiful coves and its fine diving locations. Innumerable olive trees and cypresses dot the countryside. The west coast has picturesque cliffs and numerous caves. Even a few of the highly endangered monk seals make their home here. The east coast runs along gently and has quite pretty pebble beaches. There is a Venetian fortress from 1423 as well as the former Panagía Monastery on an island just offshore of the harbour and main town of **Gáios**. In the far north of Paxí lies **Paxí**

> ! **Baedeker** TIP
>
> ### Boat trip to the beach
> Tourists come to Antípaxi first and foremost because of the delightful beaches of Vríka and Voutoúmi. During the high season, half a dozen boats come here daily between 10am and 3pm from Gáios, the principal town on Paxí, and then return to Paxí from Vríka Beach between 2.30pm and 5pm. If requested, they also stop at Voutoúmi Beach.

Lákka, the island's **water sports centre**. The **sea cave of Ypapánti** on the north coast served as a hiding-place for submarines in the Second World War. It can only be entered from the sea.

Located to the southeast of Paxí is its smaller, rocky »sister island«, Antípaxi, with beautiful, isolated beaches, especially Vríka and Voutoumi on the east coast. The 20 or so permanent inhabitants raise sheep and produce a fine wine. **Antípaxi**

★★ Corinth/Corinthos· Κόρινθος

H 9

Prefecture: Corinthía
Population: 23,000

Altitude: Sea level

The ruins of ancient Corinth, once the bridge between the European and the Asian worlds, a metropolis with a population of over 300,000, lie some 7 km/4.3 mi southwest of the modern coastal city of the same name at the foot of Acrocorinth mountain.

← *Sunbathing on the sandstone cliffs near Sidári on Corfu Island*

New old city Córinth, the modern city of Corinth on the just 6 km/4 mi wide isthmus between the Greek mainland and the Peloponnese, came into being when it was moved away from the site of ancient Corinth after a severe earthquake in 1858.

History Corinth owed its importance in ancient times to its location. The city controlled the only land access to the Peloponnese, thus dominating the trade in the Corinthian or Saronic Gulf with its two harbours, **Lechaion** and **Kenchreai**. Dorian settlers made their home here around 1000 BC. The city entered a period of prosperity under the **Bacchiad dynasty** (from 747 BC). **Kypselos** succeeded this dynasty after 600 BC, followed by his son, **Periandros**, who is ranked among the Seven Sages. Corinth was destroyed in the year 146 BC by the Roman general **Mummius** and it remained in ruins until **Julius Caesar** had it rebuilt in 44 BC. The apostle Paul preached in the city, which was notorious for its »loose morals«, in the years AD 51 / 52. The city was levelled by a severe earthquake in 521 and thereafter only Acrocorinth remained inhabited, until a settlement developed again on the site of the ancient agorá in the 10th century. Corinth was never again able to regain its significance, neither under Frankish nor Turkish rule.

▶ **CORINTH**

INFORMATION

Tourist Police
Ermoú 51/Platia Kendriki
Corinth
Tel. 27 41 02 32 82

Opening hours of the excavation sites:
Apr – Oct daily 8am – 7pm
otherwise daily until 5pm or until
nightfall

✶ ✶ Ancient Corinth

Museum The museum provides a comprehensive picture of art and culture in Corinth, from the Neolithic up into the Byzantine period. The pottery collection is particularly significant, presenting, as it does, the unbroken line of development of ancient Corinthian pottery. One of the outstanding exhibits is a statue of (presumably) Lucius Caesar, a grandson of Emperor Augustus, which was copied from a Greek original. Also on display is a remarkably well preserved floor mosaic, with the picture of a head of Dionysus, from a 2nd-century Roman villa.

Temple of Octavia To the right of the museum is a flight of steps leading to a temple assumed to have been dedicated to Octavia. Excavations south of this area have unearthed several layers of settlement, as well as a floor mosaic dating back to around 500 BC. North of the museum and west of the row of shop lies the temple precinct of **Héra Acraia** (?) and, behind it, the so-called **Fountain of Glauce**. According to

Ancient Corinth *Plan*

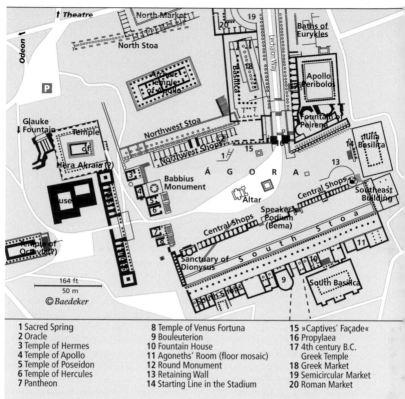

1 Sacred Spring
2 Oracle
3 Temple of Hermes
4 Temple of Apollo
5 Temple of Poseidon
6 Temple of Hercules
7 Pantheon

8 Temple of Venus Fortuna
9 Bouleuterion
10 Fountain House
11 Agoneths' Room (floor mosaic)
12 Round Monument
13 Retaining Wall
14 Starting Line in the Stadium

15 »Captives' Façade«
16 Propylaea
17 4th century B.C.
   Greek Temple
18 Greek Market
19 Semicircular Market
20 Roman Market

legend, Glauce, the daughter of the Corinthian king, Creon, threw herself into the spring. On the day of her wedding to Jason, she had put on a poisoned dress, a »gift« from Medea, whom Jason had deserted, and had started to burn. Desperate to ease her pain, she jumped into the water. But Glauce died, and Creon, who rushed to the aid of his daughter, did not survive the assassination attack either.

Standing on the highest spot in ancient Corinth are the remains of the Temple of Apollo with seven monolithic columns, a section of the entablature, the rock bedding and part of the foundation. The building had 6 : 15 columns of massive size. The cella was divided into two rooms, both having two rows of columns. The austere monumentality of the temple, erected around 540 BC, a classic example of early Doric temple construction, can still be seen in the ruins.

Temple of Apollo

The Apollo Temple in Corinth is a masterpiece of Doric temple-building.

Agorá A broad flight of steps on the west side of a Roman basilica lead down to the agorá. It was the focus of political and economic life and was once surrounded by columns. The pavement from Greek times has survived in the lower-lying eastern section, otherwise the whole complex is almost exclusively Roman. The north side is lined to the west by a row of shops, adjoined in the east by the **Captives' Façade** and the propylaea.

Sacred Spring ▶ Lying in front of it is the Sacred Spring, a fountain house dating from the 5th century BC. with seven steps leading down into the chamber with the spring, which was connected to the Temple of Apollo by a tunnel.

Podium temples ▶ The narrow west end of the agorá is bordered by the pantheon, the circular Babbius monument and a row of Roman podium temples dedicated to Hermes, Apollo, Poseidon, Hercules and Venus.

Southern Agorá Across the square is the row of so-called **central shops**. Rising up in the middle is a podium for speakers to address the people. It was here that the **Apostle Paul** had to stand trial before Proconsul **Gallio** in AD 52. A few remains are reminders that later a church stood here. The southern side of the agorá is bordered by the 165 m/180 yd long **South Stoa**, which had 33 shops. A Roman floor mosaic can be seen in a roofed room. Behind the South Stoa lies the **South Basilica** and adjoining it on its east end are the Southeast Building and the **Basilica Iulia**, built by Emperor Claudius about AD 45, a court and meeting hall.

Poppy blossoms in front of the gates of medieval Acrocorinth

The north propylon opens onto the ancient paved road leading to **Lechaion Road**
the harbour of Lechaion. Herodes Atticus had the **Peirene Fountain**
rebuilt as a magnificent marble building in the 2nd century AD. To
the left of the road lies a basilica dating from 1st / 2nd centuries, to
the right is the Precinct of Apollo followed by the 2nd-century
Roman **Baths of Eurycles**, which has a public latrine. Standing in
front of the entrance to the excavation site, west of the carpark, is
the small Roman **odeon** from the 1st century. The rows of seating,
carved from the rock, accommodated 3,000 spectators. To the north
is the theatre (5th century BC – 3rd century AD) with 18,000 seats
and an asclepieion.

✳ Acrocorinth

The fortress of Acrocorinth is among the most spectacular sights in **Unique fortress**
the wider area of Athens: a scenic as well as historic vestige of the **complex**
past. The Byzantine fortress was taken in 1210 by the Franks after a
five-year siege, fell to Venice in 1358 and to Mystras in 1394. It was
in Turkish hands from the 15th century until 1822. A road leads to
the lowest gate on the west side. A moat built by the Venetians is followed by a gate built in the 14th century by the Franks and a wall
erected in the 15th century. The third gate is framed by square towers; to the left a Byzantine tower, to the right a Hellenistic tower
from the 4th century BC. Higher up on the castle grounds are the
ruins of a mosque (16th century), followed by the north gate. Higher

yet, past the stump of a minaret and a cistern, is the medieval Frankish **Villehardouin castle**. To the east is the ancient **Peirene Spring** and, to the northeast, the 574 m/1,883 ft summit of the castle rock. There is a magnificent view from there out across the isthmus to Attica, Mt Parnassus and the mountains of the Peloponnese. Visible to the southwest, perched on a cone of rock, is the Frankish fortress of **Montesquiou / Pendeskoufi**.

Around Corinth

Lechaion

The ancient harbour of Lechaion, 3 km/2 mi to the north of Corinth, is completely silted up, but the bay can still be recognized. The remains of a 5th century Christian **basilica** were discovered on the west side. At 220 m/722 ft it was for a long time the longest in the whole of the Mediterranean region.

★ ★
Corinth Canal

The Isthmus of Corinth is cut through by a canal built between 1882 and 1893 by a French company. It is exactly 6,343 m/20,810 ft long and 25 m/82 ft wide and its walls are up to 80 m/262 ft high. As it is only 8 m/26 ft deep, only small ships can pass through it. In essence, it follows the same route determined by the notorious Roman emperor **Nero** for the construction of a canal which eventually failed. The submersible bridges at the ends of the canal are interesting. In order to avoid the long trip round the Peloponnese, a paved portage road, the **Diolkos**, on which boats and small ships could be loaded onto wagons and transported across the isthmus was constructed as long ago as the 6th century BC. Some remains of the Diolkos, which was still used in the 12th century, can be seen at the west end of the canal.

Isthmia

Some 2 km/1.2 mi west of the small town of Isthmia, south of the southeast end of the Corinth Canal, the ruins of a **Shrine to Poseidon** lie unearthed. The **Isthmian Games** – verifiable from 582 BC – were held here every two years. The prize of honour was a wreath of spruce or celery. Today, the venerable site is surrounded by industry.

Temple of
Poseidon ►

The Temple of Poseidon, a Doric peripteros with the classic proportions of 6 : 13 columns, was built around 460 BC. The site of the starting point of the races in front of the temple has survived. To the northeast of the temple is the theatre and to the southeast the stadium dating from the 4th century BC.

Fortress ►

During the reign of Emperor Justinian (6th century) the ancient buildings were used as a source of building material for the construction of a fortress, the remains of which can be found east of the theatre. The castle was part of the fortifications of the isthmus, which were continually renewed. The defensive wall ran roughly parallel to

The Corinth Canal, in places up to 80 m/260 ft deep, →
separates the Peloponnese from the mainland.

the present canal and was six Roman miles long (just less than 9 km/ 5.6 mi). The name of the village of Examília is a reminder of it today. The earliest traces from the Mycenaean period (13th century BC) were found south and southeast of the Shrine of Poseidon. More substantial wall remains date from the years 480 / 479 BC

Kenchreai Some 2 km/1.2 mi south of the Shrine to Poseidon lies the small village of Kechriás on the site of the ancient Corinthian port of **Kenchreai**, which the apostle Paul mentioned in his epistle to the Romans (16:1). The harbour is today partly under water. North of the harbour are the ruins of a temple from the classic period and, to the south, an early Christian basilica.

Sicyón The ancient city of Sicyón, home of the sculptor **Lysippus** (4th century), is located on an elevation above the coastal plain, 25 km/15.5 mi west of Corinth, near the modern village of the same name. Visible to the left of the access road are the foundations of a temple to Apollo or Artemis and, to the south of it, the remains of a stoa, a bouleuterion and, in addition, a gymnasium. On the slopes of the acropolis lies the theatre. To the right of the road is a museum housed in a Roman bath complex in which floor mosaics and sculptures are displayed.

✶ Neméa The ancient site of Neméa is set in a pretty countryside with vineyards, olive trees and cypresses, 35 km/22 mi southwest of Corinth

The athletes raced through this tunnel into the stadium of Neméa.

near the wine-growing village of Archéa Neméa. It was here that the seer **Amphiaraos** founded the Pan-Hellenic **Nemean Games** in the year 1251 BC on the occasion of the funeral ceremony of the king's young son, Opheltes, who was bitten by a snake and died. The Nemean Games were held every two years and in the 2nd century BC they were moved to Árgos. They were revived in 1996. Participants from all over the world can take part; the programme includes sports events and a supporting cultural programme. In the 4th century BC, a Doric peripteros temple with 6 : 12 slender columns was built on the site of an Archaic temple. A crypt has survived from the Archaic temple and four of the Doric temple's columns still stand upright and are visible from far away. There was a long guesthouse south of the temple, above which a Christian basilica was built in the 5th / 6th centuries as well as a palaistra and a Hellenistic bath, the earliest to have survived in Greece, and a relatively well-preserved stadium (500 m/550 yd to the south, on the road leading to national highway 7). The **museum** presents a show on the history of the excavations, along with coins, pottery and Mycenaean finds from the region (opening hours: Tue – Sun 8.30am – 4pm).

Another 25 km/15.5 mi further to the west is Lake Stymphalus, known for its interesting birds and plant life. It is the scene of the myth of the man-eating »Stymphalian birds« that were killed by Heracles.

★
Lake Stymphalus

★ ★ Crete · Κρήτη

K – P 13 - 15

Area: 8261 sq km/ 3,189 sq mi
Population: 750,000

Altitude: 0 – 2,456 m/8,058 ft
Capital: Heráklion · Iráklion
(pop. 116,000)

White beaches under an azure sky, waves breaking along the coast and the trickling of water in the fertile interior, yawning gorges and karst caves, shimmering heat and the chirping of crickets in olive groves are only a few of the facets of the country's largest island, on which Zeus, the father of the gods, grew up in a cave in the mighty Ídi Mountains.

Crete, the largest of the Greek islands and the fifth largest in the Mediterranean, forms Europe's southernmost outpost. It is an extraordinarily attractive island with its varied landscape, its beautiful beaches and its famous monuments of Minoan culture, and one of Greece's most important tourist attractions. The island varies between 12 and 57 km/7.4 and 35 mi in width and extends over 260 km/161 mi in an east-westerly direction. It is segmented by three karst mountain massifs. Reaching an elevation of 2452 m/8,045 ft in

km/4.3 mi long and in parts even narrower than Samariá Gorge. The hike from Imbros to Komitádes takes about three hours.

Lying off the western south coast of Crete is the flat, wooded island of Gávdos, Europe's most southerly point. It is also mythical Ogygia (Odyssey VII, 244), the **island of Calypso**. The island is under nature protection, is inhabited by 40 people and is a paradise for ornithologists. Tour boats from Paleochóra and Chóra Sfakíon sail to the island in the summer.

Gávdos

A German military cemetery was laid out at Máleme, 16 km/10 mi west of Chaniá, with 4,465 graves, mostly of paratroopers who were killed during the German airborne operation during World War II from 20 May to 1 June 1941.

Máleme

The road branches off to the north to **Kolimbári**, 8 km/5 mi west of Máleme. Rhodópou Peninsula begins here. Its landscape is impressive; magnificent and bleak, it extends to the north, rising up to an elevation of 750 m/2,460 ft. The fortress-like **Goniás monastery** north of Kolimbári, was founded in 1618 and owns some valuable 17th century icons.
The **shrine of the Nymph Diktynna** was unearthed at the northeast end of the peninsula, near Cape Skala. She was the protectress of fishermen and their nets (diktyon = net). Not far from the excavation site, with the remains of a temple (2nd century AD), cisterns and other buildings, is a picturesque cove inviting visitors to take a swim. The excavation site is best reached by boat from Chaniá or Kolimbári.

Rhodópou Peninsula

◄ Diktýnnaion

The little town Kastélli Kissámou is 20 km/12 mi west of Kolimbári. A rewarding excursion can be made from here to the island of **Gramvousa** off the peninsula of the same name in the extreme northwest of Crete. There, towering above the steep cliffs of the western coast, is a 17th-century Venetian castle. The remains of buildings, the harbour facilities, graves and sculptures have survived at the site of the ancient port of **Falásarna**, 9 km/5.6 mi west of Kastélli Kissámou. The town was founded in the 5th/4th century BC and presumably abandoned in the 6th century AD when the coast rose by 8 m/26 ft. There is a fine view of the Gulf of Kissámou from the ruins of the Dorian city, **Polirheneia** (8th century BC). The excavation site, located 6 km/4 mi south of Kastélli Kissámou, can be reached by foot in 30 minutes from Polirinía village.

Kastélli Kissámou

A visit to the small, white 17th-century Chrisoskalítissa monastery, 40 km/25 mi southwest of Kastélli Kissámou, is worthwhile because

Moní Chrisoskalítissa

← *A hike through the spectacular Samaría Gorge is part of a holiday on Crete.*

A stroll through town   Standing near the harbour is a beautiful 17th-century Venetian Renaissance-style Loggia, once a gathering place for Venetian aristocracy. From there, Odós Paleológon leads to the pretty **Arimondi Fountain** from 1629. Now head south to Vernárdou Street, where the Nerandses Mosque (not open to the public) with a minaret can be seen next to Venetian houses with Turkish superstructures of wood. Down Odós Ethnikís Antistáseos are the former monastery church of **San Francesco**, with a beautiful Renaissance portal, and the 16th-century Venetian city gate, **Megáli Pórta**.

> ! **Baedeker TIP**
>
> **»Extreme« Bar**
>
> AC/DC, Rory Gallagher or Metallica – Bar Xtreme at Odós Neárchou 27 by the Venetian Harbour is just the thing for rock fans.

Around Réthymnon

★ **Arkádi monastery**   Set impressively on a plateau 23 km/14 mi southeast of Réthymnon is the fortress-like complex of the Arkádi monastery, the **national shrine of the Cretans** and an outstanding historic as well as scenic

Arkádi Monastery – the national shrine of Crete

attraction. In 1866, some 1,000 Cretans – men, women and children – fled here and, after fighting a hopeless battle against 15,000 Turks, blew themselves up with a powder magazine on 8 November. The monastery, inhabited by a few monks, was probably founded as early as the 10th / 11th centuries. The present buildings date largely from the 17th century. The façade of the monastery church from 1587 displays Italian Renaissance and Baroque elements.

Located in an impressive setting on the south coast, 38 km/24 mi from Réthymnon, is the monastery of Píso Moní, founded around 1700. The monastery played a crucial role in the numerous revolts against the Ottoman Turks and most recently against the German occupation in World War II. The monastery church has an iconostasis with many antique icons and a carved pulpit. The magnificently decorated golden cross on the altar in the south nave is said to contain a miraculous splinter from Christ's cross. Stretching out on the Megálou Potámou estuary below the monastery is a fantastic, extremely popular beach on a clear blue-green sea.

Píso Moní

✷
◄ Beach

Framed by mountains, Kournás Lake, **Crete's only lake**, extends not far from Georgioúpoli Bay, 23 km/14 mi east of Réthymnon. Take a swim or hire a paddleboat, a couple of tavernas are there to provide the refreshments.

Kournás Lake

Heráklion

Heráklion (pop. 134,000), Crete's largest city, situated roughly in the middle of the north coast, is the island's administrative centre and principal port. The city's historical substance was largely lost in the Second World War so that today it looks on the whole less attractive. Still, Crete's tourist hub does have a few pretty spots to offer. The old town, still lying within the mostly well-preserved town walls, is of interest. The best place to get a feel for the atmosphere of the bustling city is on Platía Venizélou with its Morosini Fountain and its many restaurants and cafés.

Capital of the island

In Minoan times, Heráklion was the site of the harbour of Knossós. It went into decline in Roman times but was given new life by the Saracens after 824. The Venetians started calling the town Cándia in 1538, had architect Michele Sanmicheli build a long and massive fortified wall around it and made it the island's capital. After the Ottoman Turks took Crete in 1648, they laid siege to Heráklion until 1669. Heráklion lost its economic importance with the exodus of the Christians until its union with Greece in 1913.

History

The most important attraction in the city is the Archaeological Museum; the country's most significant museum after the National Archaeological Museum of Athens. It gives a comprehensive picture of

✷ ✷
Archaeological Museum

Neopalatial (New Palace) Period (1700–1400 BC) are the three so-called **snake goddesses** from the treasure-chamber of the main shrine of Knossós. The **steer rhyton**, one of the most import finds from the Minoan culture, is a masterly work in steatite; the eyes are of quartz and jasper; the golden horns are reconstructions. Clay objects with pictures of cultic scenes came from the necropolis in the area around Knossós and Festós. The Ring from Isópata with three dancing girls and a figure, probably a goddess, floating down from the sky, is a masterpiece. Another of the museum's highlights is the Harvesters or **Reapers Vase** of steatite with a very life-like depiction of men singing on the way home after finishing harvesting grain. As well as the Chieftain's or **Prince's Cup** also worked from steatite and decorated in beautiful reliefs that show a dignitary with a sword over his shoulder followed by three men wearing animal skins, all standing in front of a young man with a sceptre. Another masterpiece came from the palace of Káto Zákros from the Neopalatial Period (1700–1400 BC), the beautiful **quartz rhyton** with a handle of quartz beads and decorated with a gilt pearl wreath. Although the magnificent **frescoes** from central and eastern Crete, also

A beautiful quartz rhyton

dating from the Neopalatial Period, are largely reconstructions, they give a very good picture of the refined Minoa culture. The famous **sarcophagus of Agía Triáda** (c. 1400 BC) is the only Minoan stone coffin. It probably contained the body of a king. The remarkably well preserved frescoes show scenes of cult ceremonies with women recognizable by their white colour and men by their brown. A priestess is seen making an offering on an altar in front of a ceremonial building decorated with double horns. The bird on the double-headed axe next to it symbolize the presence of the deity. Another priestess is performing a bloody sacrifice of a bull, accompanied by a flute player. A further scene is of a funerary building with a dead person in front of it, recognizable by his lack of arms. Three men are bringing him two animals and what appears to be a funeral barge. Moving towards the group from the right-hand end are two women and others bearing offerings.

Koules castle, built from 1523 to 1540, can be found at the Venetian harbour north of the old town. The **Venetian Loggia**, built from 1626 to 1628, is in Odós 25 Avgoustou that leads south into the town centre. The former armoury (17th century) next to it is today the town hall. **Morosini Fountain** (1628), with lions dating from the 14th century, can be seen further south on Venizelos Square. Also there is the former church of St Mark (1239), which is decorated with important Cretan frescoes; a mosque from 1669 until 1915, it is used today as a venue for events. Standing northeast of the square is **Titos Church**, named after Titus, a companion of the apostle Paul and first bishop of Crete. A reliquary containing his skull is preserved in a small chapel, accessible from the portico. The building dating from the 11th / 12th centuries was made a mosque in 1862 and later an Orthodox cathedral. At the southern end of Odós 1866 is **Bembo Fountain** from 1588, with ancient spolia built into it. The Turkish fountain house next to it now serves as a kiosk. Standing on Catharine Square is the 19th century **Minás Cathedral**, the city's central church.

The Byzantine Museum is housed in the former 18th-century church of Agía Ekateríni. The most important exhibits are six icons by **Michael Damaskinos** on the south wall of the nave, which were painted

The liveliest part of town is around Morosini Fountain.

Festós

After Knossós, Festós is the most important Minoan palace on the island. The ruins of the city, according to legend founded by **King Minos**, lie on the foothills of the Ídi mountain range – with a magnificent view across the Messará plain. The new palace was built on terraces after 1700 BC on the site of a building constructed around 1900 BC and destroyed by an earthquake some 200 years later, before being gutted around 1450 BC by a catastrophic fire. The surviving sections of the palace, which were grouped around a central court, are the ruins of the west and north wing, while the south and east wings collapsed during an earthquake. The remains of the old palace can be seen on the western and northern sides of the still existing sections.

Opposite the entrance in the north courtyard is a stairway leading down. Recognizable to the right are the seating steps of a theatre and to the left is a monumental propylaea stairway leading to the palace. Among the things to be seen are a peristyle (a courtyard bordered with columns), royal chambers, a corridor, rooms with alabaster benches, a columned hall and a magazine (opening hours: April – Oct daily 8am – 7.30pm).

Vóri

Vóri , located 5 km/3 mi north of Festós, has Crete's finest and most interesting **folk art museum**. The didactically well-organized collection, containing objects up to 500 years old, illustrates the subjects of fishing, farming, forestry and handicraft (opening hours: April – Oct daily 10am – 6pm).

Agía Triáda

About 2 km /1.2 miwest of Festós – and at one time linked to the palace by a paved road – lie the remains of the Minoan Villa Agía Triáda, named after a Byzantine chapel standing on a neighbouring hill. Like Festós, it primarily dates back to the 16th century BC, but was rebuilt after a fire around 1450 BC. and remained occupied into Doric times. There is a magnificent view of the sea and the Ídi Mountains from the west side of the palace. Visible from to the south of palace is the Venetian chapel of Ágios Geórgios from the 14th century. Beyond the gate at the northeast corner of the ruins is a necropolis with two tholos tombs and a shaft tomb in which the famous **sarcophagus** was found (opening hours: April – Oct daily 10am – 4.30pm).

Ágios Ioánnis

In Ágios Ioánnis' cemetery, located just south of Festós, is the church of **Ágios Pávlos**. Its architecture is remarkable. The church consists of three building phases with the eastern, domed cubic section being the oldest; it was probably once a baptistery dating back to the 4th / 5th century The middle section with the high tambour dome was added in 1303 and the open, Venetian-style narthex was added in the 15th / 16th centuries. The fresco remains date back to 1303 / 1304. There is a small charnel-house on the inside of the east wall of the church's courtyard.

The beach at Mátala is framed by rocks honeycombed with caves.

On the sea some 8 km/5 mi southwest of Festós is Mátala, which in Minoan times was probably the harbour serving Festós, while in Roman times it served Górtys. Caves have been dug in the rock faces of the shallow harbour bay that served as tombs in early Christian times. This is where the Saracens landed in 826. According to legend, Zeus also landed here in the shape of a bull with the abducted Phoenician princess **Europa**. Today, the caves are fenced off from the beach (open to the public daily 8am until 8pm). Mátala is a very popular bathing resort. And a large number of day-trippers add to the throng during the day. The tourist site has numerous tavernas and souvenir shops.

✱ ✱ Knossós

Lying near **Makritíchos**, some 5 km/ 3 mi southeast of Heráklion, is the excavation site of Knossós, the oldest capital on the island, with the partially reconstructed Minoan palace. The palace, covering an area of 2 ha /5 acres, once had three to four floors, and was destroyed several times, presumably by earthquake. The palace existed between about 2000 – 1400 BC and was rebuilt in three phases: the first palace around 2000 – 1800, the second palace about 1800 – 1700, and the third palace around 1700 – 1400 BC. The remains visible today belong largely to the third palace.

Its complicated floor plan gave rise to the assumption that the palace might be identical to the legendary labyrinth of King Minos, particularly since the double axe symbol (»labrys«), a symbol of Minoan Crete, is often found here.

KNOSSÓS

★★ Knossós, the most important Minoan palace, is a vivid testimony to Europe's first civilization. With an area of 2 ha / 5 acres and consisting of more than 1,000 rooms, it was the largest palace of this unique culture. In its prime, more than 10,000 people are thought to have lived in the palace and its surrounding area.

Opening hours:
Daily 8.30am – 7.30pm

① Throne room
Taking a central position in the Throne Room is an alabaster throne, flanked by benches and set off by frescoes depicting gryphons. Bordering the chamber are cult rooms in which a mother goddess was venerated.

② Tripartite Shrine
It is likely that earth and fertility gods were worshipped in this, the main sanctuary, illuminated only by torch-light. The double-axe symbols, or labrys, imbue the chamber with a special sanctity.

Along with bulls' horns, the labrys was a significant cult object of the Minoan religion. In addition, there were underground cysts holding treasure.

③ Northwest Wing
In the northwest wing are cult rooms decorated with beautiful and richly detailed frescoes.

④ Hall of the Double Axes
The Hall of the Double Axes – named after the double-axe symbols decorating it – probably served as the palace's official reception hall.

Knossós *Plan*

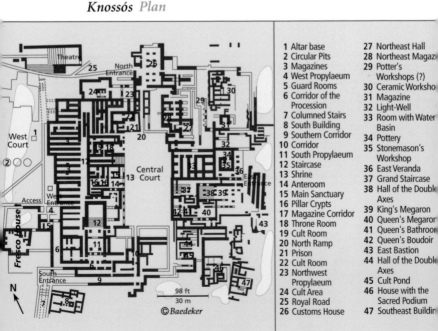

1 Altar base
2 Circular Pits
3 Magazines
4 West Propylaeum
5 Guard Rooms
6 Corridor of the Procession
7 Columned Stairs
8 South Building
9 Southern Corridor
10 Corridor
11 South Propylaeum
12 Staircase
13 Shrine
14 Anteroom
15 Main Sanctuary
16 Pillar Crypts
17 Magazine Corridor
18 Throne Room
19 Cult Room
20 North Ramp
21 Prison
22 Cult Room
23 Northwest Propylaeum
24 Cult Area
25 Royal Road
26 Customs House
27 Northeast Hall
28 Northeast Magazine
29 Potter's Workshops (?)
30 Ceramic Workshop
31 Magazine
32 Light-Well
33 Room with Water Basin
34 Pottery
35 Stonemason's Workshop
36 East Veranda
37 Grand Staircase
38 Hall of the Double Axes
39 King's Megaron
40 Queen's Megaron
41 Queen's Bathroom
42 Queen's Boudoir
43 East Bastion
44 Hall of the Double Axes
45 Cult Pond
46 House with the Sacred Podium
47 Southeast Building

© Baedeker

Tour The palace is entered from the west court. The Procession Corridor (named after the frescoes) leads to the large gateway of the south propylaea, then along a large corridor past a large number of storage rooms with clay vessels to the spacious central courtyard, where possibly bull-leaping was performed. The grand staircase and the throne room with an alabaster throne are among the things on the west side of the courtyard. On the east side are the utility and residential rooms with baths and latrines. Next to the hall named after the double-axe symbols carved on its pillars are the King's chambers and Queen's chambers. The numerous frescoes are copies; the originals are in the Archaeological Museum in Heráklion.

✳ Ágios Nikólaos

The little town of Ágios Nikólaos, charmingly set on the beautiful Mirambéllo Gulf, has an especially pleasant atmosphere. It has long been appreciated as a holiday resort because of the fine beaches in the vicinity and the many places to visit around it. Life is concentrated mainly on the harbour and at picturesque **Voulisméni Lake**.

Archaeological Museum Odós Konstantinou Paleologou leads from Voulisméni Lake to the significant archaeological museum focusing on eastern Cretan artefacts. It is worth a visit just to see the fabulous vases, the extraordinary vessels and the strange and mysterious idols. The gold jewellery in the form of bands and flowers are thoroughly enchanting. The most valuable piece is a diadem with abstract goats recognizable on it. The **Goddess of Mýrtos** from the early Minoan era is the museum's most significant exhibition piece. The greatly stylized figure consists of a bell-shaped body, an elongated neck and a very delicate head (opening hours: Tue – Sun 8.30am – 3pm).

Further Attractions There is a **folk art museum** in the port authority building. Standing on the grounds of the Minos Palace Hotel to the northeast is the 10th century **Ágios Nikólaos** church with rare frescoes from the time of the Iconoclastic Controversy.

Around Ágios Nikólaos

Kritsá 11 km/7 misouthwest of Ágios Nikólaos is the pretty village of Kritsá, spread out on a mountain slope in the midst of an olive grove. It is noted for its weaving and handiwork, not all of which, admittedly, is produced in Greece. The film, »The Greek Passion«, based on the novel by Nikos Kazantzakis, was shot here. About a mile away from Kritsá is the beautiful church, Panagía Kerá (12th

Panagía Kerá ▶ to 14th centuries), decorated with magnificent 14th and 15th century frescoes (opening hours: Tue – Sun 8.30am – 3pm).

Enchanting evening mood in the harbour of Ágios Nikólaos

The Dorian city of Lató, 3 km/2 mi north of the church, was probably established between the 7th and 4th centuries BC. There is a beautiful view of the surrounding mountainside and Mirabello Gulf from the northern acropolis .(opening hours: summer Tue – Sun 8.30am – 3pm).

★
◄ Lató
⏲

A quite delightful drive (40 km/25 mi) can be taken west from Ágios Nikólaos to the fertile, almost 900 m/3,000 ft Lassíthi plateau in the Díkti mountain range. The thousands of windmills (»Valley of the Windmills«) that once served to irrigate the intensely cultivated plateau have largely been replaced by motor pumps. There is an interesting folk art museum in **Ágios Geórgios** on the southern end of Lassíthi plateau.On the southwest edge of the plain, near Psychró, lies the impressive and much visited Diktéon Ántron cave, according to legend, the birthplace of Zeus (opening hours: daily 8am – 6.30pm).

★
Lassíthi Plain

★
◄ Diktéon Ántron
⏲

Limín Chersonísou, located on the coast north of Lassíthi plateau, is one of Crete's major tourist centres. The **Lychnostatis Open-Air Museum** to the east has a typical Cretan village with a chapel, windmill and weaving-mill that can be toured. Some 8 km/5 mi further west lies the seaside resort of **Mália**. The wide bay of the same name is, thanks to its miles of sandy beaches, one of the larger holiday regions on Crete, with a large number of hotels, restaurants and cafés.

Limín Chersonísou

There is a sweeping view of the excavation site from atop 113 m/371 ft Mt Kýnthos.

Harbours The **Sacred Harbour** was on the west side of Délos, where delegates to the festivals once came on land. Further to the south was the commercial harbour. In the 2nd century BC the coastline from the Sacred Harbour down to the Bay of Foumi was equipped with quays and warehouses, the remains of which have survived under water.

What to See on Délos

Sacred Precinct Lying between the two harbours is the Agora of the Competaliasts decorated with statues and small shrines. Competaliasts were Roman slaves and freedmen who gathered here for the cult of »lares competales«, »the patron deities of crossroads«.

A 13 m/43 ft wide processional way lead from here to the Sacred Precinct. Directly left of the 87 m/285 ft long Stoa of Philip, a columned hall open to the east and west, that, according to the dedication on the architrave, was donated by **Philip V of Macedonia** around 210 BC. East of the way stands a smaller stoa with eight business premises lined up along its rear. Spreading out beyond that to the east is the almost square South Agorá (1st century BC), once the state market. The area adjoining to the north up to Hall of Bulls was occupied by the fortifications of the Knights Hospitallers in the Middle Ages. From the south propylaea (2nd century BC) with Doric columns and a three-tiered foundation, the Processional Way runs further on to the **House of the Naxians** (7th century BC) with a base for a 5 m/16 ft statue of Apollo standing on its north side. According to the 6th-century BC inscription, the statue and its base were carved out of a single block of stone. The dedication on the west side, »The Naxians to Apollo«, was added later. Visible opposite the House of the Naxians is their L-shaped stoa (c. 550 BC) with Ionic columns. The island's »holy of holies« further north was the **Keratón** (4th century BC) dedicated to Apollo, where the famous **horned altar** once stood with ram's horns attached round about. In front of the entrance to the Keratón are the bases of a number of equestrian statues that have survived. The most northern and smallest of them was for a statue of Sulla with its inscription placed on the rear ramp. The Keratón is thought to be older than the smaller Artemision, an Ionic prostyle with a granite foundation (4th – 2nd century BC) located to the north in the courtyard. Lying at the northwest corner of the Artemision is the torso and pelvis of a statue of Apollo from the House of the Naxians. To the northwest of the Artemision is the Thesmophorion, sacred to the cult of Demeter. To the east of the Artemision stand the **three temples of Apollo**, the middle point of the precinct. The southern and largest temple, begun in 478 BC and completed in the 3rd century BC, corresponds to the layout of the Temple of Hephaistos in Athens. Following to the north are the poros limestone

The theatre located in the »residential city« provided seating for 5,000 spectators.

Ideal layout of an ancient theatre

THE THEATRES OF ANTIQUITY

Greece's first theatres built of stone were constructed during the transition from the Classical period to Hellenism; e.g., the Dionysus Theatre in Athens built about 330 BC. Up until that time, the theatre buildings had been made of wood.

The **orchestra** formed the centre of the theatre. It was a circular »dancing place« where originally the ritual dances in honour of Dionysus had been performed. Placing an orchestra at the foot of a slope or in a natural hollow made it possible to replace the audience stands with a semi-circular, open auditorium with ascending rows of seating called the **theatron** (watching place).

Seating for over 10,000 spectators

The largest Greek theatres of Antiquity could hold more than 10,000 spectators; e.g., 12,000 people in the Theatre of Epidauros and no less than 18,000 in the one in Dodóna. Opposite the theatron was the multi-storied **skene**, originally a wooden stage building that was enhanced in the post-Classic period into a stone palace with a columned façade.

The **proskenion**, a new stage or acting area above the orchestra, developed in front of the skene. The entrances for the members of the chorus were between the stage and the audience, which spread slightly beyond the bounds of a semi-circle.

The Theatre of the Romans

The Romans also used open wooden buildings at first for their theatrical performances. Later they erected large

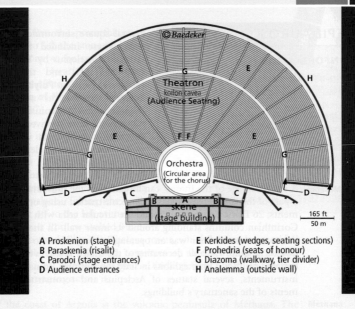

© Baedeker

Theatron
koilon cavea
(Audience Seating)

Orchestra
(Circular area
for the chorus)

skene
(stage building)

165 ft
50 m

A Proskenion (stage)
B Paraskenia (risalit)
C Parodoi (stage entrances)
D Audience entrances
E Kerkides (wedges, seating sections)
F Prohedria (seats of honour)
G Diazoma (walkway, tier divider)
H Analemma (outside wall)

stone buildings modelled on the Greek pattern, which were no longer embedded in natural surroundings but rather built free-standing. The entrances and exits for the audience were in the outside walls, accessible by stairs.

The stageless **amphitheatre**, an elliptical theatre building around a central arena for staging major events like spectator sports or gladiator contests, was a creation of the Romans. The basic form of the Greco-Roman theatre was revived in the Renaissance, but now the theatre buildings were roofed over without exception and the auditorium was increasingly more lavishly structured. It was not until the Baroque that a new form of theatre developed with the box-seat theatres.

Smaller roofed-over theatre buildings are known as **odeons**, which were primarily used for musical performances; e.g., the Odeon of Pericles in Athens, next to the Theatre of Dionysus. An especially large number of these ancient concert and lecture halls were erected during the Hellenistic and Roman periods. The term »odeon« also lives on today outside of Greece as a name for music theatres and cinemas.

Epidauros Festival

Many of the ancient theatres are still being used today. Ancient plays, including those by Aristophanes, Euripides and Sophocles, are performed as part of a festival from May through August in the Theatre of Epidauros. For those interested, the current programme is online at www.greek-festival.gr, which also gives addresses of booking offices in Athens from which advance tickets can also be obtained in Athens. At present the National Theatre, invited foreign theatres and musical events like clasical concerts and opera share the stage.

► VISITING EUBÖA

INFORMATION

Tourist Police
Chalcís
Tel. 22 21 07 77 77

GETTING THERE

There is a road link between the mainland and Chalcís; boat connections with Vólos, Arkítsa, Oropos, Agía Marína and Rafína on the mainland and the islands of Alónissos, Skíathos and Skópelos.

WHERE TO EAT

► Moderate

Gouveris
Chalcís
Tel. 22 21 02 57 69
There are tasty fish dishes in the taverna by the sea.

Lalari
Kými
Tel. 22 22 02 26 24
This taverna is distinguished by its fine seafood and friendly staff.

WHERE TO STAY

► Luxury

Eretria Village Resort
Eretria
Tel. 22 29 04 10 00
www.holidaysinevia.gr; 205 rooms
The hotel complex's swimming pool offers plenty of bathing enjoyment.

► Mid-range

Galaxy
Omirou / Odysseos
Kárystos
Tel. 22 24 02 26 00
E-mail: hgalaxy@otenet.gr; 72 rooms
Huge, modern hotel on the harbour with functionally furnished rooms.

► Budget

Beis
Northern part of the harbour
Kými
Tel. 22 22 02 28 70
Fax 22 22 02 26 04; 38 rooms
The hotel provides nicely decorated rooms with balconies and its own taverna.

fertile alluvial plains. The topography of the island is split; while the wooded north shows characteristics of low-mountain regions, the barren and arid south is reminiscent of the islands of the Aegean. Mineral deposits like magnesite and lignite form the basis for metal processing industry, particularly around Chalcís. At the end of August 2007, Euboea was ravaged by devastating **forest fires** that were abetted by the great heat and are believed to have been started by acts of arson on the part of land speculators.

History The oldest inhabitants in northwest Euboea were immigrant Ellopians from Thessaly, Abantes from Thrace in central Euboea and Dryopians in the southeast. Attic Ionians merged with the Abantes, who brought prosperity and high standing to the island from the 8th to the 6th century BC. Chalcís was subjugated by Athens in 506 BC and the possession of the fertile island soon became vital to her. The island regained independence again towards the end of the Peloponnesian War (411 BC), but later usually sided with the Athenians. Following the conquest of Constantinople in 1204, Euboea fell to the Venetians. In 1470, it came into Turkish possession. In 1830, it was finally awarded to Greece.

What to see in Euboea

Chalcís / Chalkída (pop. 80,000) is the port and chief town of Euboea, charmingly set on hills around the strait of Evrípos. Its location at the crossing-point to the mainland led to the early development of a harbour. By 411 BC, Chalcís was connected to the mainland by a wooden bridge at Evrípos' narrowest point. Today's bridge was constructed in 1962. There is a fine view of the town and the **Bay of Aulis** from **Fort Karábaba** located to the south on the mainland side, which was in service until 1856. It was from that point that the Mycenaeans set sail to Troy in mythical times. East of the bridge, the Neo-classical city hall can be seen between hotels, restaurants and cafés. Behind it is **Kástro**, the Venetian and Turkish old part of town, whose walls have partially survived.

★
Chalcís / Chalkída

Enchanting, isolated, green and blue glistening coves on Euboea's east coast

the 12th-century church, Agía Iríni, with the preceding building's free-standing columns that date back to the 4th century. There is a long beach outside of Kámpos. **Armenistís**, 15 km/9.3 mi west of Évdilos, has two beautiful beaches that are quite popular and 3 km/2 mi further on, in **Nas**, there is a pretty little pebble beach with the remains of a 5th-century BC Artemis temple lying behind it.

Foúrni Islands

The Foúrni islands are rocky islands with jagged coastlines full of coves lying within a triangle formed by Sámos, Ikaría and Pátmos. Belonging to the island group, outside of the 30 sq km/12 sq mi main island, **Foúrni** (1,000 Pop), with the town of the same name on the west coast, are the smaller islands, **Thímena** and Ágios Minás, and the islets of Ándro, Makronísi and Diapori. Foúrni and Thimena are inhabited; The only place with overnight accommodation is Foúrni, which has beautiful beaches and a couple of tavernas.

★★ Ioánnina · Ιοάννινα

D 5

Prefecture: Epiros	**Altitude:** 520 m/1,706 ft
Population: 45,000	

Ioánnina, the busy, modern capital of the province of Epiros, lies very beautifully situated on the west shore of Pamvótis Lake, surrounded by lush, verdant scenery. The old part of town on the shore, with many buildings dating from the time of the Turkish occupation, still exudes an oriental atmosphere.

History   Ioánnina was founded at the start of the 6th century by **Emperor Justinian**. It was fortified in 1085 by the Normans, and in the early13th century became the capital of the despotate of Epiros and later the seat of Serbian princes. It was Turkish from 1430 until 1913. The city's most prosperous period was 1788 to 1822, when it was the **residence of Ali Pasha**. This almost legendary figure, who has been literally trivialized into a Greek freedom fighter, was an educated and urbane as well as an unscrupulous and power-conscious potentate. It is still remembered today that in 1801 Ali Pasha had Frosini, his son's favourite woman, drowned in the lake along with 16 other women because she refused to join his harem. The Ottoman Turks besieged Ioánnina in 1820 and murdered Ali Pasha in 1822 on the island in the lake.

! *Baedeker* TIP

Typical souvenirs
Beautiful wrought-silver and embroidery work are products of Ioánnina; shops that deal in these goods can be found mainly in Odós Averof.

► VISITING IOÁNNINA

INFORMATION

Tourist Information
Dodonis 39
Tel. 26 51 04 18 68, Fax 26 51 04 91 39
www.about-ionannina.gr

WHERE TO EAT

► Inexpensive
Mavili
Located on the lake shore; a large
selection of Greek dishes.

To Manteio
Platía Neomartyros 15
Tel. 26 51 02 54 52
This simple taverna serves delicious
grilled dishes.

WHERE TO STAY

► Mid-range
Xenia
Dodonis 33
Tel. 26 51 04 73 01
Fax 26 51 04 71 89
60 rooms
Central and quiet, the hotel is located
in a nice park.

Galaxy
Platía Pirou
Tel. 26 51 02 54 32
Fax 26 51 02 50 32, 38 rooms
Quietly located hotel with comfort-
ably furnished rooms with balconies.

What to See in Ioánnina

The Citadel (Froúrio) has picturesque corners and offers fine views
of the lake and the Píndus Mountains. The **Aslan Pasha Mosque**,
built in 1619, is set up as a **municipal museum**. Standing next to it is
the Turkish library and an old synagogue. Inside the citadel in the
southeast corner is the Fetije Mosque with the **grave of Ali Pasha**
and the interesting **Byzantine Museum**.

★
Citadel

Platía Dimokratías is the centre of the city with a conspicuous clock
tower. On the neighbouring Platia 25 Martiou is the **archaeological
museum** providing information about Epiros' excavation sites. The
finds from Dodóna and the Necromanteíon Ephýras, including lead
tablets with questions for the oracle, are particularly interesting.
Modern Greek art can be seen in the **art gallery of the EHM** and the
Municipal Art Gallery.

More museums

A pretty, shady promenade leads around the Citadel along Pamvótis
Lake. The lake, with a depth of up to 12 m/39 ft, has no real outlet
but only drains through pores in the karst rock. The town sewage
channelled into the lake is a major problem, as is overfertilizing by
farmers. The boat tour across the lake to **Monastery Island**, surrounded by reeds, is rewarding. There is a little place there with a
fisherman's taverna worth recommending and five monasteries with
interesting frescoes. A memorial room has been set up in Pantelei-

Pamvótis Lake

mon monastery (16th century), where Ali Pasha was shot in 1822. It is also worth visiting Ágios Nikólaos Dílios monastery (11th century), whose catholicon is decorated with frescoes.

Around Ioánnina

Pérama Cave ✳

The magnificent dripstone cave of Pérama, one of Greece's largest caves, can be toured some 4km /2.5 mi north of the lake. A large number of stalagmites and stalactites, with graphic names like the »Leaning Tower of Pisa«, »Sphinx« and »Lion's Paw«, have formed in the 1,100 m/3,609 ft cave. There is also a stalactite in the unusual form of a cross (opening hours: daily 8am – 8pm).

Zagória ✳✳

A recommendable excursion is one to the north through magnificent mountain scenery. It is here that the **Zagorochória** are to be found, the »villages behind the mountains«, which were semi-autonomous during the period of Turkish rule. The characteristic houses with their slate roofs are reminiscent of the villages of Ticino, Switzerland, with the lush vegetation and streams spanned by arch bridges aiding the impression. **Monodéndri**, the best-known village in the Zagória region, has many old mansions and a pretty village square with huge plane trees. **Víkos Aóos National Park** stretches from Monodéndri to Kónitsa, between **Víkos Gorge** and **Aóos Gorge**. The wild, craggy landscape is heavily wooded with broad-leaf and coniferous trees, offering an environment for a wide variety of interesting flora and fauna. The spectacular 10 km/6 mi long Víkos Gorge (Farángi Víkou) is lined by rocks up to 600 m/1,968 ft in height. The magnificent and quite popular hike from Monodéndri through the gorge to the village of Víkos takes about seven hours. Both villages, **Megálo Papíngo** and **Mikró Papíngo**, are spread out particularly impressively under the rock bastion of the Týmfi massif in west Zagória.

> ! **Baedeker TIP**
>
> **If you suffer from vertigo …**
>
> … forget the short hike from the village square in Monodéndri to the abandoned monastery of Agía Paraskeví on the precipice overlooking Víkos Gorge. The trail is an extremely narrow path along the steep rock with breathtaking views down into the depths of Víkos Gorge.

Pavlos Vrellis Wax Museum

The artist, Pavlos Vrellis, worked for many years on his very life-like wax figures before his wax museum could be opened in Bizani (12 km/7.5 mi south of Ioánnina). The subject is Greece's modern history.

Métsovo ✳

Métsovo is one of Greece's most picturesque places and is now a tourist attraction with a plethora of souvenir shops, businesses and tav-

With its rugged walls of rock reaching a height of 600 m/2,000 ft, the → close to 10 km/6 mi long Víkos Gorge is one of the deepest in the world.

The Theatre of the Oracle of Zeus at Dodóna could seat 18,000 spectators.

ernas. It is located 58 km/36 mi east of Ioánnina on the 1,705 m/ 5,594 ft Katára Pass – the highest in all of Greece – in the heavily wooded mountain countryside of the Píndus. It is a wonderful place to hike in summer and ski in winter. Stone-covered houses with their balconies crowd along steep lanes with the old and new buildings hardly distinguishable from one another. A **museum of Epirotian folk art** is housed in a fabulously furnished 19th century mansion. On the main square shaded by mighty plane trees is a gallery that exhibits works by artists from the 19th and 20th centuries.

★
Dodóna

The Zeus Oracle of Dodóna lies in an impressive setting in a broad valley at the foot of the Tómaros Mountains, 23 km/14.3 mi south of Ioánnina. **Zeus Naios** was venerated here in a sacred oak. The priests would interpret the will of the god from the rustling of the tree. Later it was the sound of a bronze cauldron being struck by wind power and the cooing of pigeons in the oak tree. Dodóna was famous beyond the borders of Greece even before the 8th century BC The shrine, which was expanded by **Pyrrhos of Epiros** (297 – 273 BC) and **Philip V of Macedonia** (238 – 179 BC) – the present building dates from this period – was destroyed in AD 381 and in the 5th and 6th centuries this was the seat of a bishop. The traditional site of the oracle is marked by an oak tree planted by the excavators and by foundation walls of the **precinct of Zeus**. The walls surrounding the sanctuary, the temple of Zeus (4th century BC) next to the oak tree and the additions and alterations of the 3rd century BC can all be recognized. Three smaller temples were built a bit further west in the 3rd century BC that were dedicated to Themis, Dione and Heracles and Aphrodite. A colonnaded hall (bouleuterion) was erected west of the Zeus precinct. Dominating the area in front of the oracle precinct is the Dodóna, the **theatre** dating from the 3rd century BC. With a diameter of 122 m/400 ft, 21 tiers and 18,000 seats, it was one of the largest in Greece. Its orchestra was remodelled into an arena for animal fights in the time of Augustus. The **city wall** with its towers ran behind the theatre and visible in front of it are the rows of seats hewn from stone belonging to a **stadium**. East of the Zeus precinct lie the remains of a 6th-century Christian basilica. The finds from Dodóna are displayed in the archaeological museums of Athens and Ioánnina (opening hours: 2 June – Oct. 8am – 7pm; Winter 8am – 3pm).

★ Íos · Ἴος

N 11

Island Group: Cyclades
Altitude: 0 – 713 m/2,339 ft
Principal town: Íos Chóra

Area: 108 sq km/42 sq mi
Population: 1,600

Whoever seeks the high life, excitement and wants to live it up on the beach certainly won't be bored on this mountainous island with its wonderful, sandy beaches.

Crowded beach in the Bay of Mylopótas near the island's capital

Did the Phaeacians put Odysseus ashore here on Dexiá Bay?

ON THE TRAIL OF ODYSSEUS

Was the kingdom of Odysseus (Ulysses) at one time on Itháki? Did the hero set off from there to fight for twelve years in the Trojan War and afterwards have to go through a perilous journey lasting ten years before he could take his wife, Penelope, in his arms again?

The actual location of the places described in the two great epics, *The Iliad* and *The Odyssey* by Homer, is an ancient question. For John V. Luce, professor at the University of Dublin, the answer is clear. He states that Homer wrote *The Odyssey* and the Ithaca of mythology on the same island today Itháki in his books, *Homer and the Heroic Age* and *Celebrating Homer's Landscapes: Troy and Ithaca Revisited* – the latter with compelling photos and maps.

Facts and Myths

Although Itháki is smaller and more rugged than either Zákynthos or Kefalloniá, it is strategically much more important. The sea trade along the coast and the sea routes between Itháki, Kefalloniá and Lefkáda can be better controlled from it. Homer describes Odysseus' home island in »The Odyssey« as »low«, «narrow«, with islands »round about«, »clearly visible« and unsuitable for »steeds to romp« – descriptions that fit Itháki much better than any other of the Ionian Islands.

Odysseus' last stopover before he returned to Ithaca was the island of **Sheria**. Even in ancient times it was thought that this must be Corfu, named at the time Kerkyra. There he told the king of the Phaeacians, Alkinoos, and his daughter, Nausicaä, of his ten-year odyssey that included the adventures he experienced with the one-eyed Cyclops, Polyphemus, with the deadly Sirens and with Calypso, who held him captive on her island for seven years. With the help of the ruler of Sheria, Odysseus made it back to his home island, where, disguised as a beggar and with the support of his son, Telemachus, he

killed the suitors who had been besetting his wife, Penelope.

The Phaeacian ship that brought Odysseus to Ithaca deposited him while he was fast asleep in **Phorcys Bay** below the Cave of the Nymphs. When he woke up, he had lost his bearings and Athena, his protective goddess, appeared to him in the form of a shepherd boy and told him he was on Ithaca. John Luce identifies Phorcys Bay with today's Bay of Dexiá and the **Cave of the Nymphs** with a dripstone cave above the bay. It has two entrances, as described in »The Odyssey«, one for people and one reserved for the gods – the latter is an opening in the ceiling of the cave.

After paying a visit to the cave, where he prayed and hid his treasures, Odysseus set off with Athena in search of Eumaeus, the swineherd. He left »the haven, and took the rough track up through the wooded country« – for Luce, a footpath leading along the eastern slope of Mt Merovígli that still exists. »**Raven's Rock** above Arethousa Fountain«, where Eumaeus' hut was located, is at the north-eastern edge of the Marathiá plateau. There are still a lot of ravens at the rock, which slopes steeply down 60 m/200 ft over a length of 550 m/550 yd, and even today bears the name »stefáni tou korákou«, »Rock of the Ravens«. The **Arethousa Spring** has its source here. And the swineherd's hut and yards – »on a site which could be seen from far« – could have stood on the terrain 240 m/800 ft above the rocky shore. A nearby cave is displayed on Itháki as the place where Eumaeus lived. It was there that Odysseus met his son, Telemachus, who sent the swineherd to his parents' palace to inform Penelope.

The **palace** was probably near Stavrós on the opposite end of the island, some 24 km/15 mi away – Eumaeus needed a full day to march there and back. Luce found two other indications that the palace and the capital of Odysseus' kingdom was at Stavrós. According to »The Odyssey«, »our«

Small but effective – modern technology in the Metaxas Vinery on Kefalloniá

THE LEGACY OF CEPHALUS

Mavrodaphne and Muscat are well-known varieties of grapes. But how about Robóla, Goustolidi, Kakotrygis and Zakynthino? Wine lovers have the chance to discover new and interesting wine aromas on the Ionian Islands.

Winegrowing has a long tradition on the Ionian Islands. No less than **Cephalos**, the son of the god Hermes, is said to have brought the grapevine to Kefalloniá – which is named after him. A document from the year 1262 testifies to the importance of winegrowing for this island and the document that sealed the takeover of Corfu by Venice in 1386 indicates that wine was the island's most valuable product.

Currants and wine

Throughout the centuries, however, the production of wine lagged far behind that of **currants**. Under the Venetians, from about 1540, it developed into a lucrative branch of business and as late as 1887 Greece was still able to pay for half of its imports with the export of currants. By the late 19th century, Kefalloniá had risen to become the most impor-

tant wine island of the Ionian archipelago. The best-known were the sweet Muscat and the Mavrodaphne, which, because of its colour and flavour, was often used in northern Europe as a blending wine. Very early on, **Robóla** was considered to be the noblest grape on the island.

»Connoisseurs find it most closely matches white Bordeaux,« wrote the geography professor, Joseph Partsch, in 1890. But the two world wars and the devastating earthquake of 1953 hit the wine industry hard and burgeoning tourism drew interest away from the production of high-quality wines.

Modern times

It was not until a transformation in the wine world began in the 1980s that a new impetus was provided. Wine has been elevated to a lifestyle product that obtains high prices and

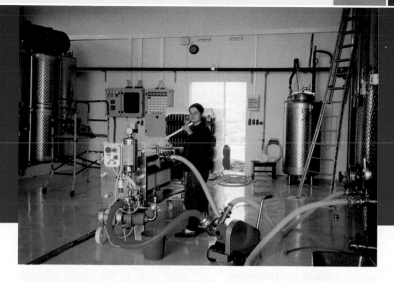

finds willing buyers all over the world. Young members of winegrowing families reconsidered their futures and newcomers switching from other professions brought fresh ideas and above all financial strength for the necessary investments. Some producers planted »international« varieties like Chardonnay, but basically the focus returned to the interesting, **old native grapes** that were, with the new methods, a treasure trove just waiting to be harvested. Moreover, the Ionian Islands were hardly pestered by the vine pest, phylloxera; which is why there are still today many old vines growing on their own rootstock (even today vine cuttings are rarely grafted). Instead of competing on the international market with a tiny production of the same wines as everybody else, they are relying on wines with defined images of their own. When necessary, new vineyards are planted to provide each variety the soil and location it needs to best develop its character – Robóla grapes, a very stony hill slope with thin soil for a

light-bodied wine; Zakynthino, which makes a full-bodied wine, deep soil on level ground.

Wines, grapes...

In 1601, more than 30 types of grape were documented on Zakyntho and in 1904 Archduke Ludwig Salvator listed more than 80. This is with only the most important ones being named. **Robóla** yields a fruity-citrus, minerally, white wine reminiscent of Riesling that goes particularly well with fish and white meat. The grape is cultivated on the larger islands, but only on Kefalloniá does it have an OPAP appellation (VQPRD, superior quality wine) for a 350 ha area; altogether, there are more than 1,400 ha planted with the grape. Whether it is identical to the northern Italian Ribolla is still debated, though it was first mentioned as »Ribola«. The fresh grape juice is fermented in cooled steel tanks and the wine is bottled after clarification without any further ripening. It is accordingly a young wine and should be drunk well

Mandraki Harbour is the heart of Kos Town

The Dodecanese island of Kos lies to the northwest of ►Rhodes off the bay of the same name that cuts deep into the Turkish coastline. A ridge of mountains that reaches an elevation of 846 m/2,775 ft extends across the 51 km/32 mi long island from east to west. Its mild climate and fertile alluvial plain allowed a lush green landscape to develop that ancient travellers described as a »floating garden«.

The island enjoyed high esteem as the oldest **cult site of the god of healing, Asclepius** and the site of a medical school, whose most famous representative was the native-born **Hippocrates** (► Baedeker Special p. 353). The Romans, Byzantines and Venetians were followed by the Knights Hospitallers from 1309 to 1523. Kos fell only a little earlier than Rhodes to the Ottoman Turks. Occupied after the Balkan War by the Italians from 1912, it was made a part of Greece in 1948.

What to See on Kos

Kos Town The **island's capital** is spread out on a wide bay on the northeast coast. The earthquake of 1933 left some medieval, Turkish and Venetian-style buildings standing that give the town a pleasant atmosphere.

★
Mandraki Harbour ► One of the most popular and most lively places in town is Mandraki Harbour. Lined with hotels, tavernas and cafés, it is set on a small, pear-shaped bay cutting deep inland. The tangled labyrinth of plane tree covered lanes in the old town with its fun-fair pot-pourri of souvenir shops, boutiques and businesses begins only a few paces from

the harbour. Towering up on the east side of the harbour is the medieval **castle of the Knights of St John or Knights Hospitallers**. The inner ring wall dates from the years 1391 to 1396; the outer was added between 1503 and 1514.

Standing on the small square near the bridge leading to the castle is the so-called **Hippocrates plane tree**, under which the great physician is said to have taught. In fact, the mighty tree, with a trunk 12 m/39 ft in diameter and now hollow, is »only« about 500 years old. The Islamic ritual cleansing fountain next to the plane tree belongs to the **Haji Hassan Mosque** that was built under the Turkish Governor Hassan Pasha from 1782 to 1786. The ancient agorá is spread out to the south of it, the largest excavation site inside the town. The Tax Gate on the west side of the agorá leads to Platía Eleftherias, »Freedom Square«, with the charming 18th century Defterdar Mosque that has been transformed into a café. The south side of the square is occupied by a market hall and on the side opposite stands an interesting **archaeological museum** that has mosaics, statues and sculpture fragments from the Hellenistic-Roman period.

In the south-western part of town, along Grigoriou Street, lie the **western excavation sites** with the remnants of a 3rd-century BC

! **Baedeker** TIP

What to do with the car?
The search for a place to park in Kos Town can sometimes become a laborious undertaking. A shady parking place can always be found – even during high season – in Grigoriou Street in a partially fenced-in, gravel-covered lot between the odeon and Casa Romana, directly across from the western excavation site.

temple to Dionysus, the remains of houses with wonderful floor mosaics and of a 2nd-century BC gymnasium and bath house (3rd century BC). Just how grand and spacious the wealthy the Kos upperclass lived in Late Antiquity is illustrated in the reconstructed **Casa Romana** (2nd/3rd centuries AD) oposite the Dionysus temple on the other side of Grigoriou Street. The villa has three inner courtyards with rooms, some furnished with mosaics, marble flooring and wall paintings, grouped about them. The largest inner courtyard is surrounded by a two-storey colonnade of Corinthian and Doric columns. Only a few steps out of town from Casa Romana is the wellpreserved 2nd-century Roman **odeon** with seating for some 800 spectators.

The sanctuary of Asclepius is very beautifully situated, overlooking the sea some 4 km/2.5 mi southwest of Kos Town. From here there is a superb view of the town, the straits and the Turkish mainland.

★
Asclepieion

The Asclepieion, erected in the early 3rd century BC, occupied three terraces. The **first terrace** is bordered on three sides by colonnades. The rooms located behind the colonnades were part of the treatment area and served as sick-rooms and treatment rooms. Thermae were

Asklepieion Plan

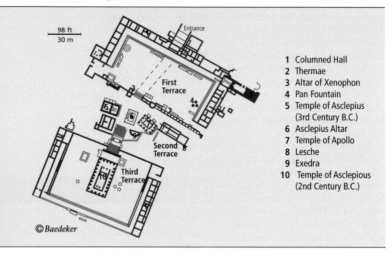

98 ft
30 m

Entrance

First Terrace

Second Terrace

Third Terrace

1 Columned Hall
2 Thermae
3 Altar of Xenophon
4 Pan Fountain
5 Temple of Asclepius (3rd Century B.C.)
6 Asclepius Altar
7 Temple of Apollo
8 Lesche
9 Exedra
10 Temple of Asclepious (2nd Century B.C.)

© Baedeker

added on the northeast corner of the terrace in Roman times. Following the asclepieion's destruction by an earthquake in 554, the Panagía tou Alsoús Monastery was built in memory of the former health centre (»sacred grove«). The first terrace ends to the south with the retaining wall of the second terrace. In a recess in the wall left of the flight of steps is the **Fountain of Pan**. Standing in a niche to the right of the steps is the altar of C. Stertinius Xenophon, the personal physician to Emperor Claudius, whom the inscription identifies as the donor.

The **second terrace** is the oldest part of the cult site. A few yards to the right of the steps stands the 3rd-century BC **temple to Asclepius**. The altar for animal sacrifices belonging to the temple can be seen next to it. Rising up to the east of the altar are seven columns once belonging to the **temple of Apollo** from the 2nd / 3rd centuries. An exedra with niches and benches was a few paces to the south.

A wide flight of steps leads to the **third terrace** with a large **temple of Asclepius**, a Doric peripteros with 6 : 11 columns built in the 2nd century BC The threshold of black marble has survived. A short 45-minute hike leads from the third terrace up the hill to the **Burinna** fountain house, which provided water for the sanctuary of the ancient city and still serves today as a water reservoir for the island's capital (opening hours: Tue – Fri 8.30am – 6.30pm, Sat/Sun until 2.30 pm).

THE FATHER OF MEDICINE

Hippocrates is one of the best-known names in human history. And yet little is known of the life and work of this man of Antiquity. Almost every physician in the last 2,500 years has had to swear an oath on his name, but Hippocrates did not even formulate the oath named after him. Nothing, however, can shake his reputation as the first »modern« physician.

Hippocrates was born around 460 BC on the island of Kos. He was descended from the Asclepiades, an ancient family of physicians who traced their lineage back to the healing god, **Asclepius**, and he was introduced to the healing arts at an early age by his father.

He came in contact with the most famous doctors of his time while travelling throughout Asia Minor and Greece practising as a physician and continued in further developing his methods of healing. After his return to the island of Kos he founded a medical school, which soon gained a high reputation. Hippocrates, whom **Plato** also mentioned as a famous doctor, died around 370 BC in Larissa, Thessaly.

The statue of Hippocrates displayed in the archaeological museum in Kos Town dates from the 4th century BC.

Legendary Physician

Naturally, a great many legends have formed around the life and work of such an outstanding personality. For example, it is said he healed the Macedonian king, **Perdiccas II**, who was suffering from headaches and loss of appetite for some unknown reason. He found out that the monarch was having a love affair, unbefitting his station, with a pretty servant girl and,

Camel Beach – one of the many great beaches along the south coast of Kos

Island tour The island's main road leaves Kos Town in a westerly direction at first. The scenic stretch heading south from the village of Zipári leads to Zia, a hill village prettily set at an elevation of 350 m/1,148 ft. It is said that the island's most beautiful sunsets can be seen here. **Paléo Pylí** (»Ancient Pyli«) can be reached via the little villages of Lagoúdi and Amaníou. It is a deserted village towered over by the remnants of a Byzantine castle from the 11th century. A little below the castle ruins is the church of Panagía ton Kastrianón (»Mother of God of the Castle-dwellers«) with fragments of 11th and 12th century frescoes.

Back on the main road, cul-de-sacs lead to the beach resorts of **Tingaki** and **Mármari** on the north coast that have developed into holiday centres because of their beautiful sandy beaches. Located close to the airport is the village of **Antimáchia**, which has the island's only surviving complete operational windmill and the »Traditional House«, a folk art museum. Crowning a mountain spur some 3 km/2 mi to the southeast, and visible for miles, is the Kástro, a castle expanded in the 14th and 15th centuries by the Knights Hospitallers.

Located about 6 km/4 mi southeast of Antimáchia on the island's south coast is **Kardámena**, another of Kos' heavily frequented holiday centres with long beaches of fine sand. Lying 5 km/3 mi north of Antimáchia on the north coast is **Mastichári**, also a tourist stronghold with corresponding infrastructure and nice, sandy beaches.

It is possible to cross over to the islands of Psérimos and Kálymnos from here. The sleepy hill village of **Kéfalos**, with its incomparably breathtaking panorama views, on a peninsula of the same name separated by a barely 2 km/1.2 mi wide isthmus, can be reached beyond the airport. The port of **Kamári**, with its sandy beach on Kéfalos Bay, is an El Dorado for sailing enthusiasts and surfers. The ruins of the early Christian **Ágios Stéfanos** Basilica, dating from the 5th/6th centuries, stands directly on the water close to the Club Méditerranée on the eastern edge of the bay. Just outside the bay is the picturesque **Kastri** rock with the Ágios Nikólaos chapel, which is always closed. Stretching out to the east of Kéfalos Bay are the island's most beautiful beaches, including fantastic **Camel Beach** and the miles-long, extremely popular **Paradise Beach**.

Neighbouring Islands

The island of Nísyros lying south of Kos is a cone-shaped volcano with its peak torn off. The almost round island has no abundance of water, yet it has lush vegetation outside of the volcanic terrain. Wine,

✷
Nísyros

The sulphur deposits and bubbling mud pots can be seen up close in the 30 m/100 ft deep Stéfanos Crater.

▶ VISITING LÉSBOS

INFORMATION

Tourist Information
James Aristarchou 6
Mytilíni
Tel. / Fax 22 51 04 25 12/3
E-mail: eotpytva@otenet.gr

GETTING THERE

Boats ply regularly between Lésbos
and Alexandroúpolis, Kavála, Piraeus,
Thessaloníki and Vólos on the main-
land and the islands of Chíos, Kos,
Límnos, Mýkonos, Rhodes, Sámos,
Samothráki, Skíathos, Skópelos and
Tínos.

WHERE TO EAT

► Moderate

Stratos
Mytilíni
Tel. 22 51 02 17 39
Taverna on the south side of the south
harbour with tasty fish dishes.

► Inexpensive

Panorama
Mólivos
Magnificent view of the sea and
countryside; serves solid, plain
cooking.

WHERE TO STAY

► Mid-range

Lesvion
P. Koundourioti 27 A
Mytilíni
Tel. 22 51 02 81 77
E-mail: lesvion@otenet.gr
34 rooms
»Lesvion« offers well-furnished rooms
and a bar with a view of the harbour.

Olive Press
Míthymna
Tel. 22 53 07 12 05
www.olivepress-hotel.com
45 rooms
The hotel, a converted olive press at
the edge of town in Míthymna, has a
very special ambience.

► Budget

Sappho
Skála Eressós
Tel. 22 53 05 34 95
www.sapphohotel.com
17 rooms
Some of the hotel rooms have a
balcony. The in-house restaurant
serves Greek food.

⏲ Ottoman times. (opening hours: July – mid-Sept daily 8am – 7pm,
mid-Sept – June Tue – Sun 8.30am –3pm).
Behind the Therapon church with its mighty dome is the **Byzantine
Museum**, which focuses on icons. Standing on the harbour is the
harbourmaster's house in which a small **folk-art museum** has been
installed. The exhibits include traditional costumes, household articles, pottery, weapons and paintings.In the southern suburb of Variá there are two museums worth visiting. First the exhibition devoted
to the painter **Theophilos** (1873 – 1934), endowed by Stratis Eleftheriadis in 1964. Eleftheriadis was born in Mytilíni and lived under
the name of Tériade as an art journalist and patron in Paris. In 1979
he also provided the funds for the neighbouring **Tériade Museum**

Variá ▶

The small port town of Mithymna is the most popular resort on Lésbos.

with graphic art by modern artists such as Joan Miró, Henri Matisse, Marc Chagall, Fernand Léger and Pablo Picasso (opening hours: ⏲ Tue – Sun 9am –5pm).

The North of the Island

Heading out of Mytilíni, the road follows the coastline to the north. **Mória** After 4 km/2.5 mi is a turnoff for **Mória**. The impressive remains of a 3rd-century Roman **aqueduct** that supplied the capital with water can be found some 600 m/660 yd west of the village.

The seaside resort of Thermís has a number of small beaches and a **Thermís** medicinal thermal spring. Some fortified tower houses from the 16th – 19th centuries still stand in the Pýrgi Thermís district. Pana-

Dístomo ► The road leading to the monastery runs through the village of Dísto-mo, which was utterly destroyed in 1944 by the Waffen SS in revenge for partisan attacks. Its 228 inhabitants, from babies to the elderly, were shot.

History ► Ósios Loukás, Blessed Luke, was born in 896 in Kastoriá, later Kastrí, and lived in various places as a hermit after 910. Between 941 and 944, the Byzantine governor of the region built a chapel dedicated to St Barbara next to his hermitage. A monastery developed out of it that now dominates the lonely, bleak landscape; here Luke died in 953, highly venerated.

✱
Central church ► The domed-crossing church erected in 1011 and dedicated to St Like is dominated by a mighty cupola, the tuff and cloisonné masonry and the windows grouped together by a blind arcade. The church's interior is agleam with stunning 11th-century mosaics fashioned by a number of different artists. Noteworthy, in addition, are the surviving marble facings on the walls and the ornate marble floor. The extraordinarily high and bright interior is dominated by the dome with the Pantocrator, Mary, John and four archangels. Beneath it in the

The Panagía Church was built during the lifetime of Blessed Luke (9th century).

tambour are depictions of 16 prophets. Frescoes have replaced the mosaics destroyed by an earthquake in 1593. There is a portrait-like image in the north aisle of Blessed Luke, who is here designated as »ágios«, although the wish for his canonization was never fulfilled.

The elaborately painted crypt was created as a tomb for Luke. Standing in it are the sarcophagus of the Blessed Luke and two other sarcophagi, traditionally said to be the last resting place of Emperor **Romanos II of Byzantium** (959 – 963) and **Empress Theophanou**.

✴
◀ Crypt

The auxiliary church dedicated to the Panagía is probably the original church of St Barbara that was built during Luke's lifetime from 946 to 955. And indeed, the way it looks, above all the plain execution of its construction, makes a remodelling in 13th century to suit Cistercian tastes quite plausible. An opening in front of the left transept of the main church leads to a narthex whose dome is supported by two columns with Corinthian capitals. The high central dome rests on four granite columns with elaborately fashioned leaf capitals. The few surviving frescoes date from the 11th and 12th centuries.

✴
◀ Panagía

In the trapeza, the dining hall, is a small **museum** in which fragments of architecture from the two churches and 17th-century frescoes can be seen (opening hours: daily 8am – 2pm, 4pm – 6pm).

◀ Trapeza

🕐

✴ Máni · Μάνη

G 11 / 12

Prefecture: Laconia

The Máni – actually the Inner (Mesa) Máni – is the middle one of three Peloponnese peninsulas that extend out to the south. Its charm lies in the rugged Taýgetos mountain landscape that rises to a height of 1215 m/3,986 ft, its villages with unusual fortress-like tower houses and their elaborately painted chapels.

What to See on the Máni Peninsula

The 80 km/50 mi drive south from Kalamáta to Areópolis on the Máni Peninsula runs through the beautiful countryside on the east side of the Messenian Gulf called Éxo Máni (»Outer Máni«). This remote, very rugged and hardly inhabited stretch of land is only now gradually being discovered by tourists. Typical of the architecture in Máni are the massively-constructed, crenellated tower houses that served as homes as well as defensive fortifications. Spread around **Avia** are out-of-the-way beaches with a family-holiday atmosphere. Beyond Almíros, the road climbs to Kámbos at the foot of Kaláthio Mountain. On a hill southeast of the village are the ruins of the 17th-century castle, Zarnáta, the most important fortification in Éxo Máni during Turkish and Venetian times. The mountain village of Kéndro, 7 km/4.3 mi away, is the starting point for a hike into the

✴
Through the
Éxo Máni

The tower houses of Váthia appear to be a single fortress.

wine-growing centre. Standing below the village is the beautiful monastery church, Dekoúlou, a basilica from 1765 completely decorated with paintings inside and with a rich iconostasis. The drive finally leads around the fabulous Bay of Ítilo that cuts deeply inland – there is a beautiful beach at Liméni – and continues on serpentine up to Areópolis.

★
Through Messa Máni

The starting point for the roundtrip through Messa Máni, the »Inner Máni«, is **Areópolis**, the most important place in the region with paved lanes, old tower houses and interesting churches. Its platía with a monument to fallen war dead is the centre of public life. Areópolis was given the name »Ares city« in honour of the Petrobey, the sultan's governor and freedom fighter, **Petros Mavromichalis** (1765 – 1848). His monument stands on the market place. A small museum was installed in one of the tower houses that illustrates Máni customs.

The wide bathing cove of Dírou can be reached by taking a turn off 7 km/4.3 mi to the south. There, also, is the impressive **Spílea Dírou cave**, Máni's most popular attraction. Up till now, a 5 km/3 mi long labyrinth has been explored with tunnels and lakes and stunning stalagmite and stalactite formations. The boat trip on the subterranean river through the effectively illuminated **Glyfáda cave** is a unique experience.

A small road 2 km/1.2 mi south of Pýrgos Dírou runs through olive groves down to **Charouda**. An 11th century Ágios Taxiarchis church can be found there in a cemetery standing behind high walls. The four columned, domed-crossing church possess a plain, Romanesque-looking bell tower and ceramic bowls worked into the masonry of the apse. The marble doorframe on the west side is particularly beautiful. The frescoes date back to the 14th and 18th centuries. The villages of Kíta and Alíka on the way to Váthia are almost deserted. Váthia itself also has just a small population but the large number of tower houses are so crowded together that they appear to be one mighty fortress. Some of the old tower houses have been converted into holiday guesthouses.

A road from Alíka crosses over the mountain ridge on Máni. A particularly stunning view of the east coast opens up past **Lagiá**, which is less barren and forbidding than the west coast. After passing a couple of bathing coves and the villages of Kokála and Nymfío, the road leads to pleasant **Flomochóri**. The road branches off back to Areópolis outside of Flomochóri.

◄ East coast

✴ Marathon · Μαραθώνας

K 8

Prefecture: Attica   **Altitude:** 52 m/171 ft

The marathon run that was first »staged« here in 490 BC and, since the start of the modern Olympic Games in 1896, the high point of every major sports event, is exactly 42.195 km/26 mi 385 yd long.

Marathon was known in Antiquity as the place where **Theseus** killed the bull of Marathon. The first major battle between the Greeks and the Persians took place here in the year 490 BC. The Persian army that had landed in the Bay of Marathon was beaten into retreat by the Greeks advancing at double time under **Miltiades**. Afterwards, an Attic warrior named Pheidippides is said to have run the 40 km/25 mi or so in full armour and without pausing to Athens to deliver the message of the victory. He reached the Areopagus with his last bit of strength, announced the victory and dropped dead from exhaustion. To commemorate this feat, the marathon race was held for the first time in 1896 in Athens during the first Olympic games in modern times.

Myth and history

▶ **MARATHON**

OPENING HOURS
Burial mound and museum
June – Oct Tue – Sun 8.30 – 6pm

What to See in Marathon

The battlefield with a 12 m/39 ft high burial mound for the 192 fallen Athenians rising up on it is located 5 km/3 mi south of the present-day village of Marathónas. There is a replica of the funerary

Battlefield

★ ★ Metéora · Μετέωρα

C 4

Prefecture: Thessaly

Towering up on the plain drained by the Piniós in the northwest of Thessaly is a 300 m/984 ft high, bizarrely shaped rock formation. Vertical walls, slender pillars of rock and massive chunks of stone loom over the town of Kalambáka and the village Kastráki. Perched on them are the famous, medieval monasteries of Metéora – the »monasteries in the heavens above«.

★ ★ Metéora Monasteries

Important Byzantine monasteries

Tá metéora monastíria, »monasteries in the heavens above«; whoever comes here for the first time understands why the monks seeking divine illumination settled on these rocks. Even today, it is impossible to escape the overpowering effect of these rock walls and pinnacles. Originally only accessible by mule-tracks, ladders and cable winches, today, the monasteries, which were designated as a UNESCO World Heritage Site in 1988, have been opened to tourists.

The road that connects the monasteries is heavy with traffic during the high season and is not suitable for pedestrians. The best way to appreciate this fantastic landscape is by exploring it on foot and also hiking to the more remote monasteries.

▶ VISITING METÉORA

INFORMATION

Tourist Services Office
28 Oktovrion 7
Kalambáka
Tel. 24 32 04 44 44

Visitors should appear in appropriate clothing. Women must wear skirts and the arms must be covered. Men may not wear shorts. There are skirts available in the monasteries for women wearing slacks. Filming is prohibited.

The various opening hours are listed at the individual monasteries.

WHERE TO EAT

▶ **Inexpensive**
Boufidis
Kastraki
At the town exit
This nice taverna specializes in grilled dishes.

WHERE TO STAY

▶ **Budget**
Arsenis
Kalambáka
Tel. 24 32 02 41 50
www.arsenis-meteora. gr
Well-tended guesthouse in a quiet and scenic setting only about 2 km/1 mi away from the monasteries.

Metéora Monasteries Map

In the early 9th century, hermits seeking solitude and inspiring surroundings settled in the caves of the Metéora rocks. The first katholikon was the church of St Mary, **Doupianí**.

In 1340, Thessaly came under Serbian rule and Simeon had himself crowned king of the Serbs and Greeks in Tríkala. During this unsettled time, the hermits sought protection and tranquillity in the heights and together formed a community.

Between 1356 and 1372, the monastery of Metéoro founded by **Athanásios Meteorítis** was built on a 534 m/1,752 ft rock. It was the first of a total of 24 »rock monasteries« that were still here in the 16th century. Today, there are only five left.

History

Ágios Nikólaos Anapafsás

The first monastery open to visitors on the road to the Metéora rock is Ágios Nikólaos Anapafsás, founded in 1368 and abandoned in 1909. The Ágios Antonios chapel still has fragments of frescoes from the 14th century. The katholikon was decorated in 1527 by **Theophanes** (opening hours: daily except Fri 9am – 3.30pm).

Roussanou

Roussanou monastery stands on a rock pinnacle and is probably the most daringly constructed of the monastery buildings. Roussanou was built around 1530 by the hermits Jóasaph and Maximos and decorated with frescoes about 1560 (opening hours: daily 9am – 6pm).

Varlaám

The Varlaám monastery was founded in 1517 on the site of a hermitage dating back to the monk Barlaam and has over 195 steps leading up to it. Its katholikon Ágii Pántes (1544) is decorated with paintings from 1548 in the style of the Cretan school that abandoned »icon-like« rigidity in favour of spatial layouts and lively scenes. The gilded iconostasis (18th century) is fascinating. In the library are some very well preserved manuscripts from the 11th, 14th and 16th centuries (opening hours: daily except Thu 9am – 5pm).

Megálo Metéoro

The traces of wooden stairs can still be seen in the rock in front of the Megálo Metéoro monastery founded in 1356, as well as the tower-like construction with its roof built in 1520 containing the old and now defunct cable winch. The katholikon is dedicated to Metamórfosis (the Transfiguration of Christ). The chapel built by the founder, **Athanasios** in 1387 / 1388 became the chancel when his successor enlarged the church. Their two tombs – with their images and a model of the church – are in the portico. The main area of the church and apse were completely decorated with paintings around 1500. The **trapeza** contains an interesting collection of antique icons, manuscripts and liturgical instruments. Also open to the public are the monastery cellar, the charnel house and the kitchen (opening hours: daily except Thu 9am –5pm).

Agía Triáda

The Agía Triáda monastery is spectacularly enthroned on a 565 m/ 1,854 ft pinnacle. Because of its extraordinary location, it was even used as a setting in the James Bond film »For Your Eyes Only«. The somewhat strenuous climb, however, is rewarded by a magnificent view. The monastery was founded in 1438. The main church, dating from 1475 / 1476, is the oldest of the monastery buildings. Its east outside wall is richly decorated with ceramics. The round Timios Prodromos chapel dates from 1682.

Ágios Stéfanos

The Ágios Stéfanos monastery, re-established in 1367 by an endowment from the Serbian prince, **Antonios Kantakuzenos**, has been a nunnery since 1961. The chapel of St Stephan, remodelled

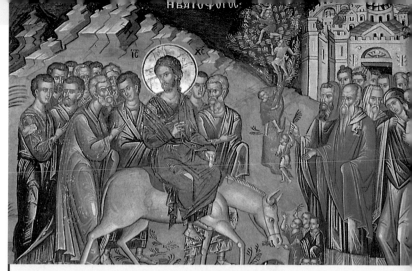

»Entry into Jerusalem« – Fresco from 1522 in the Megálo Metéoro Monastery

about 1545, is decorated with frescoes painted around 1400. The main church dedicated to St Charálambos was built in 1798 and its carved wood iconostasis in 1814. The **monastery museum** contains 16th and 17th-century icons and antique manuscripts, among other things (opening hours: Tue – Sun 9am – 1pm, 3.30pm – 5.30pm).

Around the Metéora Monasteries

The small rural town of Kalambáka, located on the Piniós River, is a good starting place for a visit to the Metéora monasteries. The name comes from Turkish and means »rock with a monk's hood«. With its hotels, camping grounds, tavernas and cafés, it essentially lives from tourism.

Kalambáka

The church located at the eastern edge of town under a vertical rock face, **Kímisis tis Theotókou**, a basilica rebuilt in 1309 by Andronikos III Palaiologos and traditionally said to date from the time of Emperor Justinian, is worth seeing. The painting in the interior was done in 1573 by **Neofytos**, the son of the famous Cretan painter, **Theofanes Strelitzas**.

It is well worth making a stop in Tríkala (pop. 35,000) before or after visiting the Metéora monasteries. The town is located about 20 km/ 12 mi to the southeast on the western edge of the Thessalian Plain with its lively bazaar district and a large square lined with pretty cafés in the centre. The place known as Trikka in Homer's »Iliad« was known in Antiquity for its horse breeding and is thought to have been the **birthplace of Asclepius**, who was to become the god of the healing arts.

Trikala

nine men, eight women and two children with burial objects of gold, such as masks, jewellery and breastplates, were found in the six shaft graves that can still be seen. Grave Circle B belonged to the end of the 17th century BC and the Grave Circle A, which Schliemann discovered, to the period after 1580 BC. The fact that shaft graves were no longer being used but rather beehive (tholoi) tombs is an indication of a change in dynasties. A few more buildings, such as the South House, the House of the Warrior Vase and the Tsountas' House, named after its excavator, lie beyond Grave Circle A.

Palace The visible remains of the largely destroyed palace, upon which a Greek temple of Athena was built in the 7th century BC, date from the 15th century BC The most important parts of the palace lie in the south; a courtyard with a surviving Mycenaean stone stairway leading up to it, as well as the throne room and megaron of the rulers of Mycenae. Below the palace, to the east, the **House of Columns** can be seen against the cyclopean circuit wall. Further to the southeast, already beyond the sally port, is the entrance to a cistern chamber lying 18 m/60 ft underground. By returning along the north wall, the north gate can be seen and, below the palace hill, a series of storerooms with clay vessels, as well.

The so-called beehive tombs that Heinrich Schliemann discovered are 3,500 years old.

Mýkonos Chóra is one of the prettiest towns in the Cyclades.

✱ ✱ Mýkonos · Μύκονος

Island Group: Cyclades
Altitude: 0 – 372 m/1,220 ft
Principal Town: Mýkonos Chóra

Area: 85 sq km/33 sq mi
Population: 6,800

The barren Cycladic island of Mýkonos, with its beaches of fine sand, is *the* holiday island in Greece and is »open 24/7« during high season. Those that come here do so to spend the days and nights of their holiday partying on the beach and on the dance floors of the discos.

With Mýkonos, it is either/or: either you are looking for a party at the beach and in the disco – or you avoid the island. It is the most popular island in the Aegean and one of the most expensive holiday destinations in Greece. It is impossible to get lodgings between June and September without reserving them long in advance. The barren island has little to offer in the way of scenery besides beautiful beaches. Among the cultural attractions are several small museums and, above all, the nearby island of Délos that is visited daily by excursion boats. The traditional architecture is attractive with its white houses, contrasting blue and red windows and white, natural cobblestone roads.

Party island

race in full armour. The winner received a branch from the sacred olive tree and they could count on considerable material advantages when they returned home. The **stadion** originally had its finishing line near the temple of Zeus, thus emphasizing the cult significance of the race. Victory was a gift of Zeus, the father of the gods. It was not until the 4th century BC that the stadium was moved to the east and out of the **Altis**, the »sacred precinct«. After their heyday in the 5th century BC, the games went into a state of decline and more and more of their religious aspects were removed, with professional athletes eventually dominating the competition. In AD 393, the games were finally banned by Emperor **Theodosius I**.

In August 2007, devastating **forest fires** rampaging through the Pelo-

Olympía *Plan*

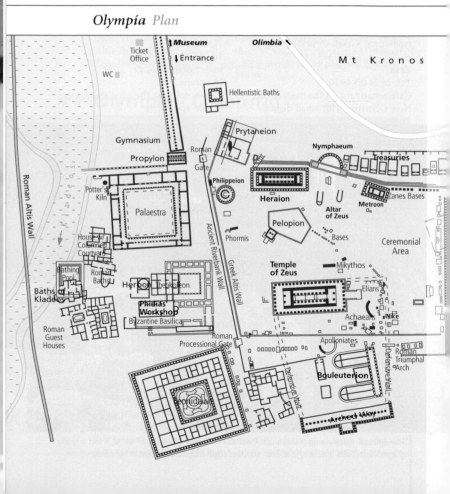

ponnese threatened the famous excavation site, whose destruction was prevented only in the last minute by a mobilization of all available help. The village of Olympía near the excavation site came into being as a result of the excavation begun in 1875 and has since become totally orientated toward tourism. A small **Museum of the Olympic Games** provides an overview of the modern games.

Excavation Site

The excavation site lies east of the village on the road to Langadia. The buildings outside the Altis walls are the first to be seen. To the left are the northern baths, followed by the Prytaneion (6th century B.C), where the victors were wined and dined. The gymnasium can be seen opposite with its 220 m/240 yd training track and the propylon to the south (2nd century BC), joined by the large, square palaistra (3rd century BC) for training boxers and wrestlers.

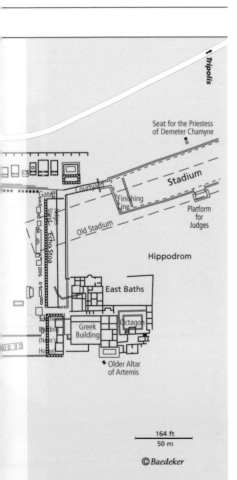

Standing behind it are the walls of a 5th century Byzantine basilica erected on the foundation of the workshop of **Phidias**. This had the exact dimensions of the cella in the temple of Zeus. It was here that the sculptor created the cult image of Zeus in gold and ivory about 438 BC. Lying next to it to the south is the Leonidaion, a large guesthouse that was erected in the 4th century BC by **Leonidas of Náxos** to accommodate guests of honour and was remodelled in Roman times so that the living quarters, lined on the outside with galleries of Ionic columns, surrounded a luxurious inner court of gardens and water fountains.

Following to the east are the southern baths, dating from the 2nd century AD, the south stoa (4th century BC) and the bouleuterion (6th / 5th centuries BC).

Sacred Precinct

Temple of Zeus The Altis is entered through a Roman gate made of shell limestone. Rising to the left are the massive ruins of the temple of Zeus. The triangular pillar for the **Nike of Paionios** (c. 425 BC), set upright again, and the bases of a number of dedicatory monuments can be seen to the east. A ramp on the left hand leads up into the temple of Zeus. The structure collapsed during an earthquake in the 6th century, but its enormous remains give an idea of the temple that **Libon of Elis** erected between 470 and 456 BC.

Massive 6 : 13 columns on high foundations stood on the three-stepped platform that has survived intact. The total height of the building was close to 20 m/65 ft. While the remainder of the building was made of stuccoed shell limestone, marble from Páros was chosen for its roof with its 102 lion-head waterspouts and the sculpturing on the metopes and pediments. The cella, in which the floor tiling from the 4th or 3rd centuries BC has survived, held the cult image created by Phidias – one of the Seven Wonders of the World – that showed Zeus sitting on a richly-decorated throne. It was taken to Constantinople sometime after AD 393 and has since been lost track of.

Heraion Located to the north of the Zeus Temple is the mythical tomb of Pelops, the **Pelopion**. This is followed by the oldest temple in Olympía, the Heraion, erected around 600 BC. It was a Doric 6 : 16 temple dedicated to the goddess Hera, with a great variety of column shafts and capitals because the original wooden columns were only gradually replaced. This resulted in thick Archaic forms being seen next to the more sleek forms of later periods. Since 1936, the **Olympic flame** has been ignited in front of the Heraion and then carried to the site of the Olympic Games.

Nymphaeum Lying to the northeast of the Heraion is the Nymphaeum that **Herodes Atticus** had built about AD 160 in memory of his wife, Regilla, a priestess of Demeter, and in honour of the Roman imperial house.

Treasuries A bit further on is a terrace at the foot of Kronos Hill, where, from the 6th into the 5th century BC, the Greek city-states erected treasuries for their offerings, usually in the form of a small ante-temple. Interestingly, the Greek motherland was represented by only two treasuries, one from Sicyon and one from Megara, while six were funded by Western Greek cities, Syracuse, Selinunte and Gela in Sicily, Sybaris and Metapontum in southern Italy and Epidamnos in present-day Albania. Not only that, Cyrene in Africa and Byzantium had their own treasuries.

Metroon

Immediately below the treasuries terrace lies the Metroon (about 300 BC), in which the mother of the gods cult was supplanted by the Roman imperial cult, and the bases for the »Zanes«, the statues of Zeus financed by the fines levied for offences against the rules of games. They stand directly in front of the entrance to the stadium.

Stadium

The stadium, which had been separate from the Altis since the addition of the Echo Hall, has been completely excavated and reconstructed in its 4th-century BC state. The starting line for the two-stade race and the stadion race can be seen. The stands for the audience have always been earth embankments without stone seating. Only the referees had a stone stand against the south wall and the priestess of Demeter, the only woman allowed to attend the games, against the north wall. The 609 × 320 m/1,998 x 991 ft **hippodrome** to the south of the stadium was destroyed by a flood back in Antiquity.

Echo Hall, Nero Villa

To the west was the 98 m/321 ft long Echo Hall, which was under construction from around 330 BC down into Roman times. Emperor **Nero** had the southeast building and the building adjoining further to the east built as his villa, the only house belonging to a mortal in the Altis.

Philippeion

Close to the west wall of the Altis lies the Philippeion, a circular building to house the five chryselephantine statues of the Macedonian royal family crafted by **Leochares**, which was funded by Philip II of Macedonia in 338 BC and completed by his son.

The Museum

The excavation site's museum is one of the most significant in Greece. The rooms are grouped in a circle around hall V with pediment figures and metopes from the temple of Zeus. In the entrance hall are models that present a picture of ancient Olympía. A model of the Nike column is also displayed here.

◄ Hall V

The east pediment from the temple of Zeus shows the father of the gods flanked by King Oinomaos, his wife, Sterope, his daughter, Hippodameia, and her future husband, Pelops, in front of one of the chariot races in which Oinomaos is said to have lost his life. The west pediment has a depiction of Zeus' son, Apollo, intervening imperiously in the battle between the Lapiths and Centaurs. The metopes from the pronaos and opisthodomos showing the Twelve Labours of Heracles can be seen at the narrow end of the hall.

◄ Rooms I and II

Rooms I and II present bronze artefacts from the Early Helladic to the Geometric periods (15th – 7th century BC), including helmets,

Restored figures from the pediment of the Temple of Zeus in the museum at Olympía.

weapons and breastplates. The large clay acroter (c. 600 BC), which once crowned the apex of the pediment of the Heraion, can also be seen here.

Rooms III and IV ▶ The reconstructions using parts of the treasury of Gela and the treasury of Megara (c. 510 BC) are worth noting. Among the outstanding pieces are the terracotta group, »Zeus abducts Ganymede« (c. 470 BC), and a helmet that according to the inscription from 490 BC was dedicated to **Miltiades**, the winner of the marathon. Fragments from the workshop of Phidias convey an impression of the great sculptor's power of expression.

Rooms VI – X ▶ The overwhelming, almost 3 m/10 ft **statue of Nike**, which Paionios fashioned in Parian marble for the people of Náfpaktos and Messene as a offering for their victory over the Spartans in 421 BC and was placed on a triangular base at the temple of Zeus, can be admired here. The famous **Hermes with the young Dionysus** (c. 350 BC) is recognized as a work by **Praxiteles**. Hermes is bringing the small Dionysus to the nymphs so that he can grow up safe from the jealous Hera. Traces can still be seen of the pigment used to paint it.

The collection of ancient sports equipment in Room X will certainly be of interest not only to sports fans.

Zeus and Hera and their family of gods sat enthroned on the summit of Mt Olympus.

★ Mount Olympus · Όλυμπος

Prefecture: Thessaly Macedonia   **Altitude:** 2,917 m/9,570 ft

Mount Olympus, sitting on the east coast between Macedonia and Thessaly, is the highest and most famous of all the mountains in Greece. Homer described it as the »home of the gods«; moreover, he named Zeus, the father of the gods, the »cloud collector«: no wonder, since even today Olympus is often hidden in the clouds.

The mountain massif that reaches its highest point, 2,917 m/9,570 ft, with **Mýtikas**, is composed of limestone and dolomite, which, along with its woods of beech, fir and Greek black pine, give it an alpine image. The large range of biotopes brought forth a diverse mix of flora with over 1,700 varieties, including more than 20 endemic varieties found only here that include the pink-blossoming Jankaea heldreichii, similar to the cowslip. Since 1938, Mount Olympus has been a **national park** with an area of 4,000 ha/10,000 acres and, since 1981, a **UNESCO biosphere reserve**. The most settled weather is recorded at the end of September and the beginning of October. In May, when the flowers are in full bloom, snow is still lying above 2,000 m/6,600 ft. A sacrificial site dedicated to Zeus was uncovered on the Ágios Antónios summit (2,817 m/9,242 ft) south of Mýtikas. A shrine to Apollo was found on the west slope at an elevation of 700 m/2,300 ft.

Home of the gods

John the Evangelist recounted his visions of the fate of mankind and of the Last Judgement in this cave.

THE REVELATION OF JOHN

»I John, who also am your brother, and companion in tribulation ... was in the isle that is called Patmos, for the word of God, and for the testimony of Jesus Christ.
I was in the Spirit ... and heard behind me a great voice, as of a trumpet ...
Saying ... what thou seest, write in a book ...« (Revelation 1:9–11)

According to tradition, John spent many years of his life in a cave on Pátmos. There he listened to the Word of God coming from a fissure in the rock ceiling and received the revelation of the future fate of mankind. He had visions in powerful imagery and words of the end of the world, of the terror and the jubilation of the final days and of the Last Judgement. The Revelation, transcribed by **Prorochos**, a disciple of John, is the last book of the New Testament. It is a work with 22 chapters built around a series of epistles to the seven branches of the church and three series of seven world catastrophes. All in all, the number seven plays a large role in the apocalyptic scenario of the Revelation. Seven is mentioned repeatedly, seven stars, seven plagues or seven golden cups of the wrath of God. The visions were addressed to the seven churches in Asia Minor as representatives the whole of Christianity in the world.

Itinerant preacher

Was this John the author of the Book of Revelation? It is historically documented that he was banished to the island of Pátmos in AD 96 by Emperor **Domitian** because of his Christian beliefs. It was traditionally

believed that this was the apostle John who wrote the Fourth Gospel and three epistles in the New Testament (the Evangelist died in AD 100). But because of stylistic and theological differences between the texts, many academics are of the opinion that the author of the Revelation cannot be identical to the disciple of Christ. It is

work itself that indicates this. Is it perhaps a compilation of the revised texts of several authors of the 2nd century AD?

In any case, the Revelation was born of a naked fear of the future and radical proselytizing zeal at a time of cruel persecution of Christians. The Apocalypse served to provide solace in

> »And the fourth angel poured out his vial upon the sun; and power was given unto him to scorch men with fire.« (Revelation 16:8)

likely that the author of the Revelation – now furnished with the epithet, **the Theologian** – was a Christian of Jewish origin who fled to Asia Minor after the destruction of the temple in Jerusalem in the year AD 70 and spread the new teachings as an itinerant preacher.

Was the Apocalypse actually written on Pátmos? There is nothing in the

martyrdom. There were a great number of apocalyptic visions at the time and many texts have survived from the 2nd century BC to the 2nd century AD that describe the end of the world. But to this day, none of these texts have so frightened and fascinated mankind as do John's apocalyptic prophesies, which have never been fully understood.

Like a defiantly fortified castle, the monastery of St John towers over the island's principal town, Chóra.

marble taken from a 4th-century basilica. The narthex (12th century) is decorated with frescoes from the 12th and 17th centuries. The church is the oldest part and has the floor plan of a Greek cross. The Russian tsar paid for its furnishing in the 19th century, including an iconostasis from 1820 with richly detailed carvings. The paintings are frequently of John and his apocalyptic visions. The silver-plated sarcophagus (18th century) of the founder of the monastery, the Blessed **Christodoulos**, is in the first chapel to the right. Important 12th-century wall paintings were discovered in the second chapel, dedicated to the Panagía, beneath frescoes from 1745 – which were removed and can be seen in the trapeza, the old dining hall.

★ ★
Museum ▶

Icons and valuable liturgical instruments, most of them from the 17th century, are stored in the monastery's **treasury**. The **library** has some unique materials, 890 codices and 35 parchment scrolls, a good 2,000 old printed works and an archive with over 13,000 documents. The library and the treasury, probably the most important ecclesiastical collection outside of the Holy Mountain of Áthos, are not open to the public. Some pieces, however, can be seen in the monastery museum, including **Alexios I Komnenos'** golden bull of 1088, said to have been over 5 m/15 ft long, 33 pages of the Gospel of St Mark (Codex Purpureus, 6th century), a manuscript of the Book of Job with 42 miniature illustrations (8th century) and a collection of sermons by Gregory of Nazianz from the year 941 (opening hours: daily 8am – 1.30pm, Tue, Thu, Sun also 4pm – 6pm).

Lying to the north of Skála are Meloi (2 km/1.2 mi) and Agriolivado **Beaches**
(4 km/2.5 mi) beaches. The beautiful bay of Kampos, in the northern
part of the island, has a flat, sloping pebble beach. The Bay of Lampi
is known for its multi-coloured pebble beach. Grígos, southeast of
the Chóra, is the second most important tourist spot after Skála and
has the best beach on the island, **Psili Ammos**.

Neighbouring Islands

The 7 sq km/2.7 sq mi island of Arkí lies 14 km/8.7 mi northeast of **Arki**
Pátmos. Its 50 or so inhabitants live essentially from fishing and rais-
ing cattle. There are some private guestrooms and beaches, the most
attractive being Tiganaki Beach with fantastically blue water. Arkí is
surrounded by numerous smaller islands and rocks, some used to
pasture goats.

Lipsí lies 12 km/7.5 mi east of Pátmos and has, besides a modest but **Lipsí**
pretty harbour village of the same name on the south coast, an **idyllic
landscape** with a couple of beautiful beaches. The few islanders live
from farming, fishing and tourists. They have a fine type of cheese
here and a strong, »black« wine. The village, reminiscent of the Cyclades, has two nice squares and a small archaeological and folk art
museum.

Pátras · Πάτρα

F 8

Prefecture: Achaia   **Altitude:** 5 – 103 m/16 – 338 ft
Population: 172,000

**The region's most important ferry terminal is only a stopping-off
place for most holiday-makers. But the university town and European Capital of Culture for 2006 has a lot to offer besides its
smartened up squares, including a wide range of cultural and en-
tertainment programmes.**

What to See in Pátras

Pátras is the largest city and principal port of the Peloponnese, as **Principal port of**
well as the capital of Achaia. It was destroyed by the Turks in 1821, **the Peloponnese**
right at the start of the War of Independence. It was afterwards rebuilt with Neo-classical buildings. Towering up in the east of the city
is the **acropolis** with a castle on it that was erected by the Byzantines
in the 6th century and enlarged by the Crusaders in the 13th century
and later by the Ottoman Turks. Below it, to the southwest on Platía
25 Martiou, is a renovated **Roman odeon** (c. AD 160), with seating
for 1,800, used for events. The archaeological museum displays arte-

Rhodes Map

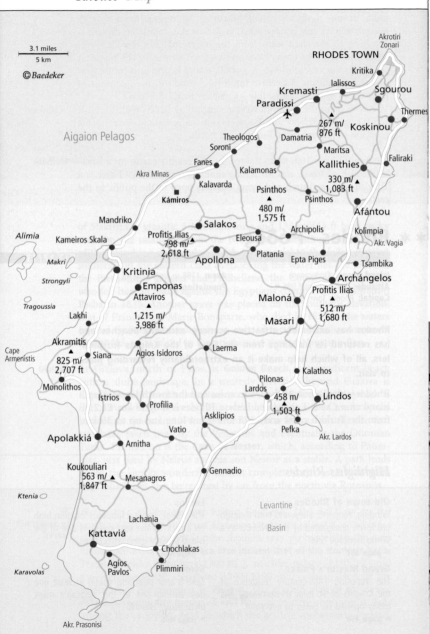

3.1 miles
5 km
© Baedeker

Aigaion Pelagos

RHODES TOWN
Akrotiri Zonari
Kritika
Ialissos
Kremasti Sgourou
Paradissi
Thermes
267 m/
876 ft **Koskinou**
Theológos Damatria
Soroni Maritsa
Fanés **Kallithies** Faliraki
Akra Minas Kalamonas
Kalavarda Psinthos 330 m/
Kámiros Psinthos 1,083 ft
480 m/ **Afántou**
Mandriko 1,575 ft
Salakos Archipolis Kolimpia
Kameiros Skala Eleousa Akr. Vagia
Alimia Profitis Ilias
798 m/ Platania
2,618 ft **Apollona** Epta Piges Tsambika
Makri
Strongyli **Kritinia** **Archángelos**
Emponas Profitis Ilias
Tragoussia Attaviros **Maloná** 512 m/
1,215 m/ 1,680 ft
Lakhi 3,986 ft **Masari**
Akramitis Agios Isidoros Laerma
Cape 825 m/
Armenistis Siana 2,707 ft Kalathos
Monolithos Pilonas **Lindos**
Istrios Lardos
Profilia 458 m/
Asklipios 1,503 ft
Vatio Pefka
Apolakkiá Akr. Lardos
Arnitha
Koukouliari
563 m/ Gennadio
1,847 ft Mesanagros
Ktenia Levantine

Lachania Basin

Kattaviá Chochlakas
Agios Plimmiri
Karavolas Pavlos

Akr. Prasonisi

Pure Middle Ages without disturbing neon advertising – The Street of the Knights with the former hospice of the Knights Hospitallers

18.6 mi wide. A long mountain ranges runs across it that reaches an elevation of 1,215 m/3,986 ft with Mt Atáviros. The land slopes gradually down to the coasts, is abundant with water and woods and is used for farming, particularly in coastal regions. One of the largest concentrations of hotels in Greece has built up in and around Rhodes town and between the island's capital and Líndos. But away from the tourist attractions, particularly in the south, the island is still today relatively unspoiled.

The island of Rhodes had already been settled by the Neolithic period, but its cultural heyday only began after its colonization by Dorian Greeks. Their three cities, Líndos, Ialysós and Kámiros, belonged to the Hexápolis (»Six Cities«) that fell under the domination of the Persians around 500 BC. Rhodes was a member of the Delian League in the 5th century BC. About 408 BC, the famous town planner, **Hippodamus of Miletus** laid out a plan for the new capital, which in the 4th century BC became a trading hub that surpassed even Athens. The wealthy, independent island-state's landmark, the **Colossus of Rhodes**, a bronze statue about 34 m/111 ft high of the sun god Helios, was one of the Seven Wonders of the World. It is thought to have served as a lighthouse in the Mandráki harbour of Rhodes, on the site of the Nikólaos castle. With the expansion of Roman domination in the Orient, Rhodes' economic importance declined, but the city continued to be a cultural centre with well-known schools of rhetoric – attended by Cicero and Caesar – and a major school for sculptors. The famous **Laocoon group**, which can be seen today in the Vatican Museum in Rome, was produced here during the reign of Emperor Tiberius (AD 14 – 37). Rhodes was fought over during the Middle Ages by the Arabs, Byzantines, Venetians and Genoese until it was finally taken by the Knights of St John in 1309. The »Knights of Rhodes« built up Rhodes Town into a huge fortress and defended the island against the Egyptians and Ottoman Turks until they had to relinquish it to the Ottoman sultan, Suleiman the Magnificent, in 1523. After almost 400 years of Ottoman rule, the island was occupied by the Italians in 1912 during the Italo-Turkish War and in 1947 was made a part of the Kingdom of Greece.

✳ ✳ Rhodes Town

Incomparable medieval Old Town
The town of Rhodes has been the capital of the island since its founding in 408 BC and is today also the administrative centre of Nomos Dodekaníssou. It was once generously laid out according to the principles of Hippodamus of Miletus in a system of streets intersecting at right angles and stretched from the heights of the acropolis in the west down to the east coast. Some of the streets in the considerably smaller medieval town – Street of the Knights, Omirou Street, Ippodamou Street and Pythagoras Street – still follow the ancient street grid. The **Colachium**, the district of the knights, with the Grand Master's Palace, the hospital and domiciles, occupied the somewhat rectangular northern section of town. The larger southern section of the walled city, called the **Burgus**, was home to the Greeks. The western part became the Turkish quarter and the eastern part was the Jewish quarter, which existed up into the Second World War. The old town, declared a UNESCO World Heritage Site in 1988, presents a unique image of a medieval town with its impressive Knights Hospitaller buildings. Turkish buildings, above all the mosques, add a further charming accent. Despite mass tourism, the old town, with its restaurants, shops and beautiful squares, possesses a fascinating atmosphere.

Town Wall
The impressive town wall, dating from the 15th / 16th centuries, with its towers, bastions and moat, encircles the old town, where no Christian was allowed to live during the Turkish occupation from 1523 to 1912. The **Amboise Gate**, built in 1512 under Grand Master Emery d' Amboise in the northwest, and the **Harbour Gate** from 1468, with reliefs of St Mary, in the northeast at the commercial harbour are particularly beautiful. The defence of the individual sections of the town wall was assigned to the eight »tongues«, i.e. the geographic-cultural subgroupings of the order. There is a superb view of the Grand Master's Palace and the old town from the wall between Canon Gate and Koskinou Gate (entrance at the Grand Master's Palace).

▶ VISITING RHODES TOWN

INFORMATION
Tourist Information
Alexandrou Papagou 31
Rhodes Town
Tel. 22 41 04 43 35 / 6
Fax 22 41 02 69 55
www.rodos.gr

GETTING THERE
Boat services to and from Alexandroupolis and Piraeus on the mainland and the islands of Amorgós, Astypálea, Chálki, Chíos, Donoussa, Kálymnos, Kárpathos, Kos, Crete, Léros, Lésbos, Límnos, Megísti, Mílos, Mýkonos, Náxos, Nísyros, Páros, Pátmos, Sámos, Sými, Sýros and Tílos.

EVENING OUT
Indulging in the nightlife in Rhodes Town is hardly a problem. Bars, discos and nightclubs are lined up one after the other, particularly along Odos Orfanidi in the new part of town.

SHOPPING
Souvenir shops crowd the alleyways of the old town, especially in Odós Soukratoú. The city is known for its jewellery, fur and leather goods and many shops selling them can be found here. Food commodities are mainly on offer in the Néa Agorá, the covered new market with an oriental flavour on Mandráki harbour, and fashion can be found in the area around Platía Kiprou.

WHERE TO EAT
▶ Expensive
① Kontiki
Mandráki harbour
Tel. 22 41 02 03 02
www.kontiki.gr

Elegant restaurant / café on a two-storied, floating pontoon in the harbour; two Dutch Michelin-starred chefs run the kitchen; fantastic view of the Grand Master's Palace and the sea.

Souvenir hunting in the old town

▶ Moderate
② Romeo
Menekleous 7 – 9
Tel. 22 41 07 44 02
The idyllic atmosphere in the 500-year-old house with its beautiful courtyard and fine food always make a visit in »Romeo« appealing.

▶ Inexpensive
③ Oasis
Platía Dorieos
The good, plain cooking in this eatery opposite the Redjeb Pasha Mosque is enjoyed beneath shady trees.

▶ Inexpensive

④ *Socratous Garden*
Odós Socratou 126
Tel. 22 41 02 01 53
Pretty garden restaurant, where, in a pleasantly calm atmosphere, you can take a coffee break or have a drink in the evening.

The small Andreas guesthouse in a 500-year-old building

WHERE TO STAY

▶ Luxury

① *Grand Hotel Rhodes*
Akti Miaouli 1

Tel. 22 41 05 47 00
www.mitsishotels.com
400 rooms, 10 suites
A hotel rich in tradition with very spacious rooms, a well-tended garden, a generously-sized swimming pool, a shopping arcade and a nightclub located across from the beach on the coastal road in the new part of town.

▶ Mid-range

② *Andreas*
Odós Omirou 28d
Tel. 22 41 03 41 56
www.hotelandreas.com
11 rooms
This little guesthouse is distinguished by its lovely setting in a medieval house and the view out over the roofs of the old town enjoyed from the breakfast terrace.

▶ Budget

③ *Via-Via*
Odós Pythagoras 45
Tel. 22 41 07 70 27
www.hotel-via-via.com
Small, quietly situated guesthouse with individually furnished rooms, attractive roof terrace and sumptuous breakfast buffet.

Platía Símis Eleftherías or Arsenal Gate leads into the bustling old town with its maze of narrow lanes, its domes and minarets set between palms and plane trees. Símis Square with the remains of a temple to Aphrodite (3rd century BC) and a collection of contemporary Greek paintings in a historic building is where its starts.

Platía Argyrokástrou Adjoining to the south is picturesque Argyrokástrou Square. Standing in its centre is a small fountain made from pieces of early Christian baptismal fonts and on the west side is the old hospital dating from the 14th century. The Hotel de la Langue d'Auvergne, built at the end of the 15th century, has a romantic inner court. A passageway leads to the southeast to the 13th-century church of Panagía tou Kástrou in which the **Byzantine museum** is found. On the south side

Rhodes Old Town Map

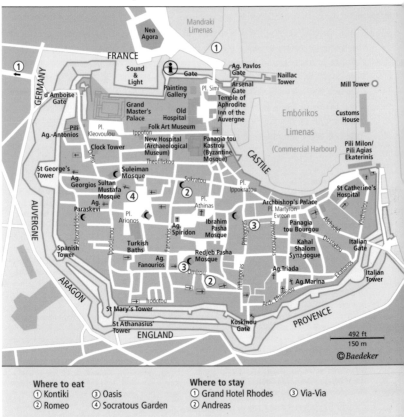

Where to eat
① Kontiki   ③ Oasis
② Romeo   ④ Socratous Garden

Where to stay
① Grand Hotel Rhodes   ③ Via-Via
② Andreas

© Baedeker

of the square, the **folk arts museum** presents exhibits from the Dodecanese Turkish period.

Standing obliquely opposite the Byzantine museum on Platía
Mousíou is the massive hospital of the order, built in the year 1440,
where today an archaeological museum is housed. From the inner
courtyard, a staircase leads up to the imposing infirmary on the
upper floor divided in two by a series of arcades. Worth noting about
the interior are the plain late Gothic chapel niches and decoration
on the capitals as well as the tomb slabs. Among the most significant
exhibits in the museum are the two Archaic kouroi (6th century BC)
and the grave stele of Krito and Timarista (late 5th century BC), a
life-size Aphrodite, the famous Hellenistic head of Helios (2nd cen-

★
**Archaeological
museum**

tury BC) and a small crouching figure of Aphrodite (1st century BC). Some of the rooms contain a fine collection spanning all periods, from the Mycenaean onwards (opening hours: Tue – Sun 8.30am –7pm).

Street of the Knights ✶✶

One of the major attractions on Rhodes is Odós Ippotón, the Street of the Knights, which begins north of the new hospital, because it still looks much as it did in the 15th / 16th centuries. Most of the inns were in this street, i.e., the meeting houses of the individual »tongues« of the Order. The most beautiful is the **Auberge de France**, built between 1492 and 1503. Above the door are the coats of arms of the order and of the grand master, Emery d' Amboise.

Grand Master's Palace ✶

Towering up on the highest point of the town, at the end of the Street of the Knights, is the Grand Master's Palace. The 14th-century castle with a triple ring of defensive walls was rebuilt after the earthquake of 1481 by Grand Master **Pierre d' Aubusson**. The palace was almost completely destroyed in the year 1856 when the gunpowder stored in the neighbouring church of St John exploded. The palace was reconstructed during the Italian occupation (1912 – 1943), but not true to the original plans. Nor do the furnishings correspond to their original state. Above all worth noting are some of the floor mosaics from the island of Kos, for example, in the Arcade Room. There is also a copy of the Laocoon Group, created in the 1st century, one of the most famous works in the tradition of Rhodian sculpture. Exhibits on the ground floor and lower floor illustrate the history of the island (opening hours: May – Oct Mon 12.30pm – 7.30pm, Tue – Sun 8am – 7.30pm; Nov – April Tue – Sun 8.30am –3pm).

! ***Baedeker* TIP**

Want your own Greek antique?
If you always thought a Greek antique would look good in your home, then take a look around the shop in the archaeological museum on Platía Simis. Replicas of well-known Greek schulptures, icons, coins and reliefs can be purchased there (opening hours: Mon – Fri 8am – 2.30pm, Sat 9am – 2.30pm).

Clock Tower

To the south of the Grand Master's Palace stands a prominent clock tower (1852), which can be climbed. To the southeast is the Suleiman Mosque, which was built in 1808. It has a beautiful Renaissance portal. Opposite is the Turkish library (1794).

Ágios Geórgios ✶

The Ágios Geórgios church, west of the mosque, is one of the most beautiful on Rhodes. The tetraconch was constructed at the close of the 14th century and, in 1447, was turned into a monastery church with a western narthex and a northern portico. The typical Rhodian arrangement of the niches in the tambour both inside

Ippókratou Square, the heart of the old town, lies in the Turkish quarter.

and out is worth noting. The Turks used the church as a madrasah (Islamic school).

The **Odós Sokrátous**, one of the town's most beautiful and most popular shopping streets, leads from the Suleiman mosque to Platía Ippókratous, the pulsating heart of the old town, with its tavernas and cafés. The square is dominated by the **Castellania**, which was built in 1503 and once served as the market administration building and as a court of commercial disputes and today houses the municipal library.

Platía Ippókratous

Further to the southeast is the atmospheric Platía Evréon Martýrion, the »Square of the Jewish Martyrs«, which was given this name to commemorate the Jews deported from Rhodes during the Second World War. Also standing there are the **Seahorse Fountain** and the 15th century **Palace of the Admiralty**, which was probably once the palace of the metropolitan (archbishop).

Platía Martýrion Evréon

Sprawling out to the south of Sokrátous street is a picturesque maze of lanes flanking Fanouriou street, Omirou street (both arched over by flying buttresses) and Pythagorou street. A couple of mosques provide a Turkish flair, including the Sultan Mustafa Mosque (1765) on charming Platía Ariónos. Opposite is a magnificent Turkish bath. Kahal Shalom Synagogue, in Dosiadou street south of Efréon Martírion Square, was once in the heart of the Jewish quarter and was

South of the Old Town

church. There are nice beaches to the east at Stégna. Further south is St Theodore church with valuable frescoes (1377).

Malóna   Malóna, located away from the main road 6 km/4 mi southwest of Archángelos, is a pretty village in the midst of orange and lemon-tree groves. The route runs past Mássari and the well-known 14th-century church of Ágios Geórgios Lórima, with its remarkable frescoes, and then on through picturesque countryside to Lárdos and beyond to the southwest in the direction of Gennádi. A detour can be undertaken from Kiotári to Asklipío, in the northwest, where the impressive church of Kímisis tis Theotókou (13th / 14th century) can be found.

Lachaniá   A turn-off 3 km/2 mi outside of Gennádi leads to Lachaniá, with its idyllic platía. Located at the southern edge of the village is Agía Iríni church, featuring a Baroque tower and an early Christian baptismal font from the 6th century. Lying on a wide, sandy beach, 6 km/4 mi further to the south, is Plimmíri. The abandoned monastery of Ágios Pávlos lies on the road to **Kattaviá**, which is the site of Kímisis tis Theotókou church, whose earliest parts date back to the 14th century.

★ ★ Líndos

UNESCO World Heritage City   Líndos is one of the major attractions on Rhodes, and for good reason. The town, with its low, white houses loomed over by a medieval castle and an ancient acropolis, is stunningly situated on a high rock between two bays. Drivers must stop their vehicles on Platía Eleftherías at the town's entrance and proceed on foot or by donkey. Odós Akropoleos, lined by cafés, souvenir shops and travel agents, leads into the heritage-protected town. The houses in its poetic lanes all date from the 17th / 18th centuries, except the Turkish one from 1599. The Captain's House, with its natural stone façade decorated with characteristic reliefs in the southern part of town, is a landmark. Archaeological evidence dating from the Neolithic period has confirmed that this site on the island's only natural harbour has been occupied since the 3rd millennium BC. During the Dorian period, Líndos was the most powerful city-state on the island and owned over half of it. It reached its full flouring in the 7th and 6th centuries BC under the tyrant **Kleoboulos**, who was one of the Seven Sages.

Anthony Quinn Bay near Ladikó is one →
of the most beautiful spots on the Aegean Islands.

The acropolis offers a wonderful view of the Bay of Líndos.

Construction was started on a Byzantine castle on the acropolis in the 6th century, which was enlarged into a massive bulwark in the 15th century by the Knights of St John.

Panagía church Along the way to the acropolis is the beautiful Panagía church, built in the 14th century and enlarged in 1489 / 1490. Its richly-decorated and gilded iconostasis and its kochláki floor are both magnificent. It barrel vaulting and dome were decorated with paintings in 1779.

Ágios Geórgios
Chostós ▶ Not far to the northeast stand the oldest church on Rhodes, the Ágios Geórgios Chostós. It dates from the 8th / 9th centuries and has very rare frescoes from the time of the Iconoclastic Controversy.

✶ ✶
Acropolis A staircase just inside the entrance to the acropolis leads to a small square with three cisterns and a Byzantine tower looming up on its east side. Next to it is an exedra with a plinth on which a consecrated figure probably stood (3rd / 4th centuries). The inscription on the back says that a priest, Aglochartos, decorated the acropolis with olive trees. The relief of a warship next to it on the right was created in honour of Admiral Hagesander Mikkion in the 2nd century BC. A vaulted gateway leads into the ground floor of the Knights of St John building. In the vault to the left are steps cut into the stone, dating from the Archaic period. Outside is another exedra (3rd century BC). It says in the inscription that the priest, Pamphilidas, had commissioned a statue of himself from the famous sculptor, **Phyles**. The temple behind it (3rd century) is dedicated to the prophesying de-

mon, Psithyros. The 87 m/285 ft long stoa, one of the most out-standing Hellenistic structures in Greece, was built at the close of the 3rd century BC. Standing to the right of the stoa is the 13th-century Byzantine church, St John's. A wide stairway leads to the propylaea built in the early 3rd century, patterned after those in Athens with five doorways in its back wall opening into the **sacred precinct**. The precinct consists of a courtyard lined with columns, with an Ionic columned hall added in the 2nd century, and a comparably modest **temple to Athena Lindia**, which was built as an amphiprostyle on the site of a previous building from the 7th century BC after a fire in 342 BC (opening hours: summer Tue to Sun 8am – 7pm, off season: Tue – Sun 8.30am – 2.30pm).

Below the town is the beautiful **Pállas Bay** and on the other side of the acropolis is the almost completely enclosed **Ágios Pávlos Bay**. The apostle Paul is said to have sought refuge here from a storm while sailing from Ephesus to Syria in the year 51.

★
Beaches

From Rhodes Town to Apolakkiá

The 82 km/51 mi drive to Apolakkiá follows the coastline along the west side of the island. Head out of Rhodes Town in a southwest di-rection. There are some icons worth seeing in the church of Panagía Kremastí in the little holiday village of Kremastí. A side road branch-ing off at Kato Kalamónas leads (7 km/4 mi) to **Petaloudes**, the idyllic »Valley of the Butterflies«, where at one time at the height of summer thousands of orange-and-brown Jersey Tiger moths could be seen, a rare variety that spends the day sit-ting on tree trunks. The moths were regularly startled by hand-claps in order for tourists to see the colours clearly, which eventu-ally drove most of them away (open to the public 8.30am to sunset). Lying 4 km/2.5 mi west of

Kremastí

> **!** *Baedeker* TIP
>
> ### Trip to an ostrich farm
>
> About 2 km/1.2 mi before coming to Petaloudes is a road leading off to the right to an ostrich farm less than a mile away. There you can not only see the huge birds, but try an ostrich burger as well and purchase goods hand-made from ostrich leather, such as handbags and belts (opening hours: daily 9am to 7.30pm).

Kalavarda is the partially excavated ancient city of **Kámiros** (6th cen-tury BC – 6th century AD) with temple precinct, agorá, cisterns, baths and residences – a typical example of the layout of a Hellenistic city in a beautiful setting (opening hours: May – Sept Tue – Fri 8.30am – 7pm, Sat and Sun until 3pm).

Not only are there good fish restaurants in the little fishing village of Kámiros Skála, but also tour boats to the island of Chálki just off the coast. Looming up some 2 km/1.2 mi to the southwest is Kastéllos Kamíros, the best preserved of the Knights of St John castles on the island.

◄ Kámiros
Skála

Émbonas   It's worth making a detour to Émbonas, the »wine capital« of Rhodes, a popular excursion destination for wine-tastings and folklore evenings.

✱
Profitis Ilías   Émbonas is the starting point for a tour through extremely beautiful scenery to Mt Profítis Ilías (highly recommended). Drive about 10 km/6 mi in a northeasterly direction to the turnoff that runs to the north along the foot of the mountain. The 796 m/2,612 ft peak, the second-highest on Rhodes, has flora unusual for Greece, including pine trees, spruce and oak, with cyclamen, arbutus and orchids. It cannot be climbed (restricted military area), but it does offer fantas-

✱
Ágios Nikólaos   tic scenery. Another 10 km/6 mi further on past the church of Ágios
Fountoukli ►   Nikólaos Fountoukli, a remarkable tetraconch built sometime in the 14th / 15th centuries, is Eleoussa, where there are Italian buildings dating from 1943. From here it is possible either to drive to the east coast via Archípoli or return to the west coast route.

✱
Monólithos   The road running above the west coast occasionally opens up to magnificent panoramas before reaching the village of Monólithos. Towering up 280 m/919 ft in a stunning setting 2 km/1.2 mi to the southwest is Monólithos rock, crowned by an imposing castle built by the Knights of St John in 1476.

Apolakkiá ►   The road finally reaches Apolakkiá, a quiet village with few tourists and lonely, wild coastal scenery.

Neighbouring Islands

Chálki   Chálki, a 28 sq km/11 sq mi rocky island off the west coast of Rhodes, is a nice place for an outing. About 300 people live permanently in the principal town, **Embório**, also called Chálki. The sandy beach in **Potamós Bay**, not far from Embório, is popular. The historic village of Chorió has two very old churches, but otherwise just a lot of ruins. Tour boats can be taken from Chálki to the uninhabited island of **Alimniá** lying to the east, where there are some enticing sandy beaches.

✱
Sými   Sými, one of the most picturesque islands in the Aegean, rises steeply out of the sea 45 km/28 mi north of Rhodes, not far from the Turkish coast, and is surrounded by a number of small islands. Its furrowed coastline is punctuated by numerous, deeply cut coves and long peninsulas. Tour boats with day-trippers arrive here several times a day from Rhodes.

✱
Sými Town ►   The island's principal town is regarded as one of the most beautiful places in Greece. The white-and-earth-coloured houses spreading up a slope at the end of a deep bay present an enchanting picture. The town of Sými consists of two parts, which have now merged together. Awaiting the visitor in **Giálos**, the lower part of town gathered around the harbour, are many cafés, restaurants and shops, in which

The principal town of Sými is one of the most picturesque towns in Greece with its old houses spreading up the slopes.

not only the usual souvenirs are sold, but also sponges and spices. Many mansions (archontiká) can still be discovered here, too, which have been renovated in the wake of increasing tourism. Several hundred steps lead from the heart of town at the rear end of the bay up the Kalí Stráta (»Beautiful Street«) to the quieter upper town, the **Chorió**, where there is a nice view of the harbour. Overlooking the Chorió is a rock with a medieval Knights of St John castle. Do not miss taking a look inside the old pharmacy (Symotikon Farmakion) in the Chorió, which still has its original furnishings. In addition, a small **museum** – the way there is sign-posted – offers displays of traditional costumes, coins and archaeological finds.

Some 4 km/2.5 mi to the northwest of Sými Town lies the old fishing village of Nimbório in a cove with a pebble beach, now more of a quiet summer resort. Tavernas and accommodations are available for tourists and nice mosaics can still be seen in the ruins of an early Christian basilica.

◀ Nimbório

Almost all excursion boats going to Sými also stop at the Panormítis monastery, dedicated to Archangel Michael, in the bay of the same name in the south of the island. The monastery that already existed in the Byzantine period was re-founded in the 18th century and is one of the most important pilgrimage sites in the Dodecanese. The focus of veneration is the richly carved and gilded iconostasis with an icon of the Archangel, Michael. Pilgrims flock to the monastery in large numbers at Whitsun and on 8 November, a feast of St Michael in the Orthodox Church.

★
◀ Moní
Panormítis

✳ Sámos · Σάμος

Island Group: North East Aegean
Islands
Population: 32,000

Area: 476 sq km/184 sq mi
Altitude: 0 – 1,433 m/4,701 ft
Capital: Sámos Town (Vathý)

It was not only its sweet red wine that made Sámos in the east Aegean a popular place to spend holidays. The green and wooded island with an abundance of water offers a wide variety of scenery with many places to hike and a ragged coastline with a large number of sandy and pebble beaches.

History Geographically, Sámos is a promontory of Asia Minor; it is only separated from the Dilek peninsula on the Turkish coast by a strait not quite 2 km/1.2 mi wide. The island rises up in the west to 1,433 m/4,701 ft with **Mt Kérkis**. The major forest fires of 1990 and 2000 destroyed about 80 % of the island's trees.

▶ VISITING SÁMOS

INFORMATION

Tourist Information
Themistkli Sofouli
Sámos Town
Tel. 22 73 02 85 82
Fax 22 73 02 85 83

GETTING THERE

Boat services to and from Alexandroupolis and Piraeus on the mainland and the islands of Agathoníssi, Chíos, Fourni, Ikaría, Kálymnos, Kos, Léros, Lésbos, Límnos, Lipsí, Mýkonos, Náxos, Páros, Pátmos, Rhodes, Sámos and Sýros.

WHERE TO EAT

▶ Moderate

Christos
Sámos Town
Good food and large servings on a small square opposite the large Platía Agiou Nikolaou.

To Kýma
Karlóvasi
Tel. 22 73 03 40 17
The best way to enjoy their delicious seafood platters is with a beautiful sunset.

▶ Inexpensive

Taverna Gregori
Sámos Town
Fast, friendly service and generous portions are the attractions of this taverna.

WHERE TO STAY

▶ Mid-range

Arion
Kokkari
Tel. 22 73 09 20 20
www.arion-hotel.gr
108 rooms
The hotel, 600 m/660 yd from the beach, consists of a main building and chalets.

Sámos Map

The island gained its greatest political and economic power in the 6th century BC under the tyrant, Polycrates. Following the uprising in 440 BC, the island was subjugated by Pericles and served as a base for the Athenian fleet until the end of the Peloponnesian War. Sámos was the birthplace of the mathematician and philosopher **Pythagoras** (► Famous People), the philosopher **Epicurus** (341 – 271 BC) and the astronomer, **Aristarchus** (c. 310 to c. 230 BC), who anticipated the Copernican model of the solar system and attempted to determine the distance between the earth and the moon and sun.

What to See on Sámos

Since 1832, when the town of Sámos (pop. 8,000) was founded, it has been the island's capital. It spreads out in a semi-circle around the harbour bay of Vathý and climbs picturesquely up the mountain slope with olive groves and grape vines to the upper town, **Áno Vathý**. The city has a central square (Platía Pythagoria) on its pretty harbour promenade with marble lions, several churches, including the bishop's church, Mitropolis, the church of St Spyridon and a Roman Catholic cathedral, as well as picturesque lanes and stairs.

★
Sámos Town (Vathý)

The archaeological museum, housed in an old and a new building by the municipal park, displays finds from the **Heraion**, including the almost 5 m/16 ft tall, colossal Archaic statue of a figure of a kouros (c. 580 – 570 BC), perhaps a dedicatory figure that stood on the Sacred Way. There is also a larger-than-life statue of a woman dating from the Archaic period (c. 570 BC). The base and three figures of the original six have survived from the archaic group by the sculptor, **Geneleos** (c. 560 BC). There are also bronze, wooden and ivory statuettes, and ceramic pottery and figurines.

★
◄ Archaeological museum

Daylight departs – blue hours in Pythagório

Zoodóchos Pigí Zoodóchos Pigí, founded in 1756, is certainly worth seeing. It is 11 km/7 mi northeast of Sámos Town, in a fantastic setting high above the sea. A superb view of Turkey can be enjoyed from there.

✱
Pythagório The pleasant port of Pythagório, 15 km/9 mi south of Sámos, lies on the eastern south coast on the site of the ancient city of Sámos. It was called Tigani until 1955, when it was renamed in honour of **Pythagoras**, the mathematician born there. With its well-preserved town centre and attractive harbour promenade, it has developed into a place often frequented by tourists. The foundations of both the harbour jetty and the **city wall** (4th century BC) that once had 35 towers and 12 gates are of archaic origin. The Metamórfosis church from 1824 stands on the kástro hill, along with the ruins of the fortress built (1822–1824) by the freedom fighter **Lykourgos Pythagório Logothetis**. A Hellenistic villa was unearthed next to it, on top of which a 5th century Christian basilica had been built. On display in the small **museum** in the mayor's office are Archaic and Hellenistic grave steles, portraits of Roman emperors and the sitting figure of Aeacus, the father of the tyrant, Polycrates. The monastery of **Panagía Spilianí**, with the cave from which it took its name, lie in the eastern area of the ancient part of the city.

✱
Eupalineíon ▶ Lying further to the north is the entrance to the 1,036 m/3,400 ft aqueduct designed by Eupalinos of Megara. The tunnel, built with a diameter of about 1.6 m/5 ft between 538 and 522 BC, channelled water into the city from the other side of the mountain in clay pipes set in separate ditches with an average incline of 0.5° and was in operation for about 1,000 years. A good 400 m/440 yd from the southern entrance, the spot can be seen where the two shafts, tunnelled in
🕐 from either side, met almost precisely (opening hours: daily 8.45am – 2.45pm).

The famous Heraion of Sámos lies 9 km/5.6 mi west of Pythagório. ★
According to tradition, the Ionian immigrants led by **Procles** found   Heraion
a wooden cult image of the goddess Hera at the mouth of the river
Imbrasos wrapped in the branches
of a chasteberry tree. The first altar
was built next to the chasteberry
tree, followed by others. The seventh was the partially reconstructed **Altar of Rhoïkos** (c. 550
BC), which was only surpassed in
size and splendour by the Pergamon altar. The Samians built the
Hera temple west of the altar. After
the first modest wooden temple
(8th century BC) and second (after
670 BC), Rhoïkos and Theodoros
built a colossal stone temple (temple III) between 570 and 550 BC,
whose double peristasis (dipteral)
consisted of 104 Ionic columns. It

> **!** *Baedeker* TIP
>
> **Folklore museum in a holiday village**
> Outside of Pythagório, in the direction of the
> airport, is the large holiday resort of Dóryssa Bay,
> built to resemble a Samian village. Along with
> Neo-classical villas and small fishermen cottage,
> there is also a village square with a church and a
> coffee-house. The tools used by farmers, basket
> makers, fishermen and beekeepers are on display
> in the folklore museum. It is occasionally
> possible to watch a potter or smithy at work in
> the historical workshops.

was destroyed soon afterwards, but Polycrates ordered a new building, temple IV. Covering an area of 112 x 55 m/367 x 180 ft, it was the
largest temple ever designed by the Greeks, but was never finished.
All but its massive foundation and the stump of a single column has
disappeared. Another peripteros temple (temple V) followed later
with 4 : 6 columns in which the cult image was placed (opening ⊙
hours: Tue – Sun 8.30am –3pm).

Predominantly agricultural Mytiliní, 12 km/7.5 mi southwest of   Mytilini
Sámos Town, has an interesting **palaeontological museum** that displays important fossils of rhinoceroses, dwarf ancestors of the horse,
short-necked giraffes, antelopes and hyenas found in the basalt tuff
in the area dating back around 10 million years.

The north coast's scenery is particularly attractive with narrow val-   Island tour
leys and terraced slopes. Drive first along the predominantly cliff-
lined north coast to the lively holiday village of **Kokkari**. Turn left beyond Avlákia to the **winegrowing village of Vourliótes**, a popular
place for outings. It is only another 2 km/1.2 mi from there to the
monastery of Vrontianí, founded in 1566. To see some fantastic scenery, take a side trip beyond the bridge at Platanákia into the shady
woodland valley of Aïdónia and on to Manolátes.
The coastal road next comes to the harbour town of **Karlóvassi**, the
economic centre of the west of the island. The west coast is picturesque but isolated and is only accessible with off-road vehicles and
on foot over steep paths. The return to Sámos Town is through the
mountainous interior by way of Marathókambos with the nearby Pythagoras' Cave and Chóra.

Hiking on Mt Kérkis A hike on 1,433 m/4,701 ft Mt Kérkis in the west of the island is strenuous but rewarding. The trail starts at the little bathing resort of **Votsolakia** and leads up past the still occupied Evangelístrias monastery (675 m/2,215 ft), then on to Profítis Ilías chapel (1,150 m/ 3,772 ft) and finally the summit, where there is a broad sweeping view of the Aegean and the mountains of Asia Minor. The trail is well marked. The ascent takes about four hours and the return about three. The descent by way of Marathokámpos, which is not as steep but takes an hour longer, is recommended.

✳ Samothráki · Σαμοθράκη

N / O 4

Island Group: North East Aegean Islands

Altitude: 0 – 1,611 m/5,285 ft

Capital: Samothráki Chóra

Area: 178 sq km/68.7 sq mi

Population: 2,900

Samothráki, Greece's most northerly island, is dominated by the mighty 1,611 m/5,285 ft Mt Fengári, whose wild and rugged mountain countryside is ideal for hiking tours.

The rituals performed in the Cabeiri Sanctuary remain wrapped in mystery.

 VISITING SAMOTHRÁKI

INFORMATION

Tourist Information
Main town, Samothráki Chóra

GETTING THERE

Boat services to and from Alexandroupolis and Kávala on the mainland and the islands of Chíos, Lésbos, Límnos and Mýkonos.

WHERE TO EAT

► Moderate

I Plateía
Main square, Samothráki Chóra
Tel. 25 51 04 12 24
If you like unusually prepared seafood, this is the place for you.

Klimitaria
on the shore raod
Kamariótissa
Tel. 25 51 04 15 35
Pleasant taverna popular with the locals offering a large selection of dishes.

WHERE TO STAY

► Mid-range

Aélos
Kamariótissa
Tel. 25 51 04 15 95; 56 rooms
Quiet hotel with swimming pool, located a bit above the town.

History

Around 1000 BC, Samothráki was populated by Thracians, who built the **sanctuary of the Great Gods** (Cabeiri). The Greeks arrived on the island about 700 BC. They enlarged the sanctuary and merged the cult with the Olympic gods. The cult began to spread in the Hellenistic world in the early 3rd century BC. Under the Romans (from 168 BC), the Cybele cult from Asia Minor became linked to the Great Gods. Despite being repeatedly destroyed by pirates, wars and earthquakes, the sanctuary continued to exist into the 4th century AD. It took Christianity to put an end to it around the year 400, but the town of Palaiópolis, lying to the east, remained populated down into the 15th century.

What to see on Samothráki

★ Samothráki Chóra

The port of Kamariótissa has little to offer besides some hotels and castle ruins. The island's beautiful principal town, Samothráki Chóra (pop. 1,600), lies to the east in the mountains, rising up two steep slopes. It is almost unique in Greece in that it has completely remained as it originally was.

★ Sanctuary of the Cabeiri

The ruins of the sanctuary of the Cabeiri, the Great Gods, are above the island's ancient capital, Palaiópolis, 5 km/3 mi north of the Chóra. They are impressively located in a scenic setting in an ascending valley cleft. The Agía Paraskeví chapel and the rubble of a Gattelusi castle on the mountain slope mark the site of the ancient harbour.

Sanctuary of the Cabeiri *Plan*

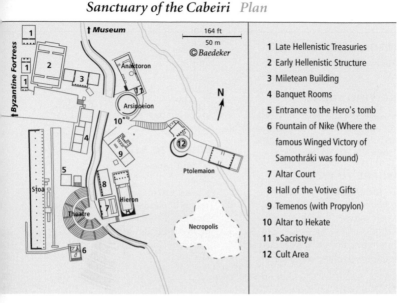

↑ *Museum*

164 ft
50 m
© *Baedeker*

↑ Byzantine Fortress

Anaktoron
Arsinoeion
Ptolemaion
Stoa
Hieron
Thuatre
Necropolis

N ↑

1 Late Hellenistic Treasuries
2 Early Hellenistic Structure
3 Miletean Building
4 Banquet Rooms
5 Entrance to the Hero's tomb
6 Fountain of Nike (Where the famous Winged Victory of Samothráki was found)
7 Altar Court
8 Hall of the Votive Gifts
9 Temenos (with Propylon)
10 Altar to Hekate
11 »Sacristy«
12 Cult Area

The fact that little is still known about the **mystery cult** is due to its nature. The initiated were sworn to secrecy. Moreover, several cults had been superimposed on each other during the course of the centuries. The cult of the Cabeiri arrived from Phrygia in Asia Minor in the pre-Greek period. Even the ancient Greeks no longer knew the meaning of the word and the deities meant by it were never exactly fixed. In the centre, at any rate, was **Cybele**, the »Great Mother« of all life, an ancient fertility goddess. Other gods were added on Samothráki, including the Thracian mother goddess, Axieros, as goddess of nature, along with Axiokersos and Axiokersa, a pair of underworld deities, and the youthful Kadmilos, god of vegetation and the phallus. They were venerated as protective gods of nature and later became more and more the patrons of sailors and those in distress at sea. The initiation into the mysteries, which took place in two steps, was open to all, Greeks and non-Greeks, men and women, free men and slaves – which undoubtedly cleared the way for the later spread of the cult.

Anaktoron ► A sign-posted walk leads to the southeast from the museum past a viewpoint to the Anaktoron (c. 550 BC), the »House of the Lords« or »House of the Gods«. The believers received here the first degree of consecration. The northern part was sectioned off as the holy of holies. Adjoining to the south is the **Sacristy**, in which a list of the names of the initiated was kept.

Arsinoion ► The Arsinoion, a place for sacrificial offerings, was built with a donation of the later queen of Egypt, **Arsinoë II**, between 289 and 281 BC and, with a diameter of over 20 m/66 ft, was the largest roofed rotunda in Greek Antiquity. It was built on the location of an ancient cult site, a stone altar of which has been uncovered.

Altars dating from the cult's early period can be found in the area between the Arsinoion and the Temenos adjoining to the south. The shrine, financed by **Philip II** and built about 350 BC, had an Ionic propylon with the archaized dancers' frieze.

◄ Temenos

The Hieron stands with its columned front up-righted again on the middle terrace. The Doric building (c. 325 BC), which had a columned portico added in the 2nd century BC, has an apse that was provided with a crypt in the Roman period, making it reminiscent of the floor plan of a Christian church.

◄ Hieron

Lying parallel to the Hieron is the Hall of Votive Gifts (6th century BC) and the Altar Court built between 340 and 330 BC, whose portico presumably served as the stage wall for a theatre built around 200 BC and largely destroyed today. Visible to the south of the theatre is the Nike Fountain, where pieces of the famous 2.4 m/8 ft Winged Victory made of Parian marble was found. It was created in 190 BC, possibly the work of the Rhodian sculptor **Pythekritos**, to commemorate Rhodes' victory over Antiochos III of Syria, and stands today in the Louvre in Paris. A replica is on display at the **archaeological museum** in the southeast of the sanctuary, south of the propylon (c. 270 BC) built by the Egyptian king **Ptolemaeus II**, and next to the ancient cemetery (7th – 2nd centuries BC; opening hours: daily 8am – 7.30pm).

◄ Hall of Votive Gifts

Lying to the north of the sacred precinct is **Palaiópolis**, the ancient city of the Aeolian colonists, whose colossal 6th century BC wall extends up to the ridge of the mountain, but only very little has survived. The ruins of a castle erected in the 15th century by the Genoese Gattelusi family lie on the ancient acropolis hill.

Winged Victory of Samothrace

Bubbling out of a 10 m/33 ft sinter cone some 13 km/8 mi east of Palaiópolis is a 55°C/131°F hot spring. Loutrá, the thermal spa with thermae that developed here, is pleasantly situated in the midst of chestnut and plane tree forests. The island's villages, especially **Profítis Ilías**, are pretty and worth a visit. The best beaches are Pachia Ammos and Vatos, both about 8 km/5 mi southeast of Lákkoma. Kípos, far to the southwest, can also be recommended.

Loutrá

★★ Santorini · Thíra · Σαντορίνη · Θηρά

G 7

Island Group: Cyclades
Altitude: 0 – 566 m/1,857 ft
Capital: Thíra

Area: 76 sq km/29.3 sq mi
Population: 7,000

Santorini or Thíra, »the Wild Island«, the most southern of the larger Cycladic islands, is one of the most attractive travel destinations in Greece because of its unique volcanic landscape.

Unique volcanic island
Entering the huge, almost closed volcanic crater on a boat is a matchless experience. The white villages are breathtakingly situated,

 VISITING SANTORINI

INFORMATION

Tourist Information
In the travel agencies on the main square of Thíra

GETTING THERE

Boat services to and from Piraeus and Thessaloníki on the mainland and the islands of Anáfi, Folégandros, Kímolos, Crete, Kýthnos, Mílos, Mýkonos, Náxos, Páros, Sérifos, Sífnos, Síkinos, Skíathos, Sýros and Tínos.

WHERE TO EAT

► Expensive
Camille Stefani
Kamári
Tel. 22 86 03 17 16
French cuisine and house produced wines are served here.

► Moderate
Flame of Volcano
Thíra
Tel. 22 86 02 52 45
This restaurant features special sophisticated grilled dishes and has a fantastic view of the caldera.

► Inexpensive
Taverna Andréas
Kamári
Simple eatery that serves Greek food in large portions.

WHERE TO STAY

► Mid-range
Atlantis
Thíra
Tel. 22 86 02 22 32
www.atlantis.hotel.gr
25 rooms
Hotel with a long tradition, on the edge of the crater with a magnificent view.

Panorama
Thíra
Tel. 22 86 02 24 79
E-mail: santorama@otenet.gr
23 rooms
This hotel on the cliffs, not far from the heart of town, offers tastefully furnished rooms, a roof garden and a fantastic view of the caldera.

Ferries anchored on the sheer cliffs of Santorini

scattered along the steep cliffs of the crater's rim. Its ancient sites are among the most important in Greece. The dark, volcanic beaches on the east side of the island are also unique in the Cyclades.

Santorini, along with its neighbouring islands, **Thirasía** and **Asproní-si**, are part of a volcanic crater that sank into the sea. The rim of the caldera projecting out of the sea forms a ring, open in the northwest and southwest, with a diameter of between 12 – 18 km/7.5 – 11 mi, around deep basin up to 400 m/1,300 ft deep. The peaks of a new volcano, the **Kaméni Islands**, appeared in its centre. Hot springs and escaping gas testify to the continuing volcanic activity. The massive layers of ash, pumice and lava lie on a mountain of argillaceous shale and greywacke, covered by limestone. In the southeast, it forms Profítis Ilías (566 m/1,857 ft), on the northern point, Mávro Vounó and on the east coast, Monólithos. The crater falls away to the inner basin in cliffs of greyish-black lava with visible strips of white pumice and reddish tuff ranging in height from 200 to 400 m/660 to 1,300 ft. The outside of the crater with its thick covering of pumice gently slopes down to the sea, forming a fertile wine and garden landscape. **Geology**

Santorini was inhabited by Carians in the 3rd millennium BC Achaean Greek settlers arrived around 1900 BC. Excavations testify to a great flourishing in the first half of the 2nd millennium BC. **History**

Santorini Map

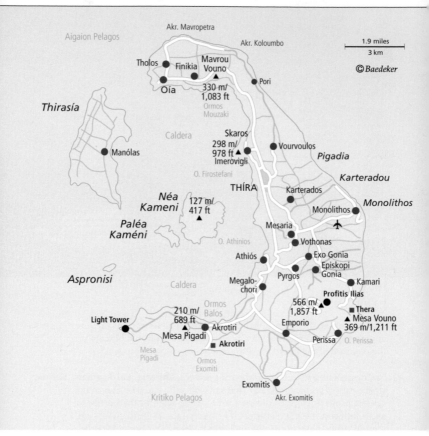

Although the island was in contact with Minoan Crete, it still developed its own culture. Akrotíri was probably not governed through a central power, but rather plutocratically administrated by merchants and shipowners, who sailed with their ships as far as Libya. The golden age ended about 1628 BC with the **explosion of Santorini's volcano**, in which more than half of the island literally burst into pieces and its centre sank into the sea (►Baedeker Special p. 478). After the volcanic eruption, the island remained uninhabited for half a millennium. It was not resettled again until the start of the 1st millennium BC, this time by Crete. A certain degree of prosperity was reached under the Egyptian Ptolemaic dynasty, who maintained a base there. The villages of Thíra and Ía were destroyed in an earthquake in 1956.

What to See on Santorini

The capital, Thíra (pop. 2,000), can be reached after disembarking at ★ ★
the port of **Skála** either on foot, by donkey along a steep path with   Thíra
almost 600 steps or by cable car. Passenger ships dock at **Athiniós**
harbour to the south. Buses travel from there to the town. Thíra is
extremely impressive with its white houses built on the rim of the
crater, its winding lanes and squares that constantly offer spectacular
new views, and the turquoise-blue domes of its churches and chapels. Towering up on the southern end of town is the magnificent
Mitrópolis church from 1956. The highlights of the new **museum of
prehistory** across from the bus terminal are some of the famous and
delightful frescoes from Akrotíri.

The **archaeological museum** shows
artefacts found on Santorini from
prehistoric to Roman times. A few
paces to the north is the Venetian
Ghisi family mansion, the **Megaron Gizi**, with interesting displays
on the island's history. It is located
in the former Catholic quarter
with cathedrals and a Dominican
convent.

i Wine tasting

■ Mésa Goniá, 2 km/1.2 mi east of Pýrgos, is
the centre of wine-growing on Santorini. In
September, anyone can take part in the
traditional wine pressing. Wineries here, and
in higher-lying Éxo Goniá, offer wine tastings.
The Boutari Winery has its visitors centre in
Megalochóri, 10 km/6 mi south of Thíra.

Sprawled out in a spectacular location on the crater's rim on the   Oía
northern tip of the main island is the tidy little town of Oía with
many tiny churches. It was rebuilt after the earthquake of 1956. The
maritime museum in an old mansion is worth visiting.

A road leads from Thíra up to the 566 m/1,857 ft summit of Profítis   **Profítis Ilías**
Ilías, which, despite being spoiled by radio masts, offers a magnificent panorama view. A path from the summit descends eastward
down to where the **necropolis of Thera** is lying on both flank of Sell-
áda ridge. Paths branch off there; the one to the left down to Kamári,
the one to the right to Baríssa and the one straight ahead runs to Mésa Vounó, past the church of Ágios Stéfanos, built on the site of an
early Christian basilica, and on to Evangelismós, a chapel with a heroon (2nd century BC) next to it.

The ruins of the ancient capital Thera are located 3 km/2 mi to the   ★
southwest of **Kamári** on Mésa Vounó, a rocky ridge with steep cliffs   Thera
on three of its sides. The city was founded about 1000 BC, was most
prosperous under Ptolemaic rule (300 – 150 BC) and was inhabited
into the 13th century. The excavations reproduce the conditions in
Hellenistic times. The **temple of Artemidoruo** (3rd century BC), a
Ptolemaic admiral, is at the start of the tour. Reliefs are carved in the
rocks, among them Artemidoros. A stepped path leads to the Ptolemaic garrison's barracks and gymnasium on the heights of Mésa

A volcano erupted in the caldera of Santorini in the 9th century (illustration from the »Illustrated London News«, 1866).

CATASTROPHE ON SANTORINI

What was most likely the greatest natural disaster in the history of mankind occurred on Santorini. It was not the last such event. Almost within living memory, there was another...

The explosion was enormous. The volcanic island flew into the air with the energy of 7,000 Hiroshima atomic bombs. In the process, a 20 cu km/4.2 cu mi cloud of ash, pumice and gas was hurled up to 80 km/50 mi into the atmosphere and two-thirds of the island was swallowed by the sea. 300 towns on the surrounding islands were destroyed and 36,000 peopled burned to death in the rain of fire or drowned in the tsunamis, tidal waves towering as high as 40 m/130 ft unleashed by the eruption, which reached Le Havre in France, 18,000 km/11,300 miles away, after 32 hours. The roar of the eruption travelled for four hours across the oceans and continents, the wave of air pressure raced around the globe several times and the ashes drifted visibly around the world for three years. The volcanic eruption of Krakatoa in the Sunda Strait between Sumatra and Java on 27 August 1883 was **one of the greatest natural disasters** in the history of mankind, but the eruption of Santorini, some 3,500 years earlier, was far worse. To gain an idea of what happened on Santorini, one has to imagine an explosion about four times as great as that on Krakatoa...

Enormous pressure

Before the eruption, Santorini was a small, round island; a number of seemingly extinct volcano cones fused together into a dome mountain that majestically rose out of the water and was covered with lush vegetation and forests. The island had been inhabited since around 3000 BC – until about 1628 BC when the volcano awoke again after a long period of dormancy. The catastrophe undoubtedly developed over a long period of time. It is likely that for weeks or months, gas explosions, fire and pumice rain and earthquakes shook the island and, as living conditions became unbearable, the inhabitants probably fled, because no signs have been found that the subsequent eruption took any human lives. The natural spectacle culminated when the inside of the volcano was torn apart by the enormous pressure of the gas and steam. This was because, as in Krakatoa, cold sea water had entered the mountain through fissures in the rock and mixed with the broiling magma, a highly explosive mixture that could no longer escape through the few vents not plugged by lava.

Ash and pumice were probably also flung several miles into the sky in this eruption. What was left of Santorini volcano was covered with a 30 m/100 ft layer of glowing ash and even on the Dodecanese, on Cyprus and in the western part of Turkey, there is evidence of a layer of pumice up to 2 cm/0.8 in thick. After the magma chamber below the vents had been emptied by the blow-out of millions upon millions of tons of lava, the great volcano collapsed, creating an enormous **caldera** into which the ocean poured. Only the sections visible today, **Thira**, **Thirassia** and **Aspronisi**, were left standing with sheer rock walls. The crater of the collapsed volcano has a capacity of about 60 cu km/37 cu mi. Whether the collapsing mountain caused a gigantic tidal wave that devastated distant coastal regions, as happened with Krakatoa in the Sunda Strait, and was the cause of the fall of the Minoan civilization in the past, as many scientists assume, is still disputed. Perhaps the magma chamber collapsed slowly without creating tsunamis.

No rest

The volcanic activity has not ended, even after 3,600 years. The latest disaster on the island took place in 1956. On 9 July, an earthquake with a magnitude of seven on the Richter scale rocked the island for 45 seconds at five in the morning, destroying 2,000 houses, injuring 200 and claiming the lives of 50 people.

Vounó. The agorá is surrounded by homes and workshops. Standing on its southeast side is the Stoa Basiliké (1st century BC), the royal columned hall; the interior hall is divided lengthwise by a row of Doric columns. A temple to Dionysus can be made out on the terrace above the northwest stoa, which was later dedicated to the Ptolemies (2nd century BC) and finally also to the Roman emperor. There are the foundations of some Hellenistic private homes on the main road and the theatre with a Roman period stage is visible, including traces of the Ptolemaic proskenion. A path branches off the main road at the theatre portal to a **rock shrine** of the Egyptian deities Isis, Serapis and Anubis.

Lying on the south-eastern end of the city is an artificially enlarged terrace (6th century BC) with the gymnopaedia square for cult celebrations honouring **Apollo Karneios**. Archaic inscriptions, some of an erotic nature, can be seen here. The temple of Apollo Karneios, adjoining to the northwest, consists of a pronaos, a cella and two chambers. On the southeast end of the ridge lies the Ephebian gymnasium (2nd century BC) with the Grotto of Hermes and Heracles, as well as Roman baths. (opening hours: Tue – Sun 8.30am – 3pm).

★ Akrotíri

Large sections of an important city destroyed by the great volcanic eruption have been uncovered at Akrotíri, 12 km/7.5 mi southwest of Thíra. Its civilisation, evidence of which has come to light here, appears to have combined the ancient Cycladic culture with the innovations of the Minoan culture. The inhabitants of the city must have fled in time because no human remains have been found. The surviving buildings date from the 17th century BC and show traces of previous earthquake damage. Unfortunately, the tour is not very exciting because the major finds are not here, but rather on display in the archaeological museums in Athens and Thíra, and the protective hall interferes with the total impression. The most important buildings of this **second Pompeii**, which is 1,700 years older than the Roman city, have been provided with floor plans and explanations (opening hours: daily 8.30am – 3pm).

Red Beach ►

A path runs down from the excavation site to Red Beach, one of Santorini's most beautiful beaches, lying beneath imposing, coloured rock walls. The volcanic island has good beaches with dark sand to offer, especially on the east coast. The holiday resorts of **Kamári** and **Périssa** are quite frequented in the high season. The beaches at **Monólithos** and further north are noticeably quieter.

Beaches and seaside resorts ►

Volcanic islands in the caldera

Tours boats from the port of Skála and the ferry terminal at Athiós visit the volcanic islands in the caldera. **Néa Kaméni**, which was first created by a volcanic eruption in 1707, is impressively bizarre with its black stone desert. There are warm, ferrous and sulphurous waters that one can bath in on the northwest coast of the smaller island of **Paléa Kaméni**.

The Kaméni Islands lie right in the middle of the caldera of Santorini.

The island of **Thirasía**, which closes off the caldera to the east, corresponds to the geologic structure of Santorini. The steep cliff edge in the east of the island, where the main town of Manólas is spread out, rises to a height of 295 m/968 ft in the south and slopes gently down in the west.

Anáfi

The 38 sq km/15 sq mi island of Anáfi, about 25 km/15.5 mi east of Santorini, has not been developed much for tourism until now. Most of its some 300 inhabitants live from farming and a little fishing. The island's epithet can be traced back to the myth of the Argonauts. Apollo caused the island to appear out of the sea with a beam of light to provide a place of refuge for the Argonauts returning from Colchis; from which the name »Anáfi« came, »the Shining Island«.

»The Shining Island«

From the little Ágios Nikólaos harbour by bus or on foot in about half an hour. Anáfi Chóra lies at an elevation of 256 m/840 ft and is towered over by a rock with the scattered remains of a 14th century Venetian castle. Or skip that and look straightaway for a quiet spot on **Klissídi Beach** about 1 km/0.6 mi further east.

Anáfi Chóra

Kastélli, a Doric city founded in the 8th century BC, was once located on a 304 m/997 ft rocky hilltop to the northeast of the Chóra.

Kastélli

Only some building remnants scattered about the area can be seen today. Kastélli can be reached on foot from Ágios Nikólaos in about an hour.

Walking tour to Cape Kálamos

A very nice walk, mostly along a coastline distinguished by its inviting beaches, leads from Ágios Nikólaos eastwards to Cape Kálamos. After 6 km/4 mi, the walk comes the abandoned monastery of **Zoodóchou Pigí** (»Life-giving Source«), built on the site of an ancient temple to Apollo. A famous icon of St Mary is kept in the monastic church and is visited by a great number of pilgrims on the 8th of September. About an hour's walk further on to the east is the monolith, Kálamos, a rock 396 m/1,299 ft high that drops sharply down into the sea on which the little church of Panagía Kalamiótissa was built in 1715.

✶ Sérifos · Σέριφος

F 6

Island Group: Cyclades
Altitude: 0 – 587 m/1,926 ft
Capital: Sérifos Chóra

Area: 73 sq km/28 sq mi
Population: 1,200

The rocky island, serrated by gorges, has beautiful beaches and a landscape that, in spots, is lush green. In recent years it has become increasingly popular with tourists.

▶ VISITING SÉRIFOS

GETTING THERE
Boat connections to and from Piraeus on the mainland and the islands of Folégandros, Íos, Kímolos, Kýthnos, Mílos, Náxos, Páros, Santorini, Sífnos, Síkinos and Sýros.

WHERE TO EAT
▶ **Inexpensive**
Platia
Sérifos Chóra
This elegantly furnished restaurant serves Greek cuisine.

WHERE TO STAY
▶ **Mid-range**
Areti
Livádi

Tel. 22 81 05 14 79
18 rooms and 3 studios
Recently renovated hotel overlooking the ferry docks; rooms with balcony and sea view; swimming pool

Maistrali
Livádi
Tel. 22 81 05 13 81
Fax 22 81 05 12 98
20 rooms
This small but nice hotel is 500 m/550 yd from the harbour and almost next to the beach; the nicely furnished rooms all have a balcony.

There is a sweeping view of the Bay of Livádi from the island's chief town.

What to See on Sérifos

The port town is the tourist centre of the island. Some very beautiful beaches can be found in the vicinity, particularly Psilí Ámmos to the north of the peninsula.

Livádi

The main town of Sérifos Chóra is located in an impressively beautiful setting 5 km/3 mi above Livádi – a footpath also leads up to it. The town is divided into two areas. The Evangelistria Church (1907) is worth seeing in **Kato Chóra** (»lower town«) ist sehenswert die Evangelistria-Kirche (1907) and the church of the Archangel, which is partly built into the rocks, and the Mitropolis, which has a beautiful wood-carved templon and an icon of St Mary, both from the 17th century, are worth seeing in **Anó Chóra** (»upper town«). A small archaeological museum is in the town hall next door with artefacts from the Roman period.

★
Sérifos Chóra

The island's oldest church stands in the pretty village of Panagía, located high up, 5 km/3 mi north of Sérifos Chóra. The church was founded about 950 and possesses two ancient marble columns, frescoes from the 13th and 14th centuries and icons from the 18th and 19th centuries.

Panagía

Some 4 km/2.5 mi further north is the fortress-like monastery of Taxiarchón (17th century), the **island's major attraction**. Its catholi-

★
◄ Taxiarchón
monastery

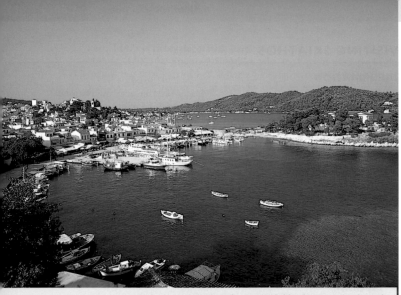

The harbour of Skiathos Chóra is divided by the Peninsula of Bourdzi.

rock on the north coast, from where there is a breathtaking view. Parts of the fortification walls with a drawbridge have survived, along with Turkish baths and three churches. The 17th century church of **Christós sto Kástro** has a large icon stand adorned with many old and valuable icons.

Monasteries About half-way there, the road passes the cave monastery of Evangelístria, founded in 1797, and beautifully situated overlooking a gorge. During the War of Independence, it served as a hiding place for rebels. Frescoes dating from 1822 can be seen in the church. Nice walks can be taken to the abandoned monasteries Charalámpos (8 km/5 mi north of Evangelístria; 17th century), Theotókou Kechriás (8 km/ 5mi northwest of Skíathos Chóra; 1540) with frescoes from 1745 and Panagía Kounístria (9 km/5.6 mi west of Skíathos Chóra; 17th century) with a magnificent, richly decorated iconostasis.

✳ Beaches The island numbers over 60 fantastic beaches, which get less crowded the further away they are from Skíathos Chóra. The most attractive beaches are **Koukounariés** (9 km/5.6 mi to the west), lined with umbrella pines, and **Lalária** (8 km/5 mi to the north), with light grey pebbles. Just offshore is a »rock arch« and next to it are two sea grottos, in which one can swim.

Tsougkria There are nine smaller islands just off the coast of Skíathos. The largest, Tsougkria, is visited by boats ferrying bathers. The main attraction is the beach with tourist facilities.

Neighbouring Islands

Skópelos, lying to the east of Skíathos, is an extraordinarily beautiful, wooded island with many excellent beaches. Almost all of the beaches, with nearby hotels and tavernas, are stretched out between Staphylos and Loutraki on the south and west coasts. A remarkable 350 churches, chapels and monasteries, some quite beautiful, have been built on Skópelos. The ancient city of **Peparethos** was supposedly founded by the Cretan hero Staphylus, a son of Dionysus and Ariadne. Staphylus (»Grapevine«) is said to have brought winegrowing here. Minoan double axes on display in the museum in ▶ Vólos were found in the so-called Staphylus grave discovered on the south coast. The **island's principal town**, Skópelos Chóra (pop. 3,000), is set very attractively in a sweeping bay, with its white houses climbing up the castle hill. The ruins of the castle on the hill date from the 13th century. The town has a **folk art museum** and about 120 churches and chapels, some of which are Byzantine. The oldest churches on the island are **Ágios Athanásio**, from the 9th century with 17th-century frescoes, and **Ágios Michaíl Synádon**, with beautiful carvings, icons, a walled-in Roman sarcophagus and an ancient grave slab. The picturesque mountain village of Glóssa in the northwest of the island climbs very prettily up the green landscape on the mountain overlooking the harbour of Loutraki and is a popular tourist destination. A fantastic view of Skíathos and the mainland can be enjoyed from there.

Skópelos

◀ Glóssa

> ! **Baedeker** TIP
>
> **Cave trip**
>
> Three sea caves – Skótini Spiliá, Galázia Spiliá and Halkíni Spiliá – are located east of Lalariá beach on Skiáthos. They can be explored by swimming into them – an impressive experience! Tour boats also enter a few yards into the caves.

The whole length of the elongated, green island of Alónnisos, to the northeast of Skópelos, is occupied by a mountain ridge that reaches up to 476 m/1,562 ft with Mt Kouvoúli. The northwest coast is steep and has few distinctive features, whilst the friendlier southeast coast has more coves. The waters around the island provide an environment for the rare **monk seal** and are therefore protected as a nature reserve.

Alónnisos

Alónnisos is suitable for holidaymakers seeking peace and quiet and who want to enjoy nature. It is particularly fine for bathing and snorkelling as the water here is considered to be the cleanest in the Aegean.

The tiny port of Patitíri, which spreads around a pretty little round bay, first came into being in the 1950s. It has a small historic museum and a folk art museum above the harbour, as well as a monk seal museum on the harbour esplanade, which provides information about the local seal colony. The island's old former principal town,

◀ Patitíri

Alónnisos Chóra, sits on a hill above Patitíri. It was largely abandoned after the earthquake of 1965 and has now been transformed into a holiday settlement. Many of the houses were acquired and renovated by foreigners, mostly Germans and British. Some 40 monk seals (Monachus monachus) live in the **National Marine Park in the Northern Sporades**, the most important colony in the Mediterranean. The European Nature Heritage Fund maintains a station on Alónnisos, which governs and implements the protection regulations. The information centre on the harbour of Patitíri provides information on the specific protection provisions and also offers tips for island walking tours.

! *Baedeker* TIP

Picnic included
The travel agency, »Ikos Travel«, on the harbour of Patitíri, offers excursions to the smaller neighbouring islands of Pélagos, Peristéra and Psathura. A picnic on the beach is included in the price.

Skýros · Σκύρος

L / M 7

Island Group: Northern Sporades
Altitude: 0 – 814m / 2,671 ft
Capital: Skýros Chóra

Area: 209 sq km / 81 sq mi
Population: 2,900

Skýros lies to the east of the rest of the archipelago and is distinctly separated from it, placing it off the beaten track – an ideal holiday refuge for people seeking peace and relaxation.

Largest of the Sporadic Islands

Skýros, is the largest island of the Northern Sporades and is divided in two. The southeast is taken up by the rugged, arid **Kóchilas** massif, which rises to an elevation of 814 m/2,670 ft. It is here that the quarries with the variegated, coarse-grained marble that was much prized in Roman times are located. The northwest, rising to 403 m/1,322 ft at its summit, **Mt Ólympos**, has a more gentle terrain, more water and is more fertile and is covered with pine forests. The two parts of the island are separated by an enclosed basin between the Achílli Bay on the east coast and the Kalamítsa Bay that cuts deep inland in the west. Lying at the foot of the steep, inhospitable cliffs on the coast are beautiful sandy beaches.

What to See on Skýros

Skýros Chóra

The main town of Skýros Chóra (pop. 2,400), in the eastern part of the island, makes a typical »Cycladic« impression. Its white, square houses rise in a semi-circle up a hill on which a Byzantine and Venetian fortified kástro once stood.

► VISITING SKÝROS

INFORMATION

Skyros Travel & Tourism
Market square
Skýros Chóra
Tel. 22 22 09 16 00,
Fax 22 22 09 21 23
www.skyrostravel.com

GETTING THERE

Boat services to and from Kárystos on
the island of Évia.

WHERE TO EAT

► Moderate

Asterias
Platia
Skýros-Chóra
Tel. 22 22 09 13 80
The »Asterias« serves delicious local
specialties.

WHERE TO STAY

► Mid-range

Skýros Palace
Grismata
Molos
Tel. 22 22 09 19 94; 80 apartments.
The hotel complex with its traditional
architecture and tasteful apartments
lies to the north of town near the
beach.

► Budget

Pension King Lykomídes
Linariá
Tel. 22 22 09 32 49
Fax 22 22 09 34 12
13 rooms
This small guesthouse lies directly by
the docks.

Sitting on a rock below the castle is the monastery of **Ágios Geórgios Skyrionós**. The church founded in 962 has a carved iconostasis and well-preserved frescoes.

The English poet **Rupert Brooke** (born 1887) died near Skýros on a French ship in 1915 on the way to the battle for Gallipoli. He is buried on the island (see below) and there is a monument dedicated to him on the Platía Brooke (1931).

In the immediate vicinity is the **Faltaits Museum**, which displays excellent Skyrian handicrafts, as well as the **archaeological museum** with artefacts dating from Mycenaean to Roman times. The closest popular beach is to the north, between Magazia and Molos.

Linariá

The port of Linariá lies some 10 km/6 mi south of the Chóra in the bay of the same name, which is protected to the northwest by the island of **Baláxa**. The best beach on the island can be found to the east at the Bay of Kalamítsa. There are also good beaches to the northwest of Linariá: Pefkos, Ágios Fokas, Atsitsa and Kyra Panagía.

Trís Boukes

Spreading out in the southern end of the island is the Bay of Trís Boukes, which is almost completely closed off from the sea by the offshore islands of Platí and Sarákino. Rupert Brooke's grave can be found in an olive grove on the eastern shore.

Remains of a theatre on the acropolis of Sparta

dations of the Athena temple that **Gitiadas** built in the 6th century BC, a mud brick construction with a wooden frame set on a stone base, whose nickname, »Chalkioikos«, derived from its bronze plate façade. Further to the east is the St Nikon Basilica (10th century), in which the saint is buried. A sweeping view unfolds of the city, of Mystrá and of the Evrotas Plain with its groves of oranges and olives.

Sanctuary of Artemis Located on the eastern edge of the city is the Sanctuary of **Artemis Orthía**, so named because the cult image was standing upright when it was found. According to Pausanias, it had been brought from Tauris by Iphigeneia and Orestes. The cruel custom of youths being bloodily flogged as part of the rites of manhood in the presence of this cult image is quite apt. The foundations of a 6th century BC temple still exist. Rows of seats arranged in a semi-circle for the witnesses to the ritual flogging were added in Roman times.

Around Sparta

Menelaion Leave Sparta in the direction of Geráki and after 5 km/3 mi turn off onto a footpath that runs past a chapel to a hill. Here are the remains of a 5th century BC heroon honouring **Menelaus**. It stands on the site of Mycenaean buildings thought to have perhaps been the residence of Menelaus.

Amyklai The sanctuary of **Apollo Amyklaios** with the »throne« above the grave of Hyakinthos is on Agía Paraskeví hill (7 km/4.3 mi to the south near Aichlés). The foundations and some fragments have survived. This throne was built around a tall bronze cult figure of Apollo.

The famous two gold goblets in the National Archaeological Museum in Athens were found in a Mycenaean tomb (15th century BC) discovered 2 km/1.2 mi south of Amyklai at the village of Vafío.

Vafío

The Taýgetos mountain range stretches a good 100 km/60 mi in a north-south direction west of Sparta, separating the regions of Laconia and Messenia from one another and rises to an elevation of 2,407 m/7,897 ft at its summit, Mt Profítis Ilías – the highest peak in the Peloponnese. The mountain ridge, made up of limestone and marble, ends in the ► Máni Peninsula at Cape Tenaro. A climb up Mt Profítis Ilías can be recommended. To undertake the hike, drive away from Sparta in the direction of Gýthio, then towards Anógia and the Taýgetos shelter. The rest of the way to the summit is on foot, which take about one hour each way.

Taýgetos

A well developed road over the pass, following the old bridal path in the west, connects Sparta with Kalamáta. This 59 km/37 mi long stretch is one of the most scenically impressive roads in Greece, particularly the eastern section through the Langada gorge between the summit of the pass (1,524 m/5,000 ft) and Trýpi.

Langada Gorge

Sýros · Σύρος

M 10

Island Group: Cyclades
Altitude: 0 – 442m / 1,360 ft
Capital: Ermoupolis

Area: 86 sq km / 32 sq mi
Population: 20,000

Despite its importance as the administrative and commercial centre of the Cyclades, as well as being an important hub for shipping traffic in the Aegean, and as it is usually just a stopping off point for island tours, tourism plays a relatively modest role on the hilly island.

After the Fourth Crusade, the island was taken over by the duchy of Náxos in 1207 and has since had a strong Catholic influence.
It was under the protection of the French monarchy during the Ottoman period (from 1537). Sýros remained neutral during the War of Independence, making it a safe haven after 1821 for refugees from Smyrna, Chíos, Psará, Crete, Ýdra and other islands, who settled here. They founded the town of Ermoupolis, which developed during the 19th century into the largest port in Greece and an important base between Asia Minor and western Europe. After the opening of the Corinth canal in 1893, the economic development of the city was adversely affected by the rising importance of Piraeus as a central port.

History »capital« of the Cyclades

Thássos · Θάσος

M 3

Island Group: Northern and Eastern Aegean Islands	**Area:** 379 sq km/146 sq mi
Population: 14,500	**Altitude:** 0 – 1127 m/3,697 ft
	Capital: Thassos / Liménas

Greece's most northerly island, with its magnificent beaches and many camping sites, has become an ever increasingly popular tourist destination.

Most northerly Greek island
Thassos is the most northerly of the Greek islands, only 8 km/5 mi off the east Macedonian coast. The appealing, round and fertile island is occupied by a densely wooded mountain range, scored by deep valleys, that reaches a height of 1,127 m/3,697 ft, **Mt Ypsário**. Its northern and eastern flanks drop steeply off into the sea, while its southern and western slopes descend more gently. The most beautiful coves and inlets with excellent sandy beaches lie on the east coast. The population earns its livelihood from farming, mining (copper,

▶ VISITING THÁSSOS

INFORMATION

Tourist Police
Thassos Town
Seafront promenade
Tel. 25 93 02 31 11

GETTING THERE

Boat services to and from Kavála and Keramotion the mainland.

WHERE TO EAT

▶ Moderate
Chrisi Amoudia
Thassos Town
This taverna at the edge of town offers a large selection of dishes along with friendly service and a terrace.

▶ Inexpensive
O Glarós
Alykí
Tel. 25 93 03 15 47
Fish and grilled specialities are best enjoyed here on the shady terrace with a view of the bay.

WHERE TO STAY

▶ Mid-range
Alexandra Beach
Thassos town
Tel. 25 93 05 24 94
Fax 25 93 05 80 04
www.alexandrabeach.gr
200 rooms
This is the best hotel on the island; directly on the sea with garden; elegantly furnished rooms with balcony and sea view; spa area attached.

Kipos
Thassos town
Tel. 25 93 02 24 69
Fax 25 93 06 01 50
www.kipos-apartments.gr
Nice apartment complex with swimming pool; each the spacious, well-furnished apartments has a balcony.

The island's capital is surrounded by lush vegetation.

zinc) and from tourism. Underground mining of red chalk, an iron ore, was taking place as early as 20,000 years ago at Limenaria – the oldest attested in Europe to date.

What to See on Thássos

The modern capital and port, Thassos / Liménas (pop. 2,300), is almost an open-air museum. It was built on the western part of the ancient capital, whose extent is attested to by the still surviving walls enclosing the naval harbour, today a fishing harbour, sections of the city wall (7th – 5th century BC), as well as the foundations of residences and shrines. The ancient city extends southeast from the harbour, rising up to the heights of the acropolis, where the Genoan Gattelusi family built their castle in 1431.

Thássos Town

The **agorá** (4th century BC to 1000 AD) with its columned halls is spread out behind the closed harbour. The archaeological museum on its west side contains artefacts found on the island, including its showpiece, a large kouros with a ram (c. 600 BC). In front of the eastern corner of the agorá, the gateway for dignitaries can be seen, whose marble walls were decorated with late archaic reliefs, now stored in the Louvre in Paris. The **sanctuary of Artemis Polo** (6th century. BC) lies further to the southeast. An odeon (2nd century) is beyond the ancient Roman road and to the southwest are the remnants of a triumphal arch erected in honour of the Roman

◀ Archaeological museum

The fantastic Alykí Bay on the southeast of Thassos

emperors, **Caracalla** and **Septimius Severus**, in AD 213 – 217, as well as a temple to Heracles (6th century BC). In the northern section of the ancient city (east of the ancient harbour) are the sanctuaries of Dionysus and Poseidon (both 4th century BC), the theatre (3rd/2nd century BC), a shrine to foreign gods, and, at the most northern point, a shrine to Patrooi Theoi (6th century BC). During the summer, performances are held in the theatre. A path leads up from the theatre to the castle and to the foundations of a temple to Athena (5th century BC) on the hill adjoining to the southwest. The way back to the city leads down the slope of a hill, where there is a niche for a shrine to Pan.

Island tour   A 100 km/60 mi road runs around the whole of the island, keeping close to the coastline, that is travelled by scheduled buses, making all the beaches and village easy to reach. Lying south of Thassos at the foot of Mt Profítis Ilías is **Panagía**, the island's capital until 1912. With its white-washed houses and slate roofs, it is one of the most beautiful villages on Thassos and a popular tourist attraction. Further to the south on the eastern slope of Ypsári is **Potamiá**, with a museum that displays works by the sculptor **P. Vagis**, who came from there. There is a fine view from here of the wooded valley down to the sea and the 4 km/2.5 mi long sandy beach, **Chrisi Ammoudio** (Golden Beach), the best on the island.

On past Kínira, whose main attraction is **Paradise Beach** is the small peninsula of **Alykí** with its two luring sandy bays. Marble quarries as